A Million Miles *from* Home

Jeanne Selander Miller

Other books by Jeanne Selander Miller—

A Breath Away
Winner of the Best Spiritual Book of 2012
London Book Festival

Honorable Mention Spirituality
New England Book Festival of 2012

Honorable Mention Memoir
Southern California Book Festival of 2012

A Breath Away is the first book of this trilogy,
A Million Miles from Home is the second, and the third
book should be out in the spring of 2014.

Editorial Direction and Coaching by Ascent
www.itsyourlifebethere.com

Cover Design by Lookout Design, Inc.
www.lookoutdesign.com

Photography by George Mallinckrodt
www.georgemallinckrodtphotography.com

ISBN: 1480127280
ISBN: 13: 978-1480127289

Through the dark night of the soul
I emerge
Strong and whole
To those who held my hand
Listened to my tales of woe
Offered comfort and wise counsel
And the encouragement to endure and persevere
With the knowledge that there would be better days
ahead for me

I offer you this story with my heartfelt gratitude

To Mom and Dad for your abiding presence

To Cullen and Gillian for your forgiveness

To Janice for your daily presence and wisdom

To Jill who sees only the best in me

To Margie for your fire and your friendship

To the cast of many who provided light in my
darkest days

And to my dear sister Susan for being my safe
place to land and to begin anew

Dearest Reader and Companion on the Journey,

This is a story about how I lost my way
How I moved away from a place of peace and well-being
to a place of pain and darkness
and how I found my way home

This book has been difficult to write
as I have needed to re-live
some dark and difficult days
In doing so I have been graced with a light
That has illuminated the way home

There may be moments in everyone's life
When all you see is darkness and no way out
This is when we most need to nurture the light within
As distant and far away as it may seem
Breathe a little life on the spark
Ignite the fire within your heart
Listen to the longings of your heart
Your heart will guide you home

Jeanne

To Karen,
Follow your heart
... your heart will
lead you home.
Jeanne Selander
Miller

CHAPTER 1

We're Not in Kansas Anymore

Everyone has a story to tell and this one is mine.
I now understand how Dorothy felt in the Wizard of Oz. Once upon a time, my life was picked up in a great gust of wind and was twisted and turned upside down. I found myself in a strange and bewildering place that I never expected to be.

In so many ways the Oz analogy fits. I have been through a deep, dark forest complete with unimaginable monsters, and like Dorothy, my goal was to find my way home. But for Dorothy home was her farm back in Kansas, and for me home was not a physical place, but rather I seek to be at home with myself, once again.

My experience is not unique except perhaps in the details. There are plenty of people, just like me, who marry fully expecting their spouse will be their lover, their partner and their very best friend, but instead discover that the person they married is someone else entirely. Instead they terrorize you just like the Floating Head of Oz.

There are people who appear to be one thing and once you buy into the illusion … you find yourself leaving behind that which you know to be true, what you wanted for yourself and for your life. These masters of deception and illusion can lead you out into unknown territory on a very frightening path. The further down this path you go the more lost you become until *home* is a distant memory lost in the mist behind you.

Some of us lose our way entirely and on this journey we lose ourselves and perhaps even our lives. But do not lose heart for if you are honest enough to look about you, to take stock of where you have traveled, and to own your part of it, then there can be an awakening. But it is in these darkest of moments, in the darkest of places that you realize that you have been deceived and led astray. You may question yourself and your judgment. You may beat yourself up for ever letting this happen. You may even hate yourself.

But The Great and Powerful Oz, in reality, is just a little tyrant behind the curtain, complete with pain and issues all his own.

⌒

This is my story. I am reclaiming my life. This is about my journey home, back to the authentic me.

I was one of the very lucky ones. I knew it then. But the years of time and space for reflection have only served to magnify the depth of what I had ... and what I lost.

I met my first husband, Fred, in 1984 and we fell fast and furious for one another. It was an all-consuming love and we were engaged in less than a year and married three months later.

Fred was a tall and handsome man with curly brown hair, sparkling eyes and a winning smile that I lost my heart to. He was smart and clever and funny and he made me laugh every single day we were together. He was strong and athletic and I felt safe and secure in his presence. He was my lover and husband and my very best friend. He was the father of my children and my heart's delight.

Fred was an attorney who made his career in the Prosecutor's Office in Oakland County. Now I know there are attorneys who are held in disrepute and rightly so, but Fred was not one of those. He was admired and loved by those who knew him. To quote Circuit Court Judge Mester, "Fred had the tenacity of a good prosecutor and the compassion of a good human being." He was the best man I have ever known. In every sense of the word, he was the best.

Ours was a storybook marriage. But consistent with all fairytales, there was tragedy and loss.

After a few short years of wedded bliss and the birth of our two children, Fred was diagnosed with an aggressive form of bone marrow cancer. I watched Fred go from playing championship tennis to becoming so weak that he was no longer able to walk. But as his physical body deteriorated, his beautiful luminous spirit shone bright, as he had an uncanny way of speaking from the heart, and making a soul-to-soul connection with those he came in contact with. After eight years of the torturous daily battle with the disease, my beloved died of complications of his second bone marrow transplant.

I had Fred's headstone engraved with this verse.

The verse was encircled with ivy and stargazer lilies, because they were his favorite.

May you always walk in sunshine
And God's love around you flow
The Happiness you gave us,
No one will ever know
It broke our hearts to lose you
But you did not go alone
A part of us went with you
The day God called you home
A million times I've needed you
A million times I've cried
If love alone could have saved you
You never would have died

I loved him from the core of my very being and I always will.

A little bit about me …

I had been blessed to be loved and cared for all of my life. I had the good fortune of being born into a home where my parents loved me unconditionally, every day of my life. Although I suffered a few hard knocks with relationships when I was in my twenties, I went on to marry Fred, the love of my life.

I know what Fred and I had was rare and unique and beautiful, and as uncommon as finding a perfect diamond in a gravel mine. But I lost my beloved despite my best efforts to keep him, and his best efforts to stay.

I know what love is.

I know that love is all there is.

I know that love is all that really matters.

Fred had left me all too soon. The reality is that he was gone and I remained. I was left here without him. But in his love and care for me and our children, he left us in a place of inner safety, and with a very real sense of being cherished, respected, worthy and loved. He left us emotionally secure and financially sound. He had provided for us and for our future.

The kids and I lived in a little white 1920's bungalow with dark green shutters on a dead end street that was a short walk to the historic village. The back of our house had been added onto. There were many large windows and French doors that opened up to a big backyard on Lake Bella. It was aptly named for it was picture postcard pretty. I loved our home. Fred and I had spent nine years there renovating, refurbishing, and making it our own before he passed. We bought the house when our daughter, Gillian, was five months old, and Freddy died there, in our great room that overlooked the gardens and the lake. It was my sanctuary. It was our home.

But prior to this next chapter of my life, although I was grieving I had also found an inner sense of peace and well-being that comes with the knowledge that one is loved and thus worthy of love. Fred was gone but his love for me was not. He left me with a good sense of myself and of my innate worth. I was a good home for my soul to take rest in. I was a woman who was comfortable in my own skin.

Fred was gone but I was not without love. I had the love of my children, the love of my parents, and the love of my sister. Fred's sister, Shelley and her husband, Joel, lived two houses away and I saw them regularly. I had the love of my neighbors, and love of my friends. I had money in the bank and meaningful work.

I thought I was pretty well-grounded.

So how was it that I could have been swept so far from my place of peace?

So the story unfolds ...

The sun had set, and the light was gone from my life. If I had allowed myself, I would have stayed home and wallowed in my grief, but that was not an option as I had two children who needed me. So I tried my best to get on with the business of living and family life. If I am to be absolutely honest with myself, those days after Fred died were unimaginably long and the nights interminable. Fred's death left me with an unspeakable loneliness, and yet true to my stoic Nordic constitution that is exactly what I did. I did not speak of it. I glossed over the pain, the loss, and loneliness, just as I was expected to do.

I continued to wear black for quite some time. Black became my uniform. I had no interest in yellow, greens, and blues. I just could not find a way to wear the bright colors anymore. It was easy and required little effort on my part to just wear black. I was grieving, and it was all that I could manage. One spring I was shopping for a couple of new summer things, and I took my selections in black to the cashier. This older woman looked me in the eye and asked me, "How long have you wanted to be invisible?"

It was as if Fred were speaking to me through this kind and gentle saleswoman. I was dumbstruck as I looked at her, and eventually all I could do was laugh. I responded, "You may have just saved me years of psychotherapy."

I was grieving. I had lost the love of my life. I had lost my cherished role as a wife, a wife to Fred Miller. I did not know my grieving and feelings of irrelevance were so obvious to total strangers. But apparently I was wrong. I thought perhaps if no one noticed me, if I was indeed invisible, no one would notice if I continued to live my life in the past. Lost in memory, in a time when I felt loved, complete and whole. Unlike now …

Losing love is like a window in your heart
Everybody sees you're blown apart.

-Paul Simon

I had started to slip away.

In the early days of widowhood everyone surrounds you with love and treats you with the utmost care. But even the best of friends cannot hold this kind of love and concern indefinitely. These personal resources are precious and although they are doled out generously, they are also time limited. The reality is that people are expected to get on with the business of living. So I did my best to re-engage with life.

My children were growing up. Cullen was entering his middle school years complete with all the high jinxes and shenanigans that accompany those years, as well as the demands of a rigorous afterschool sports schedule. Gillian was soon to be ten and was no longer completely enthralled with the prospects of entertaining her dolls in the playroom. They needed their mother, not this vacant shell of a woman who now filled that role.

So I stepped back into the land of the living. I spent my days working as a teacher and a nurse, and I immersed myself in caring for other people's children. My evenings were filled with domesticity: dinner, laundry, and homework. My greatest joy was at the end of the evening. When all our work was finished my children humored me and allowed me to read to them. They were good readers and they didn't need me to read to them. But it was something that I needed and somehow they understood this, as we would snuggle in on the couch.

So over the next few years I began to read the *Harry Potter* books aloud to my children, complete with different voices for all the characters. But I finished the series alone as my children lost interest as they were growing up.

Between days immersed in work, and evenings with my children, I filled a great deal of empty time. But there was that place in my heart that ached with the constant pain of loneliness. Fred, my love and my partner, had been taken from this world. He had dropped my hand, and he had traveled on without me.

I had been at home with him. I had been complete with him. He had been my sanctuary and now I was adrift.

It was only a couple of weeks after Fred's death that the kids were actively negotiating with me to host our annual Halloween party. This was the last thing I wanted to do. I just was not up to it, but Halloween ranked right up there with Christmas for my kids. When it didn't look like the negotiations were going in their favor, Cullen played *The Dad Card.*

"You know Mom, Dad would want us to have the Halloween Party."

And then they both looked up at me and all I could do was laugh because they were absolutely right. They grabbed onto one another and started to shout as they jumped up and down because they knew … they had won. It was the first time I had seen this unrestrained joy in their faces in weeks. The truth was that Fred also loved Halloween and everything about it.

So it began, "Fred would say this … " or "Dad would like that … " And you could almost imagine him chiming in, and putting his two cents in. The kids and

I would speak of their father like he was sitting in the next room. These conversations and remembrances helped us keep Fred's memory alive. I know this kind of talk helped us, but it also created a distance between us and other people. I know this made some people uncomfortable. In fact, there probably were a lot of things about us ... about me ... that made people uncomfortable.

And so the days turned to weeks, and the weeks to months, and there we were in the dead of winter.

There were continual reminders that our life had changed.

A few years ago at Christmas, Fred had been eyeing an automatic bread maker. The kind where all you had to do was add the ingredients and the machine would knead the dough, heat it to the appropriate temperature so the dough would rise, punch it down so it would rise again, and then bake it. He thought the idea of having freshly baked bread every morning was a wonderful one. I thought it sounded like another thing on my already overflowing plate. So I beat him to the punch and bought the bread maker for him.

This was how Fred became *The Bread Maker*. We had fresh bread every morning when he was able, and he gifted bread regularly to our friends and his colleagues. This bread affectionately became known as *Fred Bread*.

But now the bread maker stood idle on the kitchen counter. I just could not bring myself to use it. It was Fred's bread maker and Fred was the baker of the bread. So I took the machine to the basement.

I couldn't bear to look at it. The memories were just too painful.

The children were also stinging from the loss of their father. I remember Cullen had been invited to go to a hockey game with his friends and their fathers and I was encouraging him to go along.

He turned to me in tears, "I don't want to go. They're all trying to be my Dad. I have a Dad. He's just not here!"

My heart was breaking for him. I didn't know how to help him. I know these men were trying to be helpful, but the wounds were just so raw, just so damn raw for all of us. All I could do was hold him, and we both cried until there were no more tears ... at least for now.

Later that winter Gillian would have a similar experience when she told me that she wanted to quit Brownies. I launched into the typical parental diatribe about finishing things that we start and not being a quitter ... blah, blah, blah. But she saw what I did not, "I'm not going to the Daddy-Daughter Dance. My Daddy is not here." Again we both cried as I thought about the realities of the modern American family. Clearly my little girl is not the only child who doesn't have a daddy. Why do we as the adults conspire to inflict this kind of pain on children whose families don't fit the stereotype? Why must we make life just that much more difficult when there is no valid reason to do so? It was just one of those inconsequential events that people don't consider until someone you love is hurt by the exclusion.

So she quit Brownies and with my blessing. Our loss permeated our lives. There was no denying it. Everywhere we turned we faced the painful reality … Fred was gone.

My mid-winter break from school rarely corresponded with my children's break. I would have liked to have gotten away and traveled with the kids, but at least this year, 1999, it was not to be. So I tried to make the best of it, and instead used this as an opportunity to see some of my girlfriends who still had the luxury of being *stay at home* moms when I had returned to the world of paid employment.

One bleak Wednesday morning in February after dropping the kids at school, I crossed the parking lot and went to morning Mass. The faculty and the students at St. Sabula's attended Mass every Wednesday. I used to go regularly before I went back to work. But at this point in my life, I was here only once a year, during my mid-winter break. I saw old friends across the church and they gave me a welcoming smile. My children caught sight of me as they entered silently, in single file with their classmates, as their teachers led the procession. They gave me a quick underhand side wave and smiled without actually turning their heads. They had learned how to avoid the strong arm of the law from clamping down on them for the egregious offense of acknowledging one's own mother in the house of the Lord. They were learning to play by the rules, and though I find the spontaneity of children delightful, in the long run the discipline served my children well.

I knew so many of these children, the teachers and the parents. It gave me great comfort to sit there in the sanctuary of St. Sabula's. In that moment I felt the love and a real sense of peace and belonging.

Fred had been a sanctuary for me, my safe haven. Our marriage and our family life had been the walls in that refuge too.

While the liturgy went on, ironic as it was, I tried not to let the spoken words destroy the feeling, the feeling of peace, safety, and belonging.

After Mass my friends gathered in the narthex as we had already made plans to go for coffee. I had known most of these women for 6 or 7 years. Our children were growing up together and I loved these women. I felt a real sense of camaraderie based on shared purpose. We were the village. We were raising the children. We toted one another's children from point A to point B, we fed them when they were in our care, did their laundry, corrected language and behavior, shared their joys and sorrows. These women were the foundation of my inner circle. We were the mothers and we were doing our best to raise our children.

So we met at the coffee shop just down the street from church and inhabited the large table in the back as was customary. The gathering was larger than usual. All the girls were there. I knew that I was the reason. My life had taken some twists and turns and my path had deviated from the paths of my friends. We used to meet here every week.

This particular morning I was feeling pretty grounded emotionally, but it didn't take much to upset me and expose my vulnerabilities.

As I took my seat every one was admiring Ellen's new ring.

Ellen smiled with pride as she extended her hand in my direction to show me her 2-carat diamond in an elegant platinum setting. "Patrick took me out to The Rochester Chop House for our anniversary. Anyway, he surprised me with this upgrade. Fifteen years. I can't believe it."

"Ellen, it's beautiful. Congratulations to you and Patrick." I leaned in to give her a kiss on the cheek. The ring sparkled.

Fifteen years. I couldn't help myself. The thoughts came unbidden, Fred and I would have been, and should have been, married 15 years next spring. I tried to push the thought from my head.

There were moments like this when an internal shift took place and I became the observer of my own life. I found myself listening and watching from somewhere beyond.

I was no longer a central character, but rather a visitor to this coffee klatch. I was once where they are now, a happily married, stay at home mom, but no longer. I am now a single working mother, and the difference between my past and present life made me feel like an outsider, even amongst the people I loved.

"We're taking the kids and driving to Florida to see Will's parents over Easter," Liz vied for the girls' attention as I felt myself disconnect even further. It was as if I were watching this drama unfold from a great distance away. "I'd like to go somewhere else, just once, but every year it's the same. Three kids and my husband in the car for 24 hours to see my in-laws; what can I say … it's not exactly my idea of a vacation." She stopped talking long enough to take a swallow of coffee and began to look at the menu.

"We were going to fly this year. Mike had been secretly stashing away some money for airline tickets." Tricia now had the floor, and we turned our attention towards her. She had four kids and money was tight. "But I was cleaning out our drawers and I took a stack of old clothes to Goodwill. I didn't know that Mike had saved about $800 in the pocket of his old baseball pants," she paused for effect, "yep, the baseball pants he couldn't get his big toe in anymore … they were in the stack of things that went to Goodwill." She laughed good-naturedly. "I guess we will be driving again this year."

I tried to think of something to say. I quoted a friend. "Road trips with the whole fam damily. In the words of Charles Dickens, 'It was the best of times, it was the worst of times.' I'm not certain but I don't think he was talking about driving to Florida. But then again, maybe he was."

That got a laugh.

Soon everyone was chatting casually about their plans for the upcoming Easter holiday. I had nothing to add and so I just listened. I listened as my friends collectively bitched about the long car rides with their husbands and their children. They bitched about staying in cheap roadside motels along the interstate and eating fast food in the car, and the necessity of frequent potty breaks in filthy gas stations, and the hours and hours of prolonged togetherness only to be greeted by their in-laws who found their children ill-mannered and noisy.

The chatter began to shift as others chimed in about their plans for the Easter holiday … and then on to summer and family vacation plans. I was slipping away. I couldn't stay with the conversation. I couldn't stay there in the moment. It was just too painful. The distance between my dear friends and me was expanding exponentially. And yet, no one even noticed that I was gone. I became lost in my own thoughts.

I had nothing to offer as that year Easter was late in April and I would be working. My spring break was on the calendar for two weeks earlier, and didn't correspond with the weeks my children would have off. No, we wouldn't be going away. My husband was dead, and for that matter, so were my in-laws. We wouldn't be visiting them in Florida over Easter, at least not in this lifetime.

No. I had nothing to offer … except perhaps that single tear that escaped and slid silently down my right cheek. It went unnoticed or at least no one commented. It wasn't anyone's fault. It was the simple reality; I was no longer a member of this club.

I don't remember how that morning ended, but I'm certain that we promised to see one another more often. We professed our love for each other before we parted.

From that day on, I had an awareness that my friendships had begun to slip away. The demands of their own lives took precedent, as well they should. I knew I couldn't expect anyone to feel the magnitude of my loss and wallow in my grief with me. This was a part of life's journey I had to travel on my own.

As I drove home in the car the tears flowed freely as they often did when I was alone. The home that I once had –not a physical structure, but the home in someone's heart –was gone. I wanted that again. I wanted what my girlfriends still had, the security of belonging in someone's heart and in a shared life. I wanted my membership in that club renewed. I wanted to be both wife and mother. I didn't sign up for this single parenting, but here I was –a single working mother.

No, I couldn't be angry with my friends for their lack of understanding. There is really only so far someone can walk in another's shoes. They'd carried me long enough and the load was heavy, and my guess is, they were tired of it. They'd picked my children up from school when I was at the hospital with Fred. They'd filled my freezer with casseroles when Fred was dying at home. They dried my tears and prayed for us when our world was falling apart. They'd absolutely been there for me and for us. In any case, I needed to figure this out for myself. That is what adults do.

How was I going to get back in the game of life? –That was the question. My children needed me to, even though in some ways I was ambivalent. I didn't know if I was ready. I felt I'd earned the right to grieve the loss of my husband –the man who had been the love of my life –but the more I indulged my grief the longer it kept me from rejoining the journey of life, and the full range of joys with my children, my family and my friends.

As I made my way up the highway towards home, I felt I was being nudged. Or perhaps it was more like a shove from the great beyond. The voice from within spoke without words but I understood the message loud and clear.

Do not allow the past to ruin the present. You will not get these moments back.

So I began to take baby steps to re-enter my life. Driving home along the snow-covered streets of my hometown I made a decision.

I thought, I might not be able to get away for Easter because my school will be in session, but I will not let circumstances and calendars take from me that which I have left.

I remembered what Mark Twain said, *"Don't let school interfere with your education."*

I decided to take the kids to Colorado skiing during my spring break. What the hell, we'll find a way to make this work.

In the days and weeks after I made that decision I felt a little more light-hearted.

Now the reality was that I had no shortage of friends. They would call to see if I wanted to have coffee or lunch. But on Friday or Saturday nights, I was always alone. I don't know why I hadn't noticed before, as it may have been that way for quite a while. After Fred died I'd been just fine staying home. I didn't really want to go out anyway.

Later it would dawn on me, Friday and Saturday nights are reserved for husbands and getting together with other couples. It took me by surprise, as I can be a bit obtuse. Oh, now I see how it's going to be. I just didn't get the memo. Now I get it. I am the odd woman out, that's me.

And I began to realize that another force was at work, keeping me in the *outsider* position. I recognized it when one of my friends, Cathy, started to refer to her husband as *My Keith,* as if that was his given name. She began claiming him, in my presence.

I recall the first time I noticed that she had begun referring to Keith as *My Keith.* Their son Brad and Cullen were classmates and it was not uncommon for the boys to hang out together after school or on the weekend. I remember going to their home to pick up my son. The boys dilly-dallied while gathering up Cullen's belongings, which somehow had been scattered hither and yon. I stood in the garage chatting to Keith about some inconsequential thing when Cathy came out. "Jeanne, whatever are you doing in the garage with *My Keith?*" Implying nothing nefarious but more that this was a man's domain. So she slipped her arm through mine and escorted me into the kitchen while I was still mid-sentence. Keith just smiled as Cathy swept me into the house for a glass of tea, which I neither needed nor wanted.

In that moment I realized that this was a subtle reminder, just in case I had forgotten, Keith belonged to her or at least with her. I'm fairly certain she meant no offense but it drove home the point that I did not have a partner and she did.

Initially, I thought I was imagining this. But as I listened carefully I gained an awareness that she spoke of *My Keith,* only in my presence.

Did this woman that I counted as a friend really think of me as a threat to her marriage? Keith and I had always been friendly to one another, I really liked him as a person –but Cathy, she was my friend. I had a hard time believing it. But she was like the dog peeing on the bushes. She was clearly marking her territory. Okay I got it. Somehow I sensed a need to tread lightly with Cathy. There was something fragile about our friendship, particularly where Keith was concerned.

I was outside the circle.

Occasionally I would get a call, "Hi Jeanne." This was followed by the perfunctory chatter about the kids or my job or some little old piece of gossip worthy of exchange. And then –the real reason for the call, "What are you doing this weekend?"

I brightened eagerly. The answer was always the same, "Nothing much really. I'll be home with the kids."

"Oh, Dave and I just got an invitation to go skiing in Aspen with Jackie and Jim. It's just for a long weekend, only four days … "

Silly me. I'd thought perhaps this was going to be an invitation to some wonderful gathering or event or at least an opportunity to get out of the house … but instead I had just left the door wide open.

"Do you think you could possibly watch the kids?" Her voice was dripping with sweetness and her hopefulness was palpable even through the phone.

Damn. Of course. I had already indicated that my social calendar was clear from now until eternity.

I wanted to say, "No, I can't. Not this weekend. Busy." Or "No, I don't want to." Why was it always so hard for me to speak up and speak my truth?

My mouth opened and I heard myself say, "Sure. When are you leaving?" and we entered into a lengthy discussion of what a doll I really was –but every time she said "doll" or "sweetheart" or "lifesaver," I substituted sucker.

This was unfair. I know. These people were really good to me when Fred was sick and dying and now it was payback time. The truth was I didn't mind, all that much, because I really didn't have anything else going on in my life, and my kids liked to have friends spend the weekend. So why not? It was okay with me.

And yet on another level it wasn't. I had become the reliable one. I was always available to watch someone else's kids so my friends and acquaintances could get away for a romantic weekend or vacation with their spouse. It wasn't okay because once upon a time I too had a full calendar, but widowhood left me all alone in the social wilderness.

And so I said yes when I meant no –not if it meant being the nanny while other couples had romance and fun. I wanted to be included and yet I didn't want to be included –not if I was made to feel like a widow on the prowl for someone else's husband. I was not that woman.

The other confusing thing was on some level I wanted to be married again. I was happy when I was married and still I wasn't in a hurry to move on.

At night, once my children were asleep, I would crawl into my bed alone again. I rarely had trouble falling asleep and yet every night my last conscious thought was always of Fred. Regularly I would wake in the night all alone. Fred's side of the bed was cold. No one breathed quietly into the night except for me. There were many long and lonely nights when I would finally drift off to sleep just before dawn only to awaken just before the alarm sounded to announce the beginning of another ... long ... day ... on my own.

CHAPTER 2

The Wonderful
World of
Mid-Life Dating

If I really was going to take a chance on life and get back in the game I had a few things I needed to look at. I have no time for people who at this stage of life are bringing nothing to the party. So just what was I looking for? If it was my expectation that others be healthy, smart, interesting, capable of giving and receiving love, I guess I'd better take a good long look in the mirror. Was I damaged goods or did I still have something to offer?

I'd endured a great deal in the eight years that Fred was ill, but the flip side of hardship is that I'd also developed some hard-core competencies.

So here was my self-appraisal. Sometimes these were my strengths, but not always:

1. I'm smart and hardworking.

2. I generally have my act together.
3. I'm quick witted and I also have a quick tongue, and I'll be the first to say that these are not always assets.
4. I've a pretty good sense of who I am and also who I'm not.
5. I can be graceful, kind and soft-spoken when the situation requires it, as this is part of my true nature. However, I can also turn on a dime like a wild animal if I feel threatened or those whom I hold dear are threatened.
6. I'm usually well mannered and well spoken and I can hold my own in most situations but I'm not always approachable and can be dismissive when I'm just not interested.
7. I'm sassy.
8. I've a strong moral compass and I try to do the right thing and most of the time I'm successful.
9. I say what I mean and mean what I say.
10. I'm usually confident and able to size up a situation quickly.

So I ask myself how did this smart and savvy woman lose her way?

So in an effort to heal myself I took my own good advice because I knew I couldn't run from my grief, and I didn't want to. I didn't want it to come back at me later in life only to rear its ugly head, and bite me in my unsuspecting ass. I know enough about trauma and loss to know that if people don't deal with what they're feeling ... the results are not pretty.

So I looked for a grief group. The woman from the funeral home knew of one. It was specifically for widows. The one in my community was being held at the senior center. That should've tipped me off but sometimes I'm a little slow on the uptake. Okay, more than sometimes. So I went and everyone there was at least 20 years my senior but most of the women were in their 80's. They were friendly and welcomed me. The facilitator asked us to share our stories – about how long ago we lost our spouses and what we had found that helped us cope with our grief. They started on the far side of the room and made their way towards me. The women shared stories of losing their husbands.

One woman talked about how she took a helium balloon with her on daily trips to the cemetery. She leaned against her husband's gravestone and released the balloon into the sky and promised to join him soon.

The chatter in my brain played on. *Really? It could be 50 years before I joined Fred.* This wasn't an option for me.

I thought about what I would say when it was my turn. It was here before I was ready. I talked about Fred and about my children and about being widowed at 41 years old. I didn't want to cry but the tears came anyway.

As I sat down, an older woman sitting next to me took my hand to offer some well-intended kindness. "You are lucky you have the children to keep you company. I don't have anyone." I nodded in her direction but fell silent. She didn't need to know what I really thought. I bit my tongue so I didn't tell her.

No. I did not feel lucky and neither did my children. We got screwed. There had been a great cosmic fuck up and we were the victims, not the benefactors. Women divorce their ne'er-do-well husbands all the time because they're abused or neglected and they're lucky to be free of the bastards, but I did everything in my power to hold onto my beloved, and he was the one who was taken. No, I didn't feel lucky or anything else that even vaguely resembled lucky. Children are not supposed to lose their fathers before they are out of grade school. I know plenty of fathers who would never be missed in the eyes of their children because they were never around for their children anyway.

This woman was married for 60 years. Her children had their father well into their adult lives. Her grandchildren got to know their grandfather. No, I didn't feel lucky. I was pissed. I was grieving the loss of a wonderful man. It was not just my loss ... it was a loss for humanity. My anger overwhelmed me. This lovely elderly woman didn't have a clue what it was like to walk in my shoes, and I needed to remember that it wasn't my responsibility to tell her.

I thought of my wise and wonderful grandmother. Her words came to me. I could almost hear her voice, *"Poor dear, she means well."*

The facilitator suggested we break for about 10 minutes so we could get some coffee, cookies, and use the bathroom. I grabbed my purse, headed for my car and didn't return. *No, that did not go particularly well.*

These women were elderly. These women weren't my peers. What could I possibly have been thinking?

Was I so desperate for someone who might just possibly understand what I was feeling that I thought I might find them here?

I didn't belong here. I was 41 years old and in good health. I was now a single parent with two young children. I needed to get on with the business of living. I wasn't at the end of my life, and I had no intention of throwing away what remained of it. God bless them, but my issues were different from theirs, and thus my healing would need to be different as well.

I wasn't comfortable there.

I felt compassion for them, but no intimacy.

I wasn't at home.

I would need to seek my comfort and solace elsewhere.

I tried a few therapists and counselors, but always felt I was just getting started when the hour was up, and my next appointment would be a week away. It wasn't particularly helpful and I didn't feel I was making any progress. So instead of getting the professional help that I probably needed, I spent the first year of my widowhood watching sad movies, reading sad books, and crying my heart out.

I kept a grocery bag full of paperback books next to my bed. My girlfriend's mother had loaned the books to me. Marilyn's dad had pass away 20 years ago when she was in college. So the books were outdated but I didn't care. I'm a bit of a bibliophile and I read a wide variety of books. Always have. This bag was a grab bag of fiction and non-fiction, religious, and secular, but all of them dealt with love and loss. These books were a Godsend.

When sleep eluded me, which it often did, I would reach into the bag and start to read. As I read and indulged my grief I began to feel just a little less alone. There was some comfort in knowing that I wasn't the only person who felt as I did. Even if I didn't know these people personally, even if I couldn't pick up the phone and call them, their words on the printed page soothed my grief in a way that no one else had been able to. I could lose myself in their stories. I would rage with their anger and sink into their depths of despair. These authors and their stories provided me a lifeline. If they'd survived this and lived to tell about it, then maybe, just maybe, I could too. They became my sisters and I became their confidant, as they trusted me with their sacred truths.

I spent that first year in the company of my children. I needed them and they needed me.

We attended family gatherings and school events. We set the table for three instead of four and spent our evenings in one another's company.

One afternoon I was standing on the sidelines of the soccer field watching Cullen's game while Gillian went to the playground to swing on the swings. A man I didn't recognize came over to me and extended his hand, "Hi Jeanne. I'm Bill Stone."

"Hi," I reached over to shake his hand while I waited for a more complete introduction, because clearly he knew who I was, but I couldn't place him.

"I'm married to Melinda Morris and I met your ex-husband last spring." He held my hand and smiled.

I went cold. I felt like I had been kicked in the stomach. I dropped his hand and stammered, "Do you mean Fred? I don't have an ex-husband. My husband is deceased." I don't know why it hit me so hard, but it just did.

The poor guy just misspoke, but he fell all over himself apologizing. I was really shaken up. I don't think I even asked about his wife Melinda. Once upon a time she had been a very close friend of mine.

I was a mess.

What the hell was the matter with me?
Do you want the long list or the short list?

One evening I took my kids and a couple of their friends to the movies. After the show I found my two hovering near the concession stand with their heads together concocting a plan. As it turned out, they both had been invited to spend the night with their friends after the movie.

"You stayed with her last weekend. It's okay. I'll go home and be with her tonight." My nine-year-old daughter was telling her twelve-year-old brother.

Great. Now my children are actively negotiating who was going to stay home and take care of their grieving mother. It was there and then I decided that it was time for me to get on with my life. In fairness to my children, in fairness to myself, and in honor of Fred's memory, I needed to re-enter the world of the living.

Fred had been a great role model in so many ways. In the midst of dying he was able to live in the present. He had taught me this and somehow I had lost my way. I needed to relearn how to be present in my own life.

At the end of the first year, people commented on how well we were doing. However, that was merely an optical illusion, purposely devised, to let people off the hook. Others saw what they wanted to see and what I wanted them to see: We were survivors and we would be okay.

〜

One evening while I sat with my friend Cathy beside her pool watching the kids do cannon balls off the diving board, Cathy suggested I should begin to date again. "Fred wouldn't want you sitting at home in widow's tweeds," she began.

Whatever that meant … I'd never worn tweed in my life. Then it dawned on me; *oh, she means widows weeds, the mourning garb of Victorian widows.* I kept my mouth closed and just listened. This was one of the beautiful things about my friendship with Cathy. She talked and I listened. It worked well for both of us.

"Besides," as she so kindly informed me, "your beauty won't last forever." She looked me in the eye as she picked up the pitcher and began to refill my glass with sweet peach tea. "If you want another man you had best get on with it."

I didn't know what to say. No one really needed to remind me that we were all getting older, and that this gift called life has an expiration date. I knew this all too well. I was 42 years old and my husband had been dead just shy of a year.

When I was a younger woman, some people thought I was quite attractive. Not everyone mind you.

I'm a natural redhead and that alone means that I'm certainly not everyone's type. But if you like redheads with blue eyes and freckles, I was okay, even at 42.

Cathy didn't seem to notice that I hadn't responded and still she launched into her monologue. "I know a guy. He went to high school with *My Keith*. He's recently divorced, a father of two, just like you he has a son and a daughter. He's tall, blonde and handsome, and he's a lawyer, just like Fred." She was all excited. She painted a picture of a lovely man wronged by his devious ex-wife. She implied that I was about to meet the second coming of Christ.

At last she stopped talking long enough to take a breath and a swallow of iced tea. She waited for my response.

"I don't know if I'm ready." I considered her offer to set us up on a blind date. Truthfully, I was flattered that she thought enough of me to do so. But the real crux of the matter was that I was panicked at the very thought of going on a date. I did a quick calculation in my head. I was married for 13 years, dated Fred for a year and he had been gone now for a year ... that's 15 years. "I haven't had a date in 15 years." I spoke the words aloud. "I know I told you I was going to try and get out more. And I'm trying. But hanging with friends is worlds away from starting to date again." I tried to help her see. But she was having none of it.

"Trust me ... he won't last for long out there in the sea of single women. Someone will snatch him up." She said this with great confidence as if I may have already missed my chance just by taking a moment to consider.

So against my better judgment, I agreed to meet him.

A double date was planned; *My Keith* and Cathy and Mr. Roger Wright and myself. We would meet in Birmingham at the Mid-Town Café for an early dinner in late September.

But *My Keith* had to accompany his son Brad to the hospital after he turned his ankle in a soccer game. So there we were, Mr. Roger Wright, Cathy, and bachelorette #1, otherwise known as me. The dinner was a nightmare while Cathy talked incessantly and she looked lovingly between Roger and myself, smiling sweetly as if she knew we were destined to be a match made in heaven. Roger and I couldn't get a word in edgewise. And when he did speak … frankly I was underwhelmed to say the least.

Oh God, I wanted a *good* strong drink, maybe a couple, and a fairy Godmother who would whisk me away before I turned into a pumpkin. Just get me out of here.

Mercifully, the evening came to an end and we parted company without exchanging phone numbers. I was relieved. He wasn't interested in me. I was okay with that. It would have been flattering if he had been mesmerized by my scintillating conversation and stunning beauty, but that was clearly not the case.

Six weeks passed and I hadn't seen or heard from Mr. Wright, until Halloween. He showed up on my doorstep with *My Keith* and Cathy. I was hosting our annual Halloween Party complete with trick or treating for my children and all of their friends, and adult beverages for their parents. *Who invited him?* But I knew my role, and that was to be the ever so gracious hostess. So I went out of my way to make him feel welcome and comfortable amongst my guests and in my home.

And so, at the end of the party Roger Wright asked me out on a date. And then another. And then another. Did I mention that I have difficulty telling people no? I never want to hurt anyone's feelings so instead what I'm feeling gets put on ice and ignored. Over the course of the next few months I would learn firsthand that Cathy didn't know all there was to know about dear old Roger. She neglected to tell me, when she was enumerating his many illustrious qualities, that he was about as interesting as dry toast or that he had the propensity to be a stalker.

I dated Mr. Wright for a few months and by then my children had begun to lovingly refer to him as Mr. Wrong. They were right, of course, as they so often were. When I couldn't bear another evening with him I started to pull away and made myself busy when he called. He started to show up places he knew I would be. My children's soccer games, the parking lot at their school, walking down the hallway outside my classroom with a bouquet of flowers. I was getting creeped out. Then there was the morning I found him parked in my driveway at 6:00 AM. I knew I had to extricate myself from this relationship and this man who had gotten it into his head and convinced himself that I might be just perfect for him. But I had also learned something from my foray into the wonderful world of mid-life dating and it was this –I prefer solitude to boredom and if someone gives you the creeps, don't hang around to see if you are right.

I had never really had difficulty dating in my younger years. The time I spent with Roger really made me question my ability to tell the good guys from the bad. I had a hard time believing everyone who found themselves single in mid-life was going to be a creep. After all, Fred was divorced when I met him and he was my Mr. Wonderful. And here I was single again. People are single in their middle years for a wide variety of reasons.

However, in the ensuing years the applicant pool of eligible men had been severely diminished, and there were those who believed that all the good men were home with their wives. Or to quote a friend, "Where are all the handsome and sensitive men? Well they're home with their boyfriends, of course."

But I was like a US Marine Corps recruiter, just looking for a few good men. Okay, make that one good man. But I knew I was seriously out of practice. My divining rod was rusty in terms of finding men, and being able to ascertain whether or not we might be compatible. It was beginning to feel like the process of elimination. One thing could be said in my favor, I was raising the bar ... or at least I thought I was. I started to eliminate the candidates that needed to grovel on their bellies and didn't bring anything of value to the party. I'd once been pretty good at being able to read the nuances of interpersonal relationships, and yet at this point in my life, I was uncertain how to resurrect and re-engage my long dormant intuitive self.

The questions loomed large. How would I know whom to trust? And the bigger question was if and when someone did show up in my life would I have the ability to recognize him? Or was every potential suitor or lover destined to be discarded because as fate would have it … he was not Fred Miller and never would be.

Next …

Once I had crossed the barrier and had begun to date again, there was no valid reason, at least none that I could come up with, not to continue to seek love and companionship. I wanted to see what life had in store for me and so I vowed to keep an open mind, as difficult as it could be at times.

I accepted dates from the least, the lost and the forgotten. I tried to keep in mind the lessons about life I had learned from Fred. I was willing to consider people who had been through some difficult things in their lives, and I wanted to learn and see how their suffering had transformed them. I knew firsthand how pain and loss could help to build a person's character. I was looking for someone who had lived and loved, and was better for it rather than embittered by life. I was not really interested in building a relationship and a life with someone whose greatest accomplishments focused on what they had acquired, except maybe in the area of personal growth and experience.

I let my friends introduce me to their friends or friends of friends. It was slim pickin's out there and don't let anyone tell you differently. In spite of all the statistics predicting the downfall of the American Family due to the high rates of divorce, the single men who were available for a dinner date were few and far between. It was difficult to find anyone I was even remotely interested in spending the evening with, let alone a lifetime. But I persevered and said, "Yes," when I should've been saying, "No, thank you."

Let me elaborate. There seemed to be a preponderance of single men who were looking for their mommy. I have dated some of them and lived to tell the tale. There are men who have been catered to in such a way that they truly believed I was someone who was positively enthralled with every little utterance that slipped forth from their lips. They yammered on and on about every little thing that ever happened to them. I wanted to scream, but I didn't because my mother raised me better than that.

When mercifully, the evening drew to a close and I knew positively everything about my date, including where he went to grade school, when he got his first teeth, and lo and behold he knew nothing about me. He never even asked.

Women are frequently portrayed as self-absorbed and chatty. The lyrics from a Toby Keith song played through my head as my date elaborated on about this, that and the other thing of which I had not one iota of interest …

We talk about your work how your boss is a jerk
We talk about your church and your head when it
hurts
We talk about the troubles you've been having with
your brother
About your daddy and your mother and your crazy
ex-lover
We talk about your friends and the places that
you've been
We talk about your skin and the dimples on your
chin
The polish on your toes and the run in your hose
And God knows we're gonna talk about your clothes
You know talking about you makes me smile
But every once in awhile

I wanna talk about me!

–Toby Keith

So this country singer sang about the female version of my date but let me assure you, this genetic aberration is clearly not a sex-linked trait, as I have seen it manifested over and over again in males of our species.

Do I have a tattoo on my forehead that says: *Tell me your Story?*

As Mr. Self Absorbed rambled on and on about himself, the little voice inside my head started up with a competing running commentary of its own and in the end it was screaming at me to make itself heard over my date's incessant chatter—

This guy does not even pretend to be interested in you. Run while you still can!

Next ...

Then there was the date with Mr. Cheap. I should've been suspicious when he told me his favorite restaurant was Taco Bell, but I've already confessed to being a little bit slow. No sense rushing to judgment about this one, he may indeed be God's gift to women in ways that weren't yet apparent. When the server arrived at the table to see if we'd like a cocktail, this charming gent answered for both of us and asked for water. He never even inquired if perhaps I would like a drink. *What? No drinks?* There was no way I was going to get through this without a drink. My brain may not have been fully engaged but my vocal cords were. I spoke up. "May I have a glass of the J Lohr Pinot Noir?"

The server nodded to me, "Certainly." We exchanged a knowing glance. No doubt he had seen his share of first dates.

Mr. Cheap looked surprised. For here I was, a woman who speaks up and expresses her own opinion, sitting right across the table from him, right here in the new millennium. Imagine that.

He didn't look pleased. Was this because I was drinking wine or was he concerned he might get stuck coughing up the $7.50? He was already disappointed and we hadn't even ordered dinner, poor dear. So he set his sights on the menu; after carefully scouring the options he suggested we share something. "The portions here are very large," he informed me. Then he proposed the chicken that just so happened to be the least expensive item on the menu.

This poor guy looked like he was about to lose his mind when I gently reminded him, "Chicken is not a vegetable and I'm a vegetarian. Remember?" He nodded his head acknowledging he remembered hearing something about this earlier in the evening.

"Look I'm really not all that hungry." I offered up a suggestion as I took another sip of wine, "Why don't you order the chicken and I'll have the side salad that comes with it." This wasn't any great magnanimous gesture on my part. I'm a bit of a foodie and this place offered fairly pedestrian fare.

But my date smiled broadly and I could tell he thought this was a wonderful idea. "Oh that's great, I never really eat salad anyway."

Man did I score Brownie points with that one. But just wait until I order a second glass of wine.

Clearly this would be one of those one-date wonders. I had already made up my mind. There would be no second date. But there wasn't any reason to be rude. I didn't want to frighten him off dating altogether so I tried to engage and be pleasant. When at long last the check arrived I pulled out my credit card and politely suggested, "Let's split it."

He looked visibly relieved and began talking about when we might see one another again.

Was this guy for real? Never would be too soon. So instead I made up some cock 'n bull story about work and travel, and perhaps being a little bit less busy around the end of next month. When I went home I changed his contact information in my cell phone. His number now comes up as –DO NOT ANSWER on my caller ID. I wouldn't make this mistake again.

I had often joked with Fred that he could pinch pennies with one hand while throwing buckets of money out the window with the other. He spent money only on that which he valued, and he valued me. I completely understand that people need to live within their means and within their budgets. I'm not a woman who needs lavish gifts to feel of value, but neither did I want to be with someone who treasures their bank accounts more than they valued their lives or their loved ones.

I was learning. I was taking note. There were some personal traits that I could abide with and others I could not. I called it the "Ick Factor." Once the Ick had been established there was no sense prolonging the inevitable. If they didn't make the initial cut there was no earthly reason I could come up with to prolong the agony and subject both of us to a second date.

It wasn't a mystery why some of these people were single, and I would guess they were destined to stay that way or perhaps go on to make someone else miserable, but I didn't want it to be me. Oh the joys of mid-life dating.

My girlfriend, Katie, compared dating to a yard sale. Some of these folks look pretty good from the road but when you took a closer look all you found was someone else's junk that nobody really wanted. Ouch!

Next …

Then there was the guy who ranted and raved about his ex-wife and how he got screwed in his divorce. He clearly had been tainted by life and love. The real question was this: why was he here with me if he was still so angry with his ex-wife, and anyone who remotely resembled his ex-wife, and that would include anyone born female in this century?

The warning bell was ringing loud and clear with this guy. He was hostile. He thought all women cheated on their husbands. Not only did he think it, but he actually said it to me, right out loud, "All women are cold and conniving bitches just looking for a sugar daddy." Nice.

Hmmm … I'm a woman; therefore he must cast me in the same light. Let me see, would I like to have a relationship with someone who is jealous, suspicious, and angry? That would be a big no, nope, and no thank you. Not this woman. And so there you have it another one-date wonder … just keep talking buddy so I can see you for who you really are.

Next …

And then there was the guy who was a self-professed homebody. Let's call him Ward, as in Ward Cleaver. He liked to be at home. He also wanted me to hang out at home … his home. He also wanted someone to cook, clean, help him decorate his home, and care for his children, Wally and the Beaver. Perhaps he didn't notice, but I already had a home and children of my own that needed my love, time, and attention.

One evening, he told me he was looking for a traditional woman and a traditional relationship. There was something in the way he said this that suggested he saw me as something else. I pondered this and questioned: just what exactly does it mean to be a traditional woman in this day and age? I was perplexed. I ruminated on it, and the question resurfaced in my mind again and again. I felt as if this man was casting judgments on me. There are things I have grown to value and see as accomplishments in my life, but he implied that my strength and independence had somehow diminished my femininity. I don't know why this upset me so much, but it did.

When I was younger I may have been that traditional woman, but my situation had changed. My husband had died so I was no longer someone's wife. Newsflash –I was not willing to play that role for a man who didn't understand the first thing about love. This man had no comprehension about why his marriage failed or what part he may have played in its demise. Unless he woke up and smelled the coffee he was destined to repeat his past. He had no grasp of the fact that to be in a loving relationship one must actually be willing to love, and consider the needs of their partner. Selfishness and love are incompatible.

Ward also found it deeply unsettling that I knew my way around Lowes and Home Depot. He was astonished to learn I actually knew what a plumb line was and didn't need him to explain it to me. To cover

his anxiety, he made a little joke as he questioned my
sexual orientation. What an asshole. I was a single
mother, and I didn't have the luxury of turning
over every little household repair to a man, so I had
learned the very basics of home repair. This is what
capable, responsible people do. These skills are not
tied to gender or sexual preference. I reiterate, what
an asshole.

I had evolved due to the circumstances of my
life –now I played all the roles of parent. Once I
was firmly enmeshed in my role as a tender loving
caregiver, but my children also needed discipline as
well as tenderness. Like it or not, if I didn't provide
it they would be the ones that suffered. I didn't have
the option to say, "Wait 'til your father gets home!" I
didn't want to take this on, but I did the best I could
for the sake of my beloved children. I toughen up
because that was what was needed for our survival.

I knew some men found me intimidating. Too bad.
Just too damn bad.

I had learned the lessons all too well. Life is short. I
had found my inner strength and I used it. I protected
that which I held dear for I had been entrusted with
that sacred responsibility.

As I drove home from a disturbing evening of
domesticity with Mr. Ward Cleaver, I found myself
humming a little ditty from Bob Dylan and then
breaking into song at the refrain,
It ain't me babe
No, no, no it ain't me babe
It ain't me you're looking for.

Oh yes, this was my new theme song.
No more sympathy dates for me.

Next ...

My dearest friends in the world, Dave and Laura, set me up on a blind date with their friend Tim. Tim was divorced and a dentist with three kids. He lived in an exclusive neighborhood east of Detroit. His home was only 2 hours away from mine, unless you travelled during rush hour or a snowstorm. He worked four days a week in Okemos, which is about 2 hours from Saint Clair Shores. The perfect isosceles triangle, but a nightmare for a relationship. He was geographically undesirable but as luck would have it ... we hit it off.

We dated for about 18 months. The relationship worked for me, including the distance. We didn't see each other very often, but when we did it was good. It allowed both of us to have time with our growing children.

As my children moved into their teenage years, they were spending more and more time with their friends, and I had more and more time alone. If I understand anything, then it is this: time is precious; it is the real currency of our lives. How and where you spend this very precious commodity is indicative of what you value. People need to set priorities.

I was okay getting in line behind Tim's kids and his job. He was in line behind mine and we both knew it. But we had so little time together given how far apart we lived. And yet, he scheduled a week's vacation with a high school friend to go to Isle Royale and hike, and then on the heels of this vacation he went to his sister's cottage for Labor Day, without extending me an invitation to accompany him. I wasn't okay with that. I understand setting priorities. It's part and parcel to establishing a successful life.

But the summer was coming to a close and soon the football season would be starting. Tim was a hard-core football fan of his alma mater. And there was just no way I was going to stay in a relationship where I was behind Notre Dame football on any man's priority list.

Tim was good to me, but not good enough. I thought I deserved better. Fred had been the gold standard against which I compared other relationships, and this one just didn't measure up. Not even close.

I loved my friend Laura like a sister. We had been friends since our sophomore year at Michigan State, nearly 23 years. She was my closest friend in the whole world and she knew me very well. She had been there when I met Fred and was there when I buried him. I knew she wanted the best for me, but we had a difference of opinion about what that was. Laura was angry when I broke it off with Tim. On more than one occasion she had needled him about marrying me. He didn't like it one bit and neither did I. She had set us up on our first date. She thought that we were perfect together and she voiced this regularly. The problem was that I didn't. And as close as we were, she didn't get to vote. This was just the way it was. Again the wisdom of my Grandmother played on in my head ... *save me from the well intended.*

So there I was a single woman, on the outside, looking in at the marriages of my friends. Envy is not pretty. I didn't really envy any of them. There was not a man amongst them that I coveted for my own, but I missed the day-to-day ease, the partnership, and the passion that I had known in my own marriage to Fred.

The prospects for romance were bleak. Was I being too picky? I didn't think so. I was not about to settle for just any man in pants; after all I did have standards. But it was getting harder and harder to find anyone who met any of my criteria, yet alone someone who met them all. I continued to look as I scratched one after another off the list of potential partners.

I consulted the few single women I did know. Some of them hadn't had a date in years. Years? I couldn't believe my ears. These were nice, smart women with a lot going for themselves. Maybe the mid-life dating scene really was as bleak as it seemed.

My kids were growing up and I was spending more and more nights alone on the couch curled up with a book.

At one point my mother pointed out that most people never have even one great love in their whole entire life. She reminded me, and I knew she was right; I had been among the fortunate few. "Next time, you might just need to settle for something less." Mom went on to recount, by name, the people she knew personally who had remarried after a death or divorce and had settled into perfectly adequate lives.

Perfectly adequate? Is that what I had to look forward to?

I could just hear Fred's voice launch into a TV infomercial, "On one hand we have the full-bodied love, complete with romance and passion and leaving you fully satisfied, or perhaps you want to settle for *Love Lite*, satisfies your taste for something sweet but leaves you longing for the real deal. Ladies and gentlemen the choice is yours ... *Love Lite or The Real Deal?*" He was forever making jokes in a way that illuminated the heart of the matter.

Oh My God.

Love Lite?

Oh Mom, say it ain't so!

What was I looking for? I had grown up in a traditional home with a Mom and a Dad, and a brother and a sister. I was a nurse, and a teacher, and a mother. You really can't script a more traditional life for a woman. I had a fairy tale romance and love affair with my husband, complete with heartache and tragedy, and now in my forties I was widowed and a single mother ... what did I want?

I wanted a man who would know me and love me. I wanted the fairy tale but this time with a happy ending. I wanted to live happily ever after.

Was this so very wrong?

Was this too much to ask for?

Next ...

When I first heard his voice on my answering machine I was a little perplexed. Why was Paul O'Shea calling me? He called again and asked me out for dinner. I was a bit taken aback. Was this what Mom was talking about, Love Lite? Oh, what the hell, it's just dinner. Dear old Tim had just spent Labor Day weekend at his sister's and the college football season was beginning so I was feeling like the least important person on the planet. I agreed to go.

But then there was the back story–
Who is this man?
Who is Paul O'Shea?

CHAPTER 3

Who is this Paul O'Shea?

I knew Paul O'Shea. I had known him for years. Well let's say we were acquaintances because our children went to grade school together. He had a son who was in Cullen's grade and a daughter the same age as Gillian.

Now Fred and I adored our children. They were our love incarnate. But they were also a couple of free birds. There was that old nature vs. nurture question. Were they free birds because this was just part of their nature to be so or did we nurture and teach them that? The answer is probably yes on both counts. Certainly some of their personal characteristics were deeply inscribed in their genetic code. Then there was our home life. Their father and I liked to take a bit of credit for helping them on their way, but not always. Sometimes despite our best efforts they were a human handful. Secretly I delighted in them, in their entirety, even when they were naughty, I still thought they were pretty wonderful.

Cullen has always been precocious and he was born a leader. He had been like this all his young life. If Cullen had an idea of something he wanted to do, in no time at all he had a gang of many who wanted to follow along. It was not always good, but it was nearly always fun.

I can remember picking him up from preschool, and all of the children exited the classroom with their heads hung in shame. The poor preschool teacher was just about beside herself, for when she had gone into the hallway momentarily, my darling son had taken her set of Sharpie permanent markers and drawn multi-colored mustaches on all his little classmates' faces.

His antics and escapades would only accelerate, as he grew older.

By the time he was in grade school, he was the de facto head of the tribe. He and his compatriots were a force to be reckoned with. He was as smart a child as God ever put on the planet. He was handsome, quick-witted, strong, and athletic. He was so like his father and everyone loved him. They wanted to be with him and so he gathered in his friends, and they remain loyal and loving to one another into adulthood.

Now Gillian has always marched to the beat of her own drummer. While Cullen was off scoring goals on the soccer field, Gillian was taking care of every little creature that needed some love and nurturing or else she was hanging upside down by her knees on the monkey bars. She is a blonde-haired beauty with luminous skin, but as a little girl she often looked like she had been dragged behind the bus with her hair flying in all directions. Her knees were perpetually skinned and her blouses were stained with chocolate ice cream.

Her daddy sang her theme song ...

She was just about the happiest girl that I ever knew ...

—Matthew Southern Comfort

And she was.

These were our kids ... at least before their Daddy died ...

But I digress ...

My first recollection of meeting Paul O'Shea was late in autumn 1992.

It had been about one year since Fred had his first bone marrow transplant and Cullen was in second grade and Gillian was in preschool. Our kids were happy, active, and well adjusted in spite of all the drama in our lives.

Cullen was playing soccer on his first organized team and was already showing signs of athletic prowess. We would spend Sunday afternoons at various local elementary schools watching the children play, and I was learning to play the role of parent-spectator. I had never cared one iota for spectator sports so I was abundantly surprised by how much I loved to watch my son play. He played with such unrestrained joy and enthusiasm.

Gillian was four years old then, and even as a small child she had a wonderful disposition, and was always a good sport about going along and getting along. If there was some place to go, she wanted to go too. So I tried to be certain during halftime at the soccer games that she and I went to the school playground. I wanted the day to be fun for her too.

When we arrived, there was a father and his little daughter already at the playground. The little girl was about Gillian's age. She had fallen off the jungle gym and knocked out her front tooth.

I explained to the little girl's dad that sometimes a dentist could re-implant the tooth if we could find it. So Gillian and I helped the father look amongst the pea gravel for the little girl's tooth, but unfortunately to no avail.

The father offered up an explanation about the way this daughter was dressed. I hadn't asked. The little girl was dressed in shorts and a t-shirt. It was about 40 degrees, overcast, and threatening to rain. The poor little thing was freezing. She wasn't dressed appropriately for the weather. He blamed his ex-wife. She was to blame. I offered to get the little girl a blanket from our car, but he declined because they were going to leave in search of a dentist. This man was Paul O'Shea.

Paul had a son who was on Cullen's soccer team. His son was in Cullen's grade and class at St. Sabula's. Alex was that kid, who dressed for the games, but stood on the sidelines refusing to take the field with the other boys. His only participation was in the half time feeding and end of the game snacks. Fred and I, and all the other parents, had watched week after week as his father coaxed and cajoled his son to participate, but the boy refused. I can still visualize Paul as he threw up his hands in frustration and ineptitude.

My next recollection of Paul O'Shea was in the spring of 1994. It was First Communion Sunday. Again, Cullen was on the same soccer team as Paul's son, Alex. The team was short-handed because many of the children and their families were hosting First Communion parties, and were unable to attend the game. Alex had refused to play all spring, just as he had in the fall, but this situation was different. The team would be required to forfeit the game, if they didn't have enough players to field a team. This time the kids begged and pleaded with Alex to take the field. Some of the parents joined in and tried to convince Alex that he should play. I watched as Paul stood there with his hands in his pockets, and shrugged his shoulders as if to say, "I can't make him do anything."

Alex relished the position he found himself in. There was an impish grin on his face while he held this power over his teammates. Eventually, as the officials were about to forfeit the game, he agreed to take the field. But he wouldn't play. He only agreed to stand on the field, in one place, while the other boys maneuvered the ball around him.

In the end the children from St. Sabula's won the game. The kids and their parents all congratulated Alex, and he glowed with their praise. He didn't have any understanding that all the kids thought he was a manipulative loser and that his father was pathetic as a parent.

I remember thinking there was something terribly wrong with this child and with this father's ability to parent his own son. The cheering and the congratulating of Alex for standing on the field so the team wouldn't have to forfeit didn't sit right with me. I feared this kind of unearned praise would only serve to reinforce his manipulative behavior. Psych 101 – don't reinforce the bad behavior. Yikes. This kid was immobilized with fears of being inadequate on the soccer field, which was why he didn't want to play. It wasn't rocket science. How come no one took this kid in the backyard and played soccer with him to help him grow in confidence and competence? Why was everyone congratulating him for doing nothing?

The whole event would haunt me: poor, pathetic family. Where docs the word pathos come from? Oh, that would be pathology as in suffering and diseased. I'm a nurse and I'm a teacher and I have seen how these scenarios play out. I believe there are critical learning periods in the lives of children, and if certain things aren't learned during those periods, there can be a lost opportunity. Without some essential skills for living, a child builds his life without a firm foundation, and eventually the entire structure will come falling down. I had a real sense that without some critical changes in the way this boy was being raised, he would be destined for big, big problems.

But I let it go. Who was I to worry about someone else's family? I had problems in my own family as Fred struggled daily with the physical consequences of his bone marrow transplant.

Later in the spring, Cullen and the rest of the soccer team were invited to the O'Shea's for Alex's birthday party following one of their games.

After the game, Cullen was in cahoots with a couple of the other boys and their parents to blow off the birthday party and go out for pizza instead. When I caught wind of this, I put my foot down. No way. This little boy was already so socially handicapped, he certainly didn't need to have a birthday party and have no one attend.

Cullen was mad, "Mom, no one wants to go. He's a weirdo, and I don't like him."

"I don't care. You said you would go earlier in the week, the gift is in the car and you will be going. It's just not nice not to show up. They're planning on you," another lecture by mom meant to instill the essential rules of etiquette.

I was trying to encourage a sense of goodness and compassion in my son. I wanted him to learn to be inclusive and welcoming of people who were different than himself. But perhaps it was Cullen who saw more clearly than I did. There was something wrong here, and he wanted no part of it.

Once it was decided that Cullen would be going to the party, all the other boys on the team went to the party as well. They had a good time and came home with extravagant goody bags, but unfortunately no more endeared to Alex than they had been before.

Over the ensuing years I would bump into Paul at school events such as Christmas concerts, soccer games, and parent-teacher meetings. We were acquaintances, nothing more. He and his children traveled in different circles than my children and I did.

The rumor, perpetuated by the circle of mothers, was that his ex-wife, Marianne, was not very bright and not a good mother. I remember my first encounter with Paul and he was singing that song at the time. I had an inkling of a thought that perhaps it was Mr. O'Shea who was responsible for perpetuating the rumor that besmirched this woman's good name.

It was well known that Paul had been in a protracted custody battle for his children and in the end he had been designated the custodial parent. The stories circulated amongst the parents that Alex was continually in trouble for acting out at school and that little Dana had asked some of the women, "Will you be my mommy and take me home?" Clearly these kids were struggling, but Paul seemed devoted to his children even if he was inept.

I thought about how difficult it must be as single parent. I tried not to judge him too harshly. Parenting is challenging when both parents are physically present. There is no instruction manual, and let's face it, some children are more difficult to raise than others. I tried to keep my mouth shut and just listened as the women I was friends with offered up criticisms of this family. At the time I knew how very fragile Fred's health was, and at any given turn in the road I could be a single parent too.

There but for the Grace of God go I.

Spring 1997

Again I was sitting on the bleachers at the soccer game, Cassia Caputo another soccer mom, was talking about being a bridesmaid at Paul O'Shea's wedding. She was going on and on about all the fu-fu and glam of the upcoming event and her reluctance to be a bridesmaid at 45. Paul was marrying a younger woman. Tina was 20 years his junior. She was a beautiful blonde that worked in publishing for Vanity Fair.

I remember feeling happy for him, but also for his children as Cassia gossiped on and on about the wedding to all those who would listen.

Fred was very ill at the time and I lived with the nagging unspoken fear that at any time I might lose him. I pushed the notion from my head and remember feeling happy for Paul O'Shea.

These are the only conscious memories I have of Paul from the time before Fred died.

∽

Eighteen months later, on October 9, 1998, Fred would pass on into eternity. My greatest fears were realized. My kids and I would struggle to make a life for ourselves without Fred. Some days were more difficult than others.

The kids were suffering from the loss of their Dad. Still, time had moved all of us on, little by little …

Somewhere, somehow, someone must have counseled Cullen about his need to be the man of the house, now that his dad had passed. This was a big responsibility for an 11 year old to take on. But Cullen tried. He did his best in school, and in his sports, and in the first year after Fred died he really stepped up. His shenanigans didn't go away entirely, but they were held in check. He was always loving and kind towards his sister and me, but now he had redoubled his innate consideration for us and what we needed. He was trying his best to be a good boy.

I remember how badly he wanted to play on a travel basketball team with his friends from school. Now Cullen would eventually grow to be 6 feet tall, but at twelve years old, although intellectually and socially mature, he still looked like a little boy and thus didn't receive much playing time. I conceded he might benefit by playing on this team, but I was personally overwhelmed with grief and responsibility. I didn't need one more thing to do. So we compromised. I agreed he could play. I would be at all his games and bring him home if he would be responsible for his uniform and arranging his rides to the games with one of his friend's mothers, as none of them worked outside the home.

I can tell you I didn't exactly feel like *The Mother of the Year.* On one cold and snowy January evening in a drafty old gym, my 5-foot tall, 85 lb twelve year old son stood shaking on the basketball court in a soaking wet uniform. He had washed it and forgotten to put it in the dryer. It was part of our deal … he was responsible for his uniform.

He'd known of his mistake early that morning before he left for school. But he never mentioned it to me. Instead he put the wet uniform in a plastic bag and into his backpack. He voiced no complaint. He cast no blame on me. He quietly bore the consequences of his error.

I, on the other hand, berated myself greatly. He was just a little boy. He had always been precocious, but our life circumstances were pushing him to grow up even more quickly. I didn't want to hasten this. I desperately wanted to hold onto my children. I was torn with needing them to be helpful and responsible, and yet I clung ferociously to their childhood.

No, I wasn't in any position to criticize anyone else for mistakes they may have made in raising their own children.

The next summer we would celebrate Gillian's 10th birthday. Now Gillian's birthday is in August, and we lived on a lake so there was never any question where she would have her birthday party. I did my best to have her birthday party the way she wanted it, but this year things were different. They just were. After all the little girls had gone home, she just broke down and cried. She was inconsolable. She kept crying on and on, and yet she couldn't find the words to tell me why she was so sad. Eventually it all came out that she didn't want to be ten years old. She was now in the double digits, and she was getting closer and closer to 100, and then she would be dead.

She was missing her Daddy. Her Daddy was dead and she was afraid of death, and afraid of dying. I remember how she cried out in pain and anguish. My heart was breaking for her. I could do nothing to protect my daughter from this pain. Her pain and fears were not from a bad dream or an imaginary monster under her bed. No, her pain and fears were based in her reality. But I held her in my arms and rocked her like a baby until she cried herself to sleep. I so wanted her to feel safe and secure, but regardless of what I said to try and ease her fears, she knew about tragedy and injustice. She was just a little girl. She knew about death because her Daddy was dead.

But it wasn't always like this. We had good days too. The children had convinced me, "Dad would want us to have a dog." Fred had been allergic to animal dander so we couldn't have one while he was alive. But I thought they were probably right, their Dad would want them to have a dog.

So we went to the dog show and picked out a breed we all agreed on. Next we contacted a breeder and waited for a puppy to be born. We went to see the puppy and even named him, Duncan because this was Fred's middle name. The kids had already fallen in love with him.

But the day before we were to bring our puppy home the breeder called, "This particular little fellow is ever so beautiful. He has perfect conformation. He is absolutely show quality," I listened and waited for the real reason she had called. As she wrapped up the lengthy lists of merits that had been bred into this puppy, she got to the bottom line. She was going to renege on her promise to give us this puppy unless I promised to show him and not have him neutered so he could be a stud.

No possible way!

I had enough difficulty getting my children where they needed to be. Now I was supposed to go to dog shows and arrange for my dog's sexual encounters. I couldn't even arrange any sexual encounters for myself! I may be a crazy woman but I wasn't that crazy.

Needless to say the kids were disappointed. They tried to convince me going to dog shows might be fun … like I said, "No way. It's not going to happen. Not in this lifetime."

So instead of a small, non-shedding male terrier, the next day we bought a female yellow lab puppy, and we still named her Duncan. And oh by the way, labs shed like you cannot believe. My neat and clean home was now filled with dog hair. But things happen for a reason and she became our love and she loved us generously in return.

Okay, maybe I am crazy. But if bringing Duncan home was a bad decision, I hope I make many more. The kids walked her, talked to her, trained and loved that dog. And our house was filled with laughter and joy, and again the kids were right, "Daddy would have wanted us to have a dog."

When Gillian was in 6th grade she was having a particularly difficult time with some of the other middle school girls. It was like a scene right out of the book *Queen Bees and Wannabees*. Some days the girls were nice to her, and some days they were little bitches in training, not unlike some of their role model mothers.

It broke my heart to watch her suffer. In the evenings, Gillian would recount the day's events. I would hold her and dry her tears, and then we would strategize ways to make middle school less painful.

One night she received a phone call from Dana O'Shea, Paul's daughter. She had called to tell Gillian that she had a new baby sister, Fiona. Gillian was all excited. I know she was delighted to hear about the baby because she loves babies, but Dana was also on the fringes of the popular clique, and I was certain it felt good to be on the call list. Gillian indicated a heartfelt desire to buy a gift for Dana's new baby sister. I consented but I had a gnawing concern that her relationship with this gaggle of girls was tenuous at best. I was as certain as spring would follow winter they would turn on her, and exclude her, and hurt her again. The most beautiful baby gift in the world would not cement her relationship with these girls. I braced myself for more pain and suffering.

Gilly picked out a baby gift, we wrapped it and she delivered it to Dana at school. I was happy for Paul and his family.

No thank you note was ever received. The gift was never acknowledged.

The following January, Dana celebrated her 12th Birthday and all of the "cool girls" were invited. Gillian didn't receive an invitation and she was crushed. The birthday party would involve a trip to the mall where each of the girls at the party was given $50.00 to go shopping and then out to dinner at J. Alexander's. The Somerset Mall Collection includes Saks, Neiman Marcus and every other high-end exclusive shop.

I was appalled. You've got to be kidding me. Affluenza.

I recounted the story to people whose opinion I actually valued. I tried to get some perspective. Was I appalled because my daughter was hurt because she was excluded or because this was outrageous? They concurred that it was indeed outrageous, and somehow I felt vindicated.

I set it aside and I worked with my daughter to help her learn to be resilient, to learn when to walk away, to continue to be kind, and to value that which really matters. She recovered, and I moved on.

March 2002

Fred had been gone for about three and a half years. I was dating Tim, the dentist. It was mid-morning and my phone rang when I was in my bedroom putting away the clean laundry. It was Paul O'Shea. We chatted for a minute and he asked, "Do you know when the auction at St. Sabula's is?"

"I have no idea." Why was he asking me this? Surely this couldn't be the reason for his call. As I looked out the window I stepped into the mid-morning sunshine that was streaming into the room. It felt good to be warm.

I never go to those events. All those happily married couples yammering on about their perfect families. Not exactly geared towards singles. I was curious why he had called me for this information. We didn't exactly run in the same social circles. But I kept these thoughts to myself.

I hadn't run into Paul since the birth of his daughter so out of politeness I inquired, "How is Tina and the new baby? Is anyone getting any sleep at your house?" It seemed like an appropriate question to me.

But Paul's response took me by surprise, "So you haven't heard the sad story of the late, great Paul O'Shea?"

"No, is there a story?" I asked as I sat down on my bed. Something in his voice indicated he needed someone to talk to.

Over the course of the next hour he told me that he and Tina had been divorced for about 6 months now and the baby, Fiona, was not his daughter. I let him go on and on about his hurt and humiliation. My heart went out to him while he recounted the gory details of infidelity and betrayal.

He asked me about myself, and my foray into the world of singles. I told him I was dating but my kids didn't like the fact that I dated, or for that matter they didn't like anyone I chose to date. So I tried to respect their feelings by being discreet and not to put it in their faces.

As we ended our conversation, I was left to scratch my head and wonder what the whole conversation had been about.

Later that evening, I was out to dinner with Tim, and I told him about the phone call. He didn't like it one bit. He saw clearly what I did not. Tim leaned across the table and shook his head at me, "This guy has designs on you. I'm a guy and I know how guys think. He was going to ask you out. If he wanted to know the date of the auction he could have found it on the school calendar." He finished speaking and looked me in the eyes, his head still shaking. He clearly didn't like other men calling me.

I changed the subject. But in the back of my mind I had to admit he might be right.

The next day Marilyn and I had lunch together, and I brought her up to date on the weekend's events. She cautioned me to be careful, "Those kids are a mess and so is their Dad. You so don't need this in your life."

The prophecy delivered.

Why was I the last to see?

The reality is that my greatest strengths are also my weaknesses.

Somehow I had a real need to feel useful and here was poor, broken Paul O'Shea, and his motherless children. If their lives continued on this trail of neglect and abandonment, what pray tell would happen to them? Over the course of the next few months I found myself thinking of this family and their trials and tribulations, and their quest for a wholesome happy life.

August 2003

It was Gillian's 13th birthday. She was having ten girls over to the house to swim in the lake, have a cookout, and a sleepover. The girls were up all night talking, laughing, and carrying on, as teenage girls will. They woke me at dawn, because they wanted to swim across the lake. I outfitted all of them in life jackets and insisted on kayaking with them across the lake. I clearly remember thinking how different Gillian's party was from Dana O'Shea's birthday bash at the mall. I was comfortable with the choices I had made as a parent, and the people my children were growing up to be. Gillian was a happy girl and all the girls had fun at the party.

Since I had been up nearly all night, by mid-afternoon I was having a nap. I was sleeping when the phone rang. It took me awhile to surface and return to a conscious state. Paul O'Shea was on the phone.

"I've been thinking about you," he said in a slow deep voice.

"You have?" I was still waking up and was having difficulty stringing two thoughts together.

He was calling from Atlanta and wanted to take me to dinner sometime. He was vague and we didn't set a date. In retrospect, in my half-wakened state I must have given him at least some hint of encouragement or at least agreed in concept to have dinner at some point in the future. Three weeks later he called and asked me out.

I agreed to have dinner with Paul the next weekend.

What was I doing? What about Tim? This didn't feel good. I was lost in my thoughts while Paul elaborated on the pros and cons of the high end, exclusive restaurants in town.

Next thing I knew he was setting the time and was offering to pick me up.

Wait, wait, wait … I didn't do that. I like to have my own car so I can come and go as I please.

"No, that's okay. I know where The City Grille is. I'll meet you there." I tried to regain some control of this run away conversation.

"Oh, I see you're one of those independent women," he said and laughed like it was some kind of a joke we were sharing.

"It's not a joke," I assured him, "I am an independent woman." I should have seen the seeds of conflict had already been sown.

As I hung up the phone I remember thinking, "What the hell am I doing?"

I don't know why I silenced the voice that tried to warn me. It's never a good idea to disregard one's intuition. But instead I rationalized ...

Tim had been absent lately ... a lot. His summer was filled with work and juggling time with his kids. I got it. The reality was, as much as he proclaimed to love me, it no longer felt like that.

The fall was upon us and Tim could talk at length about college football and his alma mater Notre Dame. I just couldn't muster up any enthusiasm for college football. I couldn't even fake it nor did I want to. Now his football mistress was also vying for his limited time.

I'm not a stupid woman and I was tired of being his lowest priority.

Let's face it, I was 45 years old, and I wasn't getting any younger. I was lonely and I missed the day-to-day interaction of living in a loving relationship. I thought I wanted to be married again. But somehow I misunderstood what I was really missing was not marriage, but Fred. I missed Fred and I was trying to find a way to fill the empty place in my heart and in my life that belonged to him, and him alone.

Tim had put me on the back burner while he tended to other things in his life and if the truth were told, I wasn't very happy about it. So when Paul asked me to dinner, I hesitated. Tim was going to South Bend for another football weekend. So I said yes. *What the hell, it's only dinner. Right?*

≈

The Date

As we had planned I drove myself to The City Grille. Paul arrived early and secured the best table in this small intimate restaurant and was having a glass of white wine when I got there.

He stood to greet me leaning in to give me a kiss on the cheek. Totally appropriate given we'd been acquaintances and perhaps friends or at least friendly for years.

He was dressed in an expensive looking black and white checked sports coat. On closer inspection the pattern of the fabric was woven, a small houndstooth plaid. Now I don't think that patterned sports coats look particularly good on anyone, but they really don't do much for a shorter man who has a tendency to carry his weight in his abdomen. But I was able to appreciate the quality of the fabric. Perhaps it should have been reserved for an upholstered library chair. I digress.

I was wearing black slacks, black sandals and a black twin set. Black-Black-Black

It was almost all I ever wore. I liked it. It kept the wardrobe simple and easy, and rarely hopelessly and hideously out of fashion. And if that were the case, then perhaps when I was in all black, no one would notice me at all.

Paul O' Shea was shorter than I thought and heavier too. The reality was I had never really thought about Paul O'Shea all that much.

We sat and chatted for a moment before the server arrived and asked if I would like something to drink. I ordered a glass of wine and Paul's face indicated disapproval as he reached for the wine list. His reading glasses were perched on the end of his nose as he perused the offerings. The server waited. He looked up at me from across the table, "May I suggest something?" Paul asked. I nodded in agreement and he ordered a different and more expensive varietal. "I think the lady will like this better."

He was right. It was delicious. At this point in my life I knew very little about wine and never ordered expensive wine. I thought back on my date with Mr. Cheap. I savored the wine and made a conscious choice to appreciate the ambiance of the evening.

I remember being struck by his confidence and his savoir-faire. Although his manners gave every appearance of graciousness there was something about him that was amiss. Somehow his apparent kindness was tainted with a hint of arrogance. As in … *I am more sophisticated than you and know more than you.* I thought it was probably true. Maybe I should silence the inner critics that caused me to shun so many of my dates and instead try to enjoy this moment. Maybe, just maybe, I might actually learn something from him as shocking as that might seem … now who was being arrogant?

We chatted on and on … mostly about our kids until he asked, "Do you think we would have anything to talk about if we didn't talk about the kids?"

I was a bit taken aback. I didn't think at the time this was a sign he wasn't interested in my children, but rather that he might be interested in me. What a novel idea, to date a man who might actually be interested in me. I had dated men who really were not all that interested in me, and yet Paul appeared to be. He was really listening to what I had to say, and so with some hesitancy I agreed to see where this might lead, "We could try."

And so Paul asked the questions and I answered and elaborated. He made me feel like he thought my life story was fascinating. He asked me what I thought and felt, and what I liked and didn't like, and in response he filled in the gaps about his own life. Coincidently we shared similar circumstances, thoughts and feelings.

In hindsight, I believe it was because he asked me about myself first that I felt he cared about me. He was a good listener. But later I would discern the reality to be something else entirely. He had only been asking me about myself so he could manufacture a story to present himself in the best possible light. So he would appear to be exactly what he thought I was looking for. What I took for interest in me, as a person, was really just market research.

"What do you think about this?" he would ask.

And

"What do you think about that?" he artfully wove his questions seamlessly into the conversation.

My responses were frequently followed by, "Me too," and then some gratuitous embellishment.

We chatted on and he proceeded to discuss the ins and outs of his lengthy career in corporate America. Paul had been the Director of Marketing for a multinational computer company. By the end of the evening I had concluded that Paul was a successful man, had been the victim of two bad marriages, and that his poor children had suffered the ramifications of an unstable home life.

Poor Alexander and Dana. How would my children have coped if they had been abandoned? Their father died, but he never would have left them or have left me.

These poor motherless kids, my heart broke open as I thought about their abandonment. Paul painted a pretty bleak picture of pain and desertion. First their mother, and then their stepmother. How could these women possibly have been so cruel and left these children? God help them.

Only later would I put the pieces together. This is what people in marketing do ... they try to determine the needs of the market ... and I was the market. I was the potential customer and he was the goods and services that were up for sale. He had played my heartstrings. He was astute enough to ask the right questions, and determined who I was. In response he tailored his life story to match what I thought I was looking for.

So much for being a smart, savvy woman. Later people would ask, how did this happen to you? The only explanation I can offer ... I bought the marketing plan ... over- promised and under-delivered.

I just wanted someone to know me. This is the forte of the marketers. They know what their clientele are looking for, and they find a way to convince them they can deliver. I was lonely and looking for love.

As the evening ended, I thanked him for dinner and he escorted me to my car. We had parked next to one another in the lot behind the restaurant. He made no overture to kiss me, and I was glad for that as I slipped into my car and waved good-bye. I had a lot on my mind.

Paul got into the car next to mine. He was driving a silver BMW. I don't know what model, but it didn't look like the garden variety that the elite suburbanites in this community drove. It was similar, but different. I would later find out he had borrowed it from the executive parking lot where he worked. He had wanted to impress me. I'm afraid it was a wasted effort. I know and care as much about cars as I know about college football, and it has already been determined that I couldn't give a rat's ass about either.

I had barely traveled a quarter of a mile towards my home before Paul was calling me on my cell phone. There and then he confessed to being totally taken with me. "I was nearly the late Paul O' Shea. I was so distracted pulling out of the parking lot that I was almost broadsided by an on-coming car. Good night. I'll call you soon," and then the phone went dead.

Oh Shit. This guy was going to ask me out again. What was I going to do about Tim?

The problem was that I loved Tim. The relationship was highly inconvenient and our schedules rarely coincided. He was a busy man. But if I were honest with myself the reality was that some relationships are like shoes that just don't fit. You can really like them for a whole lot of reasons, but if they don't fit right, they will never really work for you. You may wear them occasionally, perhaps for special occasions, but you sure can't wear them everyday. It was like that with Tim.

I wrestled with this for a few weeks, but Paul was persistent, and Tim was busy. So in the end, I decided to call it off with Tim, and date Paul.

Tim was heartbroken and in a last gesture of futility, he asked me to marry him. Even though we both knew that neither of us were really looking to get remarried at the time. He didn't want to see our relationship end, but for all the same reasons that the relationship wasn't working before, his offer to marry me wasn't the solution. I was sad and it hurt me to know that I had hurt him, but I was moving on.

I was looking for someone who would love me. Paul was not perfect, but neither was I. My curiosity about this man was piqued, and I was willing to explore where this might lead. I know love looks different when you're in your 40's than it does when you're young and in your 20's. Life has a way of changing all of us.

I thought back to a story that I read many times to my children, the story of *The Velveteen Rabbit*. In this children's story, the velveteen rabbit had been loved so long and so well that it had lost all of its velveteen fur. It was no longer considered beautiful, but in exchange for its losses, love had caused the velveteen rabbit to become real.

I was looking for someone real so I was willing to look beyond some of the more superficial trapping of love. I was no longer a young woman. I was middle-aged and 45. I made allowances when relationships were less than perfect, and I compromised on things, because I thought maybe if I did, I might be more likely to find another real love.

CHAPTER 4

So this is
Paul O'Shea

My next date with Paul was at The River Club in the city. They were hosting a very expensive wine dinner with a *prix fixe* menu.

There were eight courses; each course was paired with a different wine. Kendall the sommelier was all over Paul. They discussed the pros and cons of each vineyard and varietal in excruciating detail. The intricacies of the conversation sought to exclude those who couldn't keep up or contribute. Myself included. But I listened with fascination as if they were discussing some great work of art. I was among the uneducated, as far as wine was concerned.

"Oh Mr. O'Shea, this 1999 Volnay is from the Cote du Beaunne region of France. The bouquet of this Volnay is light and delicate," Kendall informed Paul as he poured a tasting portion into his red wine glass. "It has acquired its bouquet much sooner than the Nuits that was served with the previous offering of charcuterie."

Paul picked up the glass and swirled it adeptly with one hand, then stuck his nose into it and inhaled deeply. "Yes, I can smell the fragrance of raspberry and violets in the bouquet. The varietal is a Pinot Noir, correct?" he asked Kendall.

"Oh Mr. O'Shea, you have such a discriminating sense of smell. You are so knowledgeable, as a Volnay is indeed made with the Pinot Noir grapes."

Paul swirled the glass again and took a taste of his roast pheasant with a sip of the wine. "This pairing is exquisite, Kendall."

Kendall turned towards Paul and bowed at the waist in a gesture of false humility. Paul was enjoying the attention and admiration but he quickly recovered, and dismissed Kendall with the turn of his hand. It was as if, all of a sudden, Paul found Kendall's presence an annoyance. Kendall's status, as the sommelier, made him unworthy of any more of Paul's time or attention.

In that instant the smile vanished from Kendall's face and he dropped his gaze towards the floor as he backed away from our table. I recognized the look on his face because I had seen it all too frequently amongst my high school students. It was the pain of rejection when people stretch beyond the rigid barriers of social class. Kendall had presumed to be Paul's equal based on his extensive knowledge of wine, but alas he had presumed too much.

I was embarrassed for this haughty wine steward who had just been so summarily disrespected by my date. In an effort to smooth things over I lifted my glass to smell the wine to see if I could detect the scent of raspberries. Paul recovered nicely as he turned his gaze towards me, "I didn't like the way Kendall was excluding you from entering into the tasting."

His comment took me back a little bit as Paul had seemed to enjoy the repartee, and so I was quick to acknowledge, "Please don't concern yourself. I wasn't offended in the least and I didn't have anything to add. As you already know, the subject of fine wine is well beyond my area of expertise."

This small incident, the way Paul had treated the wine steward, stuck with me. His arrogance had caused me to bristle. But Paul's explanation, that he was concerned with my exclusion, allowed me to view the situation in a different light. He had interpreted the wine steward's behavior towards me as arrogant, and he quickly put a stop to it. I had seen the situation differently. My perception shifted. What I had taken for arrogance was really an act of consideration. Paul had been considering my feelings and it was kind of nice to be considered.

I hate to admit to being so superficial but I was impressed with how knowledgeable Paul was about wine. As for me, I felt like the country bumpkin.

So after Paul dismissed the sommelier he took it upon himself to expound upon the virtues of each of the wines that we tasted. He consumed his wine and then finished mine; he implied that my taste in wine was not very sophisticated as I was unable to ascertain the nuances that he elaborated on. "Maybe the smell of your lip gloss is interfering with your ability to smell the wine, let alone actually taste it."

His comment stung a little bit. I felt like a bubble gum chewing teenager from the wrong side of the tracks. But then he smiled and reached for my hand across the table, and gave it an affectionate squeeze. I forgave him, because I was so certain he hadn't intended to offend me.

As one course after another arrived, he spoke with ease and confidence on everything from wine and food to the ethnic profiling at our nation's borders, the increase in homeland security, and the impact on our personal freedoms. He spoke about his need to travel internationally with his job and how the changes in security regulations since 9/11 affected him. "When Tina and I were dating she used to rearrange her schedule so she could stay with the kids when I was out of town." Taking a long draw from his wine glass, he added, "I need to go to Germany at the end of the month and I guess I'll need to drive to Akron to get my mother so she can stay with them."

I thought momentarily about how difficult it must be for Paul, to have this big job with a demanding work schedule, and also be a single parent. It couldn't be easy for him. Although I had a notion that I could have his kids stay with us, I kept my mouth closed. The truth was that we hardly knew one another. It crossed my mind that he might be fishing for an offer of assistance, but instead I asked, "What about Marianne? She is their mother."

"No fucking way! " He spat the words out as fire burned in his eyes.

Inadvertently, I had touched on a hot spot and opened up an entirely new topic of conversation.

"She's a terrible mother and terrible human being. Under no circumstances would I allow my children to spend any more time than the court requires with that awful woman." He leaned in towards me and held my gaze.

I felt a great deal of compassion for Paul and his children while he recounted instance after instance to support his accusations that Marianne was not fit to raise her own children.

I felt so bad for him and for his children. It must have been so difficult to share the responsibilities of parenting with someone who didn't put the needs of their children above their own.

And as quickly as we had gotten into the subject of his ex-wives, the conversation changed, and Paul began to ask me something about myself.

The entire evening I was a bit out of my element. I don't know if it was the arrogance of the sommelier or the attention Paul drew to it. Or perhaps it was Paul's continual elaboration about his job and his achievements, but I felt inferior.

I know that people can't make you feel anything without your implied permission. I'm an educated woman of independent means and I was acquainted with many people who held positions of power and prestige. But in the words of Shania Twain …

That don't impress me much.

I rarely felt incapable of holding my own, so what I felt that night was an uncommon experience for me.

When we left, the valet brought Paul's silver BMW around to the door. The entourage of valets was all abuzz about this particular vehicle, and Paul was wowing these young motor heads with his knowledge of the car and its features. It was lost on me ... I was not impressed. I was just concerned about getting into this car with someone who had drunk a boatload of fine wine.

On the drive home I remember thinking he drove pretty well considering how much wine he had consumed. Despite his ability to keep the car on the highway, I was still worried about his speed. I thought about all the precautions I delivered on a regular basis to my young students about getting into the car with people who had been drinking. Yet I couldn't even follow my own sage advice.

Next time ... if there was a next time ... I thought, I would be smarter. I have two kids and they needed me. I couldn't afford to be involved with this kind of recklessness.

I don't remember what we talked about, probably the car. I know he didn't hold my hand because the car had a manual transmission and he was rapidly putting the car through its paces. When Paul dropped me off at home it was late and the lights were on. My kids were still up, and so I discouraged Paul from walking me to the door. While still in the car I thanked him for a lovely evening, and then opened the car door and we parted company.

I remember offering up a little prayer of gratitude for getting home safely. No more driving with drinkers. I had way too much at stake.

After I hustled my teenage children off to bed and cleaned up the remnants of their evening snacks, I remember thinking that Paul still had not kissed me. I filled the sink with some hot soapy water and washed down the countertop.

Did I miss the memo? Had there been an edict from above that had eliminated the good night kiss. How were you supposed to know if there was any animal attraction?

I washed my face, brushed my teeth, and then slipped into a nightgown. I thought, I'd wait this out. I was actually a little relieved.

I was a little put off by his arrogance. Why did he need to act like that? As I mulled things around in my head I chalked it up to working in a corporate culture. Maybe he thought if he didn't sing his own praises loud enough that no one would notice him and he would be passed over. Was this required for climbing the corporate ladder to success?

Anyway he wasn't really my type.

The next afternoon as I weeded, mulched, cut back the flowers, and attempted to put the garden to bed for the winter, I found myself lost in my own thoughts.

I tried to get past the superficial. I didn't want to be so small-minded that I would miss the opportunity to meet someone interesting and wonderful just because of aesthetics.

The truth of the matter was I was still not over the loss of Fred, and so I had purposely chosen to date men who couldn't and wouldn't interfere with the part of my heart that would always belong to Fred and to Fred alone. I didn't want any rivals or intruders into this very sacred place in my heart.

So, the next time Paul called to see if I could go out, I responded, "Not tonight. My kids have friends in for the evening and I'm home –parent en garde!"

Instead of cancelling entirely Paul offered to come by the house. We sat companionably in the living room and shared a bottle of wine. He spoke about kissing me, and yet he kept his distance and made no attempt to do so. He said he had a cold. I thought maybe he was just being considerate, but maybe the truth was we just didn't have any sexual chemistry.

After all this hype, when he finally did kiss me a few weeks later, it was less than thrilling. Perhaps we just needed to give this some time. So patiently, I waited fully expecting maybe next time there might be fireworks. Just how naïve could a grown woman possibly be?

Paul began to notice small things around my house that had begun to fall into disrepair since Fred was gone. One afternoon he arrived, without notice, with his toolbox. He replaced the broken doorknob on my bathroom and the latch on the garden gate. I was completely taken by the simple fact he noticed something he could do for me, without being asked. A simple act of ordinary kindness meant more to me than all the fancy dinners he escorted me to.

We started to see one another every other weekend when his children were at their mother's and one night during the week. Divorced parents with children have the opportunity to date when their children see their ex's, but the widowed parent is on duty 24/7. Yes, this brings abundant joys, but it can also be difficult.

My children had a major freak-out when they realized that I was actually dating Mr. O'Shea. "He's Alex O'Shea's dad! He's not just some guy you're friends with. Alex is a creep and don't expect me to hang out with him. It's not happening." Cullen left little doubt about how he felt about me seeing Paul.

"Don't go out with him, Mommy. I just don't like him. I don't trust him, and Dana is so rude to me," Gillian also gave me her unsolicited opinion.

They clearly didn't like it that I was seeing Paul O'Shea, but initially I thought their disapproval had more to do with how they felt about Paul's kids. I listened to their concerns, but I also clearly recalled that they never liked Tim or Roger either. I rationalized they just didn't want me to date –but the reality was that the world moves in twos, and I didn't want to be left behind.

Cullen began to have some difficulty in math simply because he didn't do the homework. Paul offered to tutor him in the evenings. Now Cullen is very bright and with a bit of one-on-one instruction his grades improved, but not his feelings towards Paul.

I was irritated by Cullen's general lack of gratitude. I had raised him better than that, so to compensate for Cullen's behavior, I showered Paul with gratitude and praise for all the help he gave to my son.

As the weeks progressed, Paul's life story unfolded. But I suspected early on he didn't always tell me the truth.

One night after he'd been drinking, he was telling me a story about a woman he once knew named Sarah. As the story unraveled, I learned he had lied to me about how many times he'd been married. Somehow he had forgotten to mention he'd been married to Sarah. I learned she wasn't just his girlfriend, but had actually been his first wife. They had been married for ten years when he lived in California. *Oh, that little old decade.* When he slipped up and the truth came out, he confessed, and asked for forgiveness.

And so I absolved him from his sins. Why did I do that? I guess I felt compassion for him, because his life had been filled with so much heartache and misfortune. I guess I thought perhaps he lied to cover his embarrassment.

Then there was that second little white lie, when he lied about his age. He was actually two years older than he told me originally.

On the other hand, he peppered his stories with references to all the good deeds he had done, and his philanthropic endeavors. When I asked for details he became humble and backpedaled, "I'm just a regular guy doing regular stuff."

He helped this friend move, and helped another friend paint his house, and contributed generous gifts to a charity auction sponsored by his friend at his country club. However, I never met any of these close *friends.*

I began to suspect Paul was a little insecure. He could be a bit of a namedropper, and regularly boasted about his past accomplishments, honors bestowed upon him, places he had been, and people he had met.

In the two years we dated he obtained corporate passes for the Boyne Mountain Ski events. He took me and all the kids skiing. He bought all new ski clothing for himself and ski equipment for his kids. His kids didn't exactly take to it. Paul and his family spent most of the weekend in the lodge watching movies while my children and I skied.

Paul was forever promising to ski with me, except that he had an old skiing injury from his days of skiing with his friend, the Olympic athlete, Jean-Claude Killy, on Mammoth Mountain in California.

The first winter we were dating he signed his family up for kayaking classes in a high school pool. He wanted his kids to be ready to kayak with us when the summer arrived. Paul never did get in the kayak on the lake.

There were stories about how he was accepted to Princeton but when he was given a full scholarship at Xavier University, well, he just had to go. Now Xavier is a fine school and Paul was a smart man. Did he really think it would matter to me? Or was he just so insecure?

Early in the relationship I remember having a sense that he embellished and elaborated on aspects of his life in an effort to enhance his status or accomplishments. Usually the exaggeration had some basis in truth, but was frequently unverifiable, and related to things of little or no consequence. I don't know why, but I chose to ignore it.

There were stories about how dreadful his ex-wives were. The stories of their infidelities and betrayals, and his victorious redemptions through divorce, and I believed him.

Why wouldn't I? I didn't lie to people and it just never really crossed my mind that I was being naïve and too trusting. I felt compassion for him. He had a difficult childhood, and his adult life was filled with one tragedy after another. I minimized his boastful ways because I believed it helped him feel better about himself. I rationalized that Paul talked about his accomplishments and past glories as a way to fill the loneliness that I was so certain resided deep within him.

Why did I ignore the signs that should have shown me the truth about this man? They were all present. Perhaps I was just so lonely that I accepted things that I never should have.

Dating is different in the throes of adulthood than it was when I was a young woman. There was no guise about the preservation of innocence or virtue. What happens when you're in mid-life is clearly between two consenting adults. There is an expectation of a sexual relationship in the world of adult dating that was not necessarily present when I was younger. For this reason I was not comfortable dating more than one man at a time. I practiced serial monogamy, only involved in one relationship at a time. I didn't deceive myself I was being virtuous in any manner but I certainly wasn't a whore either. I'm a sexual person, I wanted sex, and needed it in my life. I'm not apologizing for the way I am. It's just the way I have been designed by my creator.

It was Sweetest Day and Paul had purchased a variety of gifts for me from Pottery Barn. *Ding Ding Ding ... did I not hear the bell?*

This man didn't know me. He talked to me, but he didn't listen. He didn't know or perhaps didn't care that I collected authentic antiques. I never purchased any furnishings for my home at the mall. No, I didn't heed the warning bell; instead I convinced myself he was sweet to have purchased those candlesticks for me. They were lovely, though not at all my style.

He had taken his time romancing me with a fancy dinner and the gifts. After dinner he covered my eyes with a blindfold, the type given to first-class passengers on an airplane, and then he led me upstairs to his bedroom. I thought I was in for some fun. Now, I have a propensity for the creative type, but sadly to say it was not to be. Did he really think if I couldn't see I wouldn't know? I'm sad to report that what he lacked in dimension was only exceeded by his lack of caring. Oh he cared all right, but only about himself.

The sex was abysmal. This man had his share of shortcomings, and not the least of which resided between his legs. He hadn't a clue how to satisfy a woman, at least not this woman. Did I really think I could teach this old dog any new tricks? What was I, an animal trainer? How did I ever consent to this? When he had satisfied himself with the use of my body, he instantly fell asleep and began to snore like a freight train.

I got up out of bed and dressed to go home. The lights were turned down, but in the dark I could still see that the room was a colossal mess. All his laundry, clean and dirty, was strewn about and his dressers were cluttered with weeks and weeks worth of leavings.

He had seduced me, and I had gone along willingly. But he hadn't made even the simplest preparations to treat me like an honored guest. The room was a hovel. As I picked through the laundry for my clothing, I came across a pile of business cards that were still on the bedspread.

Paul awoke as I dressed so I told him, "All those business cards that were on your bed … I put them on your dresser."

He rolled over and laughed, "You may leave yours when you go."

I should have known … the truth was revealed in this moment.

I had glimpsed his true nature and the depth of his cruelty. I should have left and never returned.

But my strengths are also my weaknesses. I am a stubborn woman who does not always see what I need to see.

What did I feel at the time? I don't really remember, as hard as that may seem to believe. I'd been so hurt by the loss of my beloved husband that the pain and humiliation of this night barely registered in comparison. I was in survival mode. If I could survive the loss of Fred, clearly I could survive this. Emotionally I was so protected that the pain of this night was somehow deflected. I wore my body armor but I would need to deal with this later.

Why did I keep quiet? Why didn't I tell him off? Why didn't I leave and never return? Long ago I had learned to swallow my voice.

No one asked my opinion. Not then. I kept my opinions to myself.

I was very much a traditional woman of my time, playing my designated role in this fairy tale. The gender rules were clearly understood. Good girls were seen and not heard. Only men were given the prerogative of freely speaking their minds.

My family had valued my counsel and my opinions but Fred was gone. There would never be another Fred for me. He was irreplaceable.

I was so lonely and maybe what Paul was offering was better than nothing.

So there I was, losing my way in an effort to find someone who would love me.

Perhaps it's a part of the human condition and knows no gender. Perhaps I was just another lost soul looking for a little human kindness, love, and compassion —looking to give and receive love, to know and to be known. So I was willing to grasp onto any little scrap of human compassion that I was shown, just something to justify my humanity and give meaning to my days and keep the loneliness at bay.

And in doing so, I forgot what I was worth.

CHAPTER 5

Ignorance is Not Bliss

So out of sheer loneliness, Paul and I began to see one another more often. We regularly invited our children to join us in what we had planned.

Gillian and Dana were starting to bond. The more time they spent together, to their surprise, they found they actually liked one another.

One afternoon, when I was home gardening, Paul offered to pick Gillian up and take the girls shopping for their Confirmation dresses. I had wanted to take Gillian, but wasn't ready to go at that time so I gave my consent and planned to meet them at the mall after I'd finished in the garden and cleaned up.

When I arrived at the small upscale women's clothing store, the girls were in the dressing room. Apparently they had been giving Paul a fashion show while he critiqued their outfits. Inside the dressing room, stacks and stacks of expensive dresses had been thrown on the floor. I couldn't believe my eyes.

"Gillian, get dressed right now and help me put these dresses back on the hangers." I was so angry. "You know better than this."

Gillian dropped her head in shame and began turning a dress right side out as she handed it to me to put on a hanger.

Dana was clueless as to why I was upset, "Won't the ladies who work here pick them up?" She asked innocently.

She really didn't understand so I began to explain as gently as I could, "Girls, these dresses are expensive and they don't belong to you. They belong to the store and someone else has already paid for them. If they're ruined through your carelessness, no one else will want to buy them, and then the store loses money. As far as someone else picking them up, you both threw them on the floor; therefore, it is your responsibility to clean up after yourselves. You can't create a mess and expect someone else to clean up after you. It's just disrespectful to the people who work here." Lecture delivered.

Paul was out wandering about the store as the girls and I carried the armload of dresses out to the sales associate. "Did you decide which ones you want?" He asked.

"Gillian will not be getting her dress here." I was still fuming. Did he have any idea what had been going on? Besides, all these dresses were way outside of my budget, and way too sophisticated for a Confirmation dress.

"Mom, can I go look next door?" Gillian asked. She knew full well that she had disappointed me, and the dresses she'd been trying on would never fly with me.

"Go ahead. I'll be over in a minute." I responded as the girls took off together.

"What's your problem?" Paul asked, as he looked me in the eye. "The girls were just having fun. You're always such a killjoy. Can't you just lighten up?"

I didn't want to get into this with him in a public place. I spoke in a hushed voice, "This wasn't what I'd expected or the type of dress I want to see my daughter in for her Confirmation. I don't think it is appropriate."

"You have no sense of style. You need to wake up and realize that Gillian isn't your little baby anymore. You're always so frugal and cheap; why don't you buy her something nice for once?" He walked out ahead of me, and I stayed behind to help the sales staff return the mountain of dresses to the racks.

I turned to leave and an older woman from the store took my hand and said, "Thank you. I heard you talking to the girls in the dressing room. This kind of thing happens here all the time. You might find something for the girls at Hudson's, they have some nice dresses in the junior department."

Paul's words rattled around in my head. Was I really a killjoy? I knew I was conservative with my money, but I didn't think I was cheap. My kids were well provided for. Perhaps Gillian did need a more upscale wardrobe. I had always felt I had a good sense of balance between value and fashion. Maybe I was wrong.

I went to meet Paul and the girls in the next store. Gillian came over and snuggled up next to me. "Sorry Mommy."

"No harm done honey," I said as I squeezed her shoulder.

"Can I show you something?" She asked as she led me over to a rack of clothing. "What do you think of this?" She pulled a pretty spring dress from the rack.

I liked it, and I could tell that she did too. I looked at the price tag and it was affordable. "Why don't you go try it on."

It fit her well. She looked beautiful, with her long blonde hair and luminescent skin. She didn't need to look like she was 30 as she was still 14 with the freshness and purity of her youth. We both were happy with this dress and so I bought it, while Paul took Dana back to the other store where he bought her an expensive, sophisticated, skirted suit in blue moiré.

The day of the girls' Confirmation, both girls looked lovely. Gillian wore the dress we purchased and Dana arrived at the church in a skirt and sweater. The blue moiré suit was never worn. It went to Goodwill with the tags still attached.

∾

That was the summer Gillian had made a very conscious choice to be a vegetarian. She was really beginning to exert her independence and make up her own mind about a whole variety of things. I was marveling at her personal growth. I did my best to encourage her to speak from her heart, and live in a way consistent with what she felt was right.

When we went out to eat Paul took every opportunity to roll his eyes and mock her choices when she spoke with the server about the preparation of various items on the menu. She thought he was an asshole. I could read it in her face. I stood in solidarity with my daughter. When Paul ridiculed her choices and her burgeoning independence, he was also mocking me.

∽

Cullen had some friends who were musicians, and he was learning to play the electric bass guitar so they could jam together. He hadn't taken music lessons since he was in grade school so he had some catching up to do. He practiced diligently, and developed a real passion for playing music. I hadn't seen him so excited about anything in a long time. I thought perhaps he and Paul might be able to find some common ground. Paul had been a musician in a band during high school. But as Cullen began to show some real aptitude and talent, Paul's encouragement began to wane.

Paul had purchased four inexpensive electric guitars and bass guitars, one for each of our kids. He wanted his kids to find some passion in their lives. I found this admirable. They had tried one thing after another. Maybe they would take to music. But Paul's kids lacked the discipline to learn to play, and really had no interest in learning.

But by this time, Cullen had developed enough skill and auditory awareness that he was dissatisfied with the sound quality of these beginner instruments. After playing around on the electric bass guitar for about an hour, Cullen asked Paul, "Do you think I could exchange this bass for a different one?"

"You need to practice and get a whole lot better than you are right now. The problem is not the instrument, but the musician," Paul responded with a snorting laugh.

Cullen laid the instrument down and walked out of the room. His words stung and clearly were untrue. But once those words had been spoken, it was impossible to take them back. So here was another rift for me to try to mend.

My children weren't accustomed to this kind of insensitivity. I remember thinking perhaps this was a learned corporate motivational strategy. Yet Paul showed no insight as to how his words landed on my children, or on me for that matter. So here comes Jeanne to the rescue. Perhaps he could learn to be less offensive and insensitive. I could show him, by example, a different way to relate to other people, where he considered their feelings before he spoke. I did this all the time with my own children and with my students. I forgot one important component in adult learning ... one must have a desire to learn. Oh that ...

∾

I needed to get some exercise every day. It was critical to my emotional well-being so Paul and I began to ride our bikes three times a week on the Paint Creek Trail. The exercise was really good for me, and it was good for Paul too. After all, you can't drink excessively and still ride twenty miles on your bicycle. Paul lost a little weight. He was sleeping better, and was feeling less anxious about work and life in general. We settled into a nice routine. It was nice to have someone to ride with. I was feeling strong. My children were keeping busy with their friends, and I was filling my time with someone too.

When summer rolled around I was free of my teaching obligations, and able to spend more time at home. I didn't really see Paul any more than I did during the school year.

I loved the summers. It was my time at home with my kids. I loved my home and my extensive perennial gardens. It was our safe haven from the outside world. It was filled with love and memories.

It was the summer of my mother's 70th birthday. I hosted the party at my home on the lake for my family. My sister Susan and her husband Robert, accompanied by their two sons, came in from New York. My brother John and his wife Diane, along with their five sons, also came to the party. It was a weekend of family. Paul came to dinner one night. It was the first time he would meet Susan. They were cool to one another.

Now Susan is a great beauty and I had told Paul this before he met her. But Paul told me, "I don't see it."

I wondered why he couldn't simply acknowledge that she was a beautiful woman.

Given that Robert was a world-renowned musician and Paul played the guitar and had been in a band while he was in high school and college, I found it disturbing that Paul refused to engage in any discussion of Robert's musical career. Paul had expounded to me ad infinitum about his musical prowess and the glory days of his greatness. Did he have an aversion to recognizing the talents, skills, and good fortune of others?

I was in the process of fabricating my own version of reality that bore no likeness to the truth. I was trying to convince myself I was in love with this man, and we could live happily ever after, and dance off into the sunset.

And so we went along. But then there were the days when I allowed myself the time and space to really look at my life; I knew I was getting restless. In my heart I knew that Paul and I didn't have what it would take to keep our relationship together. He appeared to be a nice man, but there were more than a few chinks in his armor, along with his battle scars, and personal imperfections. He had his baggage and I had mine. Most days I liked him but I didn't love him, at least not with the depth of love nor the kind of love that is needed to sustain a relationship through the twists and turns of life. We had been dating for over a year and I was entertaining the thought of leaving him, breaking up, and moving on.

I never felt about Paul the way I felt about Fred, not even close. The truth is I didn't want to. People are not replaceable.

We are more than functionaries just filling a role in one another's lives.

My children didn't like me to date, and they certainly didn't want me to marry. Sitting in our kitchen, after Fred had died, and before he was even buried, my children had attempted to extract a promise from me that I would never remarry.

"Promise us, Mommy, that you will not marry again. Daddy would never marry again if you had died." They presented a united front.

I tried to wrap my head around the basis for their fears, as I don't believe they even knew any other children who had stepparents. Then it all became abundantly clear. They had grown up with the classic childhood fairy tales of Hans Christian Anderson and the Brothers Grimm, and the retelling of those stories through Disney movies. They feared the evil stepparent. There are reasons why these are recurrent themes in children's literature, and that is because they are based in the cross-cultural experience of the human family.

I tried to be reassuring when they were little. They needed to know I would always act with their best interests at heart. But as they grew older and were still resistant to me dating, I began to feel they were being manipulative, as teenagers are capable of being. At this time in their lives, their entire world revolved around getting what they wanted, without any real understanding whether the complete fulfillment of all their worldly desires was really in their best interest. So I took some of their negativity and criticism of Paul and his family with a grain of salt. Paul repeatedly encouraged me to stand strong. "They're just trying to wrestle with you to see who will be the head of the tribe."

The truth was each of us had our own agenda and those agendas were very different.

CHAPTER 6

Upping the Ante

It was late afternoon in November 2003. I had been at my accountant's and I was in good shape financially. I was feeling lighthearted. I got into my car and flipped open my cell phone to find out that Paul had called just a few minutes before. Rather than listen to his message, I just called him back.

He launched into some story about his day. "I had a very important meeting this morning with Mr. Executive VP of blah, blah, blah." He was always name-dropping as if the names of these corporate bureaucrats meant anything to me at all. He attached their titles so I could fully appreciate their power and prestige. He wanted me to think he was a big swinging dick. This may work well in his corporate world but it was lost on me.

He was going on and on, stressing how important this meeting was. I listened on my cell phone as I negotiated my way home through the beginnings of rush hour traffic. "And so I had forgotten the report at home. I had left it on the kitchen counter. You know, it's been years since I have forgotten anything. I just don't do that." He paused to make certain I was listening.

"Uh huh." I responded.

And so he continued, "I had to go home to retrieve the report before the meeting at 10:00 AM. I pulled into the driveway and opened the garage door and Alex was in his car in the garage. All the garage doors were closed and his car was running."

"What did you just say?" I was stunned. I wanted to be certain I had understood.

"Weren't you listening? I said, Alex was in his car, in the garage, with the motor running and the garage doors were closed." He sounded exasperated with me for interrupting him just before he was about to deliver the punch line.

"Oh, Paul. What happened?" My stomach dropped as I held my breath and hung on his every word. My mind raced as I offered up a silent prayer for Alex. *Dear God. Poor Alex. Is he okay? Please dear God. Let him be okay.*

"He was groggy and slightly incoherent when I pulled him from the car. Good thing my house has a three-car garage." Paul added as a matter of fact.

The three-car garage decreased the concentration of the carbon monoxide. Okay I followed his train of thought as I waited silently for the rest of the story.

I was taken aback, as Paul recounted the incident to me. Instead of the story being about Alex and the near tragedy that was averted, somehow the story became about Paul and how he had *the power* to know things before they happened. In Paul's version of reality, he was transformed into the clairvoyant and almighty savior, who returned home at just the right time to save his son from suicide.

I was shaken. *Cut the bullshit. Just stop talking.* "Paul," I interrupted with greater volume and urgency than I'm known to project. He paused, unused to being interrupted. "Paul, where's Alex now?" I checked the clock on the dashboard. It was now 5:30 PM.

"I sent him to school." He responded as if this was irrelevant and should already have been assumed. His tone of voice registered his annoyance just when he was elaborating on his heroic role.

"You sent him to school?" I was shocked beyond words.

He continued with the recitation of the facts, "First I insisted he change his clothes because he wasn't in his school uniform." As if this was what every good parent's initial concern would be with a suicidal child. "Then I told him to drive himself to school as I was late for my important meeting."

I was no longer listening. My mind was whirling. His son attempted to take his own life, and he sent him back to school, and he hurried back to the office so he wouldn't miss a meeting. *What the hell is wrong with this man?*

I took a deep breath and tried to think. School should have been over hours ago and this child needed to be on a suicide watch.

"Where is Alex now?" I reiterated my original question. *My mind raced ... had he tried again? Was he still alive? He had to be hurting, and who was caring for this distressed child? Where for the love of God was he?*

"I don't know." Paul was quieter now. He no longer sounded like the conquering hero. The bravado and bluster were diminished now. I think this was the first time it had dawned on him that Alex may not have gone to school, and may have tried again to take his own life.

"You think he's at home, but you haven't seen or spoken with him since you sent him off to school? Is that right? Paul, that was over 7 hours ago." I tried to think. I needed to get a handle on the situation.

"Did you call the school?" I asked trying to keep the panic out of my voice.

"No," he paused and breathed audibly. "Why would I do that?"

He really didn't have a clue. This was what I did for a living. I ran a high school crisis team and we specialized in helping troubled kids. Paul and I had been dating for over a year by this time. Did he ever listen to what I said about my work and what I did? How could he be so incompetent in the raising of his own children, that he would send his suicidal child to school by himself, and not inform the school? Who would ensure Alexander's safety?

I pulled a Michigan left and turned the car around to head south on Dixie Highway. "I'm on my way to your house to look for Alex." I informed Paul and again offered up a silent prayer for Alex's safety, hoping we wouldn't be too late.

When I arrived at Paul's, I was relieved to find that Alex's car sat in their driveway. I parked behind it and I entered through the opened garage door. Paul's car was parked in his usual spot inside the garage.

I went upstairs to Paul's room where he was reclining on the unmade bed. His suit coat had been tossed on the bed and he was still dressed in his suit pants, shirt, and tie. The television played some inane show, and Paul was already sucked in and engaged in the storyline of this modern day teenage sit-com.

Really? Now?

"Where's Alex?" I asked as I turned off the TV to Paul's annoyance.

"He's in his room." He responded nonchalantly.

I started gently, "Have you gone in to talk with him?"

He looked me in the eyes for an extended moment and then admitted, "No. I don't know what to say." His voice was barely audible, just above a whisper.

For God's sake, this is your son and he attempted to take his own life today.

How about I love you! ... For starters.

He did not know what to do, but I did. "Go get Alex and bring him back to your bedroom. I will help you." And so Paul walked down the hall and returned with Alex in tow. In the interim I'd cleared some of the laundry off the bed, and pulled back the bedspread to make a place for the three of us to sit.

I felt like I wanted to vomit. How had I become mixed up in this family and why was this my responsibility? I don't like confrontation and I avoid it when I can, but I will not roll over when there is something that needs to be dealt with. This poor kid needed an adult in his life to step up and help him. If his father and his mother could not or would not, then for the love of God, I would.

In the end, I asked most of the questions and Alex answered me directly and was forthcoming about his intent to end his life. We talked on and on for hours while Paul sat and nodded appropriately, trying to be reassuring. But I could see he was lost and didn't have a clue how to deal with Alexander's pain.

In my opinion, Alex needed a psychiatric evaluation. I was not at all convinced he might not try again. Paul sat and listened to his son. He heard everything I had heard so it didn't take much prodding to convince Paul to call Harborside Psychiatric Hospital, as they have an adolescent inpatient unit.

When the intake worker heard the story over the phone, she agreed to see Alex immediately. So at 10:00 at night, Paul took Alex to the psychiatric hospital and I went home to my own children.

When I told my children what had happened their hearts broke for Alex and they were aghast at Paul's incompetence as a parent. I was emotionally worn out as I told my children, "I cannot continue this relationship."

Their response surprised me. "Mom, you can't leave him, not now. Alex needs us."

And so I agreed to stay.

Alex was hospitalized for three weeks. When he was released and returned to high school, he was so doped up on psychotropic drugs, he slept all day and did not attend his classes. He wasn't capable.

At the end of the semester, the principal informed Paul that Alex needed to find another high school. In the interim, Alex was admitted to the psychiatric day treatment hospital for ongoing daily therapy, and Paul in his infinite wisdom went on a weeklong business trip to Germany.

Who would care for this woebegone child? Oh, this responsibility would rest with me, the girlfriend.

When Paul returned from his business trip, he started to talk about marriage. There was no time frame. He was feeling me out and I was ambivalent, but I never told him so. I guess I didn't want to shut him down or hurt his feelings. So instead I listened to him talk in vague generalities about all the things we could do, and the places we would go when we were married, and so I let him go on with the fantasy.

I wrestled with the idea of marriage to Paul. Paul was not Fred, and never would be. The truth was, as much as I bought into the fairy tale and wanted someone to sweep me off my feet, I knew in my heart Paul was incapable of being that person for me. Fred had been my knight in shining armor, and no one else could ever truly be cast in that role for me, certainly not Paul O'Shea. Why did I ignore the wisdom of my heart?

Perhaps what Paul was offering would be enough: a home, companionship and love, albeit *Love Lite*. The truth was he needed me far more than I needed him. His children needed nurturing, stability, and loving discipline. They were literally crying out for it, and I had the skill set to provide what this family lacked.

In the interim Paul began to shop for me. He brought me a gift nearly every date, tokens of his appreciation: pearls, perfume, sunglasses, and clothing.

Fred and I had been busy squirreling away money from every paycheck. Fred wanted to be certain if he passed on, the kids and I would be well taken care of. He always bought me beautiful and thoughtful gifts for my birthday, and Christmas, and our anniversary but not daily extravagances like Paul lavished on me. There was a part of me that felt I should be refusing these little luxuries, but there was another part of me that felt loved and cared for by Paul's remembrances. I know I was still looking for *the happily ever after.*

It was in the dark of night, as I lay alone in my bed that I argued with myself about the wisdom of continuing on this path. Sleep eluded me and my mind turned to the words of Jesus.

> *Therefore everyone who hears these words of mine and puts them into practice is like a wise man who built his house on the rock. The rain came down, the streams rose, and the winds blew and beat against that house; yet it did not fall, because it had its foundation on the rock. But everyone who hears these words of mine and does not put them into practice is like a foolish man who built his house on sand. The rain came down, the streams rose, and the winds blew and beat against that house, and it fell with a great crash.*
>
> *Matthew 7:24-27*

My heart knew Paul was not the right man for me. In the night I saw clearly the cracks in the foundation of our relationship. My heart was uneasy. I sensed I was ignoring great wisdom and indeed was the foolish builder building a home on the sand, but in the daylight I lacked the resolve to confront the situation, and call the relationship off. I was a coward.

One night Paul and I had been out to dinner and he had way too much to drink and was not safe to drive home. To this day I am uncertain if his drunkenness was calculated or not. But I never slept with men in my own home when my children were there. It was just something I did not do. Other men I had dated understood and respected my decision to protect the innocence of my growing children and didn't push the issue. Paul however kept trying to insinuate his way into my life. He thought that since I was the adult it was my prerogative, and my children's sensitivities shouldn't dictate the behavior of consenting adults.

So in his drunkenness he fell asleep on the couch in the family room, but at some point during the night he came into my bedroom. He was fully clothed but he had his body draped over mine, when Gillian came down to my bedroom in the middle of the night. She was horrified and woke her brother. Cullen and Gillian left home in the night. They were 14 and 17 years old. In the morning I found their angry note.

My children were heartsick. Gillian sobbed uncontrollably and Cullen spared no words telling me just exactly how he felt. "You are a hypocrite. Do you have any idea how your behavior is affecting Gillian?

Daughters look to their mothers to set an example and it's a fine example you are setting for her."

It was one of the lowest moments of my life, and years later I still sting with the shame and humiliation of my selfishness and this bad decision.

ᗢ

Paul acted overtly sexual with me in public places when others were watching. His behavior made me and everyone else who happened to be around uncomfortable.

One afternoon Gillian told him, "My Mom wants to take a ride in your new car with the top down."

He responded with laughter, "Does she want her top down or the car's top down?"

He thought he was being funny, but she was mortified. She told me, "I wanted to kick him. He is such a pig. He is so disrespectful to you Mom."

He always made a big play of the passionate kiss hello and goodbye. Any observer would think he couldn't possibly get enough of me. I began to sense that these public exhibitions of affection might be a staged display to convince others of his sexual prowess, power, and ownership. But they were embarrassing and humiliating for me.

In the bedroom the sex was infrequent and marginal at best. I tried to rationalize this. Maybe the physical aspects of love were really just for the young, and now companionship was what really mattered. Polly Anna that I am, I was always looking for the silver lining. I was certain that things would improve if we only had more time together, and more privacy. *Wrong again melon head.*

I think this played a part in my decision to marry Paul. I couldn't bear to be seen as a whore in the eyes of children. I had always held them to a high moral standard, and although I didn't believe my behavior was in anyway immoral, I understood given their ages and their Catholic upbringing, even the slightest allusion of sexual behavior was seen as indecent, at least as it related to their own mother.

⌘

So one evening in December 2003, Paul and I attended an exclusive champagne dinner and an auction of high-end luxury items. Paul bid on a full-length mink coat and a large diamond ring. He bid the price up against his competitors. Paul was a man who got what he wanted. The champagne impaired my judgment. I was caught up in the glitz and glamour of it all and although I hemmed and hawed about not needing these things, I did not stop him, and in the end they were his. Or should I say ... they were mine.

It was my consent to a marriage by default. My consent was implied each time he upped the ante, showing this group of very prestigious strangers my worth and value. He was buying me and I did not stop him.

When we arrived back at the house, Paul sat down with Cullen and Gillian and asked them for their blessing. He planned to marry their mother. My son began to cry unabashedly and shook his head. He couldn't find the words, but his feelings were clear.

This time Gillian spoke her mind. She looked at me and yelled, "No! No! No! Mom, don't do it!" She and Cullen clung to one another and fled the family room in tears. They had made their feelings known.

"I think I need to be with them now. We can talk more about this tomorrow," I said as I escorted Paul to the door.

Paul put his arm around me while he gathered up his coat. Then he kissed me goodbye with great drunken passion letting me know that this was not over.

"They just need more time." He whispered in a reassuring manner leaving the house with the fur coat and diamond ring.

I was in the middle. I should be used to this position, as I was the middle child. Over the course of my life, I have played the role of the peacemaker between the various factions. I knew how to play this role and I was good at it. I played it well, but sometimes compromise is not the desired outcome. Sometimes, one must choose sides and fight for what's right. In this case, I should have stood in solidarity with my children. What kind of a mother was I? I would wage an internal war with myself for a very long time for my inability to take this stand, and say no to this unholy alliance with Paul O'Shea.

Paul was not easily dissuaded, but neither did he press the issue until he had completely disarmed me and I hadn't seen it coming.

There are none so blind as those who will not see.

After Christmas without an answer to the marriage question and the diamond ring safely tucked away in his jewelry box, we took a Saturday afternoon drive and came upon an open house. We decided to look inside. The house was extraordinary and the asking price was well over one million dollars. Swept up in the moment, the next thing I knew, Paul was making an offer on the house. It had enough bedrooms and bathrooms to accommodate all our children, his and mine.

In the end, we were outbid and didn't get the house. But at that point there was an unspoken understanding: if I would live with Paul in that house, then the implication was that I would live with him. My children's feelings about Paul ... the O'Shea Family ... and the marriage? Well, I was certain that in time they would find a way to deal with it.

Sometimes the failure to decide is a decision in itself. Since I didn't say no, then the answer must be yes.

As I reflect on all that happened, I am so ashamed. I can barely stand the sight of myself. I was totally caught up in the trappings of a life of wealth and privilege. I had never needed or desired these things before. Why now? I think I was trying to fill a big gaping hole in my heart with material things. Perhaps this would be the compensation for the loss of my beloved Fred. But no one could fill that place in my heart, not Paul, and certainly not a McMansion on the hill. I see this now, but then ... let us say ... the game was afoot.

Every weekend for the next few months we looked for houses to accommodate the needs of a blended family. By the end of March, we had opted to build, and had purchased a ten-acre plot of land on the outskirts of town.

Paul asked to look through all my financial records to determine my solvency. My finances were in order. When I questioned whether it was a good idea to build this expensive house, Paul assured me we could afford it. As proof of his love for me he asked, "How can I possibly give you less than I have given my previous wives?" He felt he needed to give me a larger and more beautiful diamond ring and a majestic home, as evidence of the magnitude of his love and devotion.

I was proud of how well I had managed my money. It was in that vein I allowed Paul to review my finances. It never really crossed my mind I might be in a better financial position than he was. After all, he was the one with the power, prestige, and position complete with a large salary. He had elaborated on how he was compensated with salary, annual bonuses and stock options. But what he didn't share with me was how he spent his money or how much debt he carried.

In the end, we decided if this was truly going to be our house, we should jointly contribute to the purchase. This seemed like the fair and equitable thing to do. I wasn't looking for someone to take care of me; I was looking for a partner, and I thought I had found one.

The most damaging lies are the ones we tell ourselves.

The night before we finalized the paperwork for the construction loan I tossed and turned all night. I was filled with apprehension. What was I doing? Was this really a good idea? When I was finally able to fall asleep I had a disturbing dream.

Fred was in our garden trimming the roses. He wore a tuxedo. His hair was long and he was barefoot. I felt that there was something he wanted me to know.

I rarely dreamt of Fred. But this did not seem like a dream, it felt like a visit.

But I had already led Paul to believe I was going to go through with this. I should have dealt with my fears and misgivings long before now. But instead of speaking up, I kept quiet.

So we signed for the construction loan for our new home and we each put our homes up as collateral.

In the interim, against my rabid protestations, my children started smoking pot with greater regularity. I would confront them, and rant and rave. One night I even sat Cullen down and shaved all the hair off his head with the caveat, "Your hippie days are over." Oh, if it had only been that easy. I wanted my kids to stop smoking pot. I wanted them to change their behavior. But my darling children had found a way to deal with what was happening in their lives. It seems so clear to me now: the one who needed to change their behavior should have been me.

Once the contracts were signed and our finances were inextricably intermingled for the building of the house, Paul asked me to marry him, and I accepted the ring he had offered. I'd hoped for a night of joyous celebration and unbridled passion, but Paul was exhausted and fell asleep on the couch. Once again, I let myself out and drove home alone.

My children were furious with me and refused to go to the wedding. So we planned a destination wedding, just for the two of us, in July, in Napa Valley.

My girlfriends, Laura and Marilyn, took a risk to tell me what they thought: this marriage was a really bad idea.

Marilyn took the gentle approach and took me to lunch. "The kids will be out of high school in four years; perhaps you should wait, for their sake." She reached across the table and held my hand. I knew her motives were pure as she always spoke with love in her heart.

But I didn't want to hear it. I wanted to be married. I didn't want to be alone anymore. I knew Paul was not perfect but over the last few months, I'd faced some pretty glaring flaws of my own. Perhaps we would be able to give all the kids a better chance of stability together than either of us seemed capable of providing on our own.

But Laura let me have it. "You're being selfish. Your children do not want this. Can't you see that you're diving head first into a big, nasty shithole? What the hell is wrong with you? Mark my words, this will not play well for you." And with this prophesy she slammed down the phone.

She was so angry with me. This was the last real conversation we would have. My decision to marry Paul ended my 28-year friendship with my best girlfriend. The loss and regrets I have are huge.

Less than two weeks before the wedding, I found a copy of a correspondence in Paul's bathroom. Paul had met a woman over the Internet, and had made a date to meet her at a local restaurant, The Moose Preserve. The details of the arrangement were spelled out on the paper I held in my trembling hand.

The muscles of my abdomen seized up. I felt like I had been poisoned. I wanted to vomit.

He had plans to meet her on Thursday at 7 PM.

I would be at Country Day's graduation that night. Attendance at graduation was not optional. It was mandatory and explicitly stated in my contract. Paul knew this. It was the perfect night for Paul to arrange a rendezvous.

I took a few deep breaths and walked out of the bathroom with the paper in my hand. I stood tall and strong as I took a deep breath. This needed to be addressed. He was lying on his bed, fully clothed, and napping. I gently nudged him on the shoulder, and he awoke. I held the paper out and asked, "What is this?"

He took it from me and adjusted his glasses as if he were seeing it for the first time. Calmly he looked me in the eyes, "Oh, I've been feeling a little neglected lately so I printed that out for you to see." He locked in on my eyes and held the stare, "I wanted you to know. You had best be attentive, as there are other women who find me interesting."

It felt like emotional blackmail. *What the hell was he doing? Was he threatening me with infidelity?*

I was confused and hurt. What was I supposed to do about this? I was on the verge of tears. He readjusted the pillow behind his head and said, "Don't worry about it, I'm not going to go." It was as if he felt there had been no offense or no betrayal since he didn't actually plan to meet this woman. Or so he said.

I was deeply unsettled. I didn't know if I could believe him or not. Graduation was over at about 10:30 PM, and there was the annual faculty-only party at Cathleen Lawson's. I didn't go. Instead I went to The Moose Preserve. He wasn't there. It was now 11:30. I drove to his house, and went up to his bedroom. He was in bed sound asleep. Sleeping off the evening's drinks. I slipped out as silently as I had crept in.

As crazy as it sounds, I didn't want him to know I didn't trust him. But I didn't. Maybe I was being judgmental and I needed to stop judging Paul by my standards. I had asked him and he told me the truth. He didn't see that woman because here he was sleeping. Was I the one who was being suspicious and sneaking around? How had I come to this?

So in spite of all of my misgivings, two weeks later we left for California to be married.

I'm a hardheaded stubborn woman. I have a hard time believing anyone knows me better than I know myself. Once I set out on a trajectory it's difficult for me to change direction, in spite of all the reasonable and rational justification to do so.

Years later, someone would ask me about this aspect of my personality as he gently prodded, "Is it because of the red hair?"

I responded, "No! ... Well ... Maybe. It's part of my complete package. The bottom line is ... there is no ala Carte."

It's the way I am, and still I struggle to make peace with my Aries, fiery warrior, and martial nature. Sometimes, it's an asset, and sometimes a curse. Sometimes, I need more of it, and sometimes less. But I still haven't been able to adequately master the control valve.

CHAPTER 7

Love Lite

July 2004

Paul and I had planned to be married in a private ceremony at a Napa Valley vineyard. We made all of the arrangements on the Internet.

While we were driving to the airport, he began to refer to me as Mrs. O'Shea. This had always been a sticking point for us. He wanted me to change my name to O'Shea, and I didn't want to. I never changed my name to Miller when I married Fred. And he couldn't have cared less. We loved each other and had a wonderful partnership. I didn't need to be Jeanne Miller to be Fred's wife. As our children got older, people assumed my name was Miller because that is my children's last name. I never felt the need to correct anyone. I know who I am and I like my name; it's my father's name and my family name.

I had made it clear to him, " I don't want to change my name."

The more Paul pushed me to change my name, the more resistant I became. This was a point of contention for us. Paul had three ex-wives: Sarah O'Shea, Marianne O'Shea, and Tina O'Shea. The name changes didn't guarantee the success of those marriages, and I didn't intend to give up my name and meld into this identity he was creating for me. I tried to laugh it off and change the subject. But he'd made it clear, he fully expected me to comply with his wishes.

A name is deeply personal. I'm an independent woman. I may have consented to be his wife, but not his property. Not his or anyone else's.

Paul and I met with the minister the day before the wedding. The minister and I hit it off. So much so I was fairly certain he and I would have been friends if we'd lived in the same town. Paul, on the other hand, acted as if the minister was wasting his time. I knew that Paul was just itching to get to the vineyards and into the tasting rooms. In the end we planned to meet the minister at the vineyard the next day for our wedding. As our meeting broke up, the minister shook Paul's hand and told him what a lucky man he was. Paul responded, "I think you have that wrong. She's the lucky woman." He offered this up like a joke. But it fell flat, and only Paul laughed.

The day was beautiful, and so was the wedding. After the wedding, the owner of the vineyard gave us a tour of the acreage in a beautifully restored old Mercedes. When we returned from the tour, thanks to the wonders of digital photography we were given a copy of the wedding proofs to peruse. Paul looked at a photograph of me walking up the aisle to meet him and he commented, "You look terrified." My body language couldn't be denied.

Paul had made arrangements for us to have our wedding dinner at The French Laundry. The French Laundry is a very exclusive restaurant. They offer only two seatings each night, and accommodate about 8 tables at each seating. There were no options as everyone was served from the 8-course prix fix menu. Each course was paired with wine and the cost was $800 per couple. People made reservations months and months in advance. We hadn't made reservations, but the concierge at our hotel had been able to work his magic, and we had the good fortune of getting a table. I thought, perhaps, it was divine providence and a good omen for our marriage.

I couldn't drink all the wine, as I'm a relatively small woman. I tasted each of the pairings, and Paul would finish his glass, and then finish mine. No sense in wasting all this good wine after all. At the end of the evening, Paul was intoxicated, and I was still relatively sober. At my insistence, we exercised good judgment and left our car at the restaurant and walked across the street to the inn where we were staying.

Let me set the stage –this is the man who had kissed me so passionately in public much to the chagrin of my children, this is a man who would pat me on the ass during Mass at the exchange of peace, and this is the man who had just publicly and legally declared his love to me as we were just married that afternoon. It was our wedding night. I took off my wedding dress, slipped into some very sexy lingerie, and climbed into the marriage bed with Paul, my husband.

As I cuddled up beside him, he pushed me away, and in his drunkenness he said, "Get away from me, you *nasty bitch.*"

I could hardly believe what I had just heard, but he turned his back to me, and rolled away to the far side of the bed. His intent was clear. He wanted nothing to do with me. I was shaken to my core. It was beyond my ability to comprehend that I had just married this man who had such disdain for me. This was our wedding night.

I spent the night in restless, fretful sleeplessness. In the morning, Paul was hung over. He offered no explanation for his behavior the night before, but neither did he make any attempt to make love to me.

He got up in the morning to use the bathroom, and when he returned, I was still in the bed.

"I could use something to eat. How about you?" He asked.

This was not at all what I wanted or needed right then. I was looking for a little human compassion and loving tenderness. I wanted someone to love me, but no, Paul wanted to eat. Since it was so abundantly clear that nothing was going to happen. I got up and got in the shower. In the solitude of the shower, the sound of the running water covered my cries of devastation. My soul cried out in anguish. I let hot water wash over my naked body, covering me and comforting me in a way this man, I had just married, was incapable of doing.

In the meantime, Paul left the room, and waited for me in a little restaurant down the street. After lunch, we walked from the restaurant to a little shop in town. Paul put his arm around my shoulders, and drew me close to him.

"I was over-served last night," he whispered in my ear.

I was hurt and confused by his behavior on our wedding night, but I held onto this halfhearted explanation, even if it wasn't an apology. Perhaps he called me a *nasty bitch* because he was drunk. I tried to convince myself this was why he had been so cruel, but my heart didn't believe it. My heart knew otherwise.

We spent the next few days eating, drinking, and shopping ... but not making love. I wouldn't approach him again, and it took three days before we finally consummated our marriage.

Maybe this is just the way it is when one settles for Love Lite. I was left empty and unfulfilled. For me making love requires a willingness to make a physical, emotional, and spiritual connection. When someone is more concerned with the pursuit of goods and services, and defines themselves by what they have and what they do, maybe they're not really available to have a soul-to-soul connection with another human being. The sexual connection suffers.

Paul tried to make it up to me. He bought two statues, the size of adult women, depicting the goddesses of the seasons. They were white and luminous and carved of Carrera marble. He said they were for me. They were very beautiful, but really they were for him. He knew the one that I really liked was the statute of the angel. But I didn't need to own any of them and had made this clear. I didn't want the statues. I was looking for a loving partner. He purchased them and throughout the remainder of our honeymoon he would tell me over and over again how expensive I was.

These statues were crated and shipped to the new home we were building in Michigan.

How would I choose to deal with this debacle I was immersed in? Part of me screamed … *Run! Get away from this as quickly as you can. Save yourself while you are still able.*

But the truth was our finances were already commingled and committed for the building of the new house. If I bailed before the house was completed, I would still lose my home, because I had used it as collateral against the construction loan. Where would I live with my children? We really got things out of order. There is a reason why conventional wisdom says you do not buy a house with someone until you have established a loving commitment.

I could've given into my fiery Irish nature, and told him off, and left him once and for all, which I should've done on numerous occasions. But I yielded and let the Nordic stoic parts of my personality reign. I was crushed. I needed to think and not be rash, because I knew our choices have consequences. My Catholic upbringing is clear on the sanctity of marriage. Even this unholy alliance? I needed to look at it, walk around it, and look at it again. I'm a proud woman who is not easily defeated. I'd married Paul, and I would make this marriage work, come hell or high water. I chose to stand and not to run. Again, my martial warrior nature, my inner fortitude, and my pride are strengths … but they are also my greatest weaknesses.

∾

Paul and I decided that when we returned from our honeymoon, I would put my house on the market as I had agreed to. My kids were still very upset with me, and they made no secret about it. We moved into Paul's house when Cullen began his senior year of high school, and Gillian entered her freshman year.

Cullen was supposed to stay with his grandparents while I was away. Instead he went to Canada with some friends. He was angry with me, as teenagers often are with their parents, but he had good reason to be. I'd taken my children's world and turned it upside down. Cullen was rapidly moving from childhood to adulthood and was a force to be reckoned with. My absence gave him free reign and he ran wild, like the young stallion he was.

My children were reeling. They had lost their dad, they had lost their home, and they had lost their sense of safety, security, and belonging. Their home was so closely tied to loving memories of their father. It was their safe haven that their father had so lovingly provided for all of us. And I decided to sell it. We moved into someone else's house in a different town. They did not want to move and they were not welcomed.

In any case, it was time to try and blend our families.

What a homecoming it was. When we returned on the red-eye, an all-night flight from California, we planned to go directly to bed at Paul's house. We both needed to get some sleep because we'd slept very little on the plane. I pulled back the bedspread to find a pair of women's panties lying in the bed. They weren't mine.

Paul hit the roof and started screaming for Alex while pulling the soiled sheets from the bed. Alex hung his head and admitted to bringing his girlfriend to his father's bed.

I changed the sheets and remade the bed. Paul was so enraged with his son that he couldn't sleep. I lay down for a little while but my sleep was fitful. As I drifted off I could hear the angry words being exchanged downstairs. Paul had resorted to name calling, "Have you no respect for anyone, let alone yourself? You brought that low-life, sleazy whore to my bed? You are just like your mother!" Paul growled, implying that Alex was as lewd and licentious as his despicable ex-wife Marianne.

When I awoke, I knew something more had happened and another major storm was brewing. The story was that Alex had taken my car out for a joy ride, and had an accident. The front quarter panel on the driver's side was smashed. Alex was uninsured, because his driver's license had been revoked for reckless driving. Great.

Paul was steamed. He verbally berated Alex. His son stood there shamefully unable to make eye contact with his father. Mistakes had been made, no doubt, but this kid was getting beaten up, and needed a little forgiveness. So uninvited, I entered into the role of the peacemaker. It felt like I was in the middle of a dogfight. Next thing I knew they were both barking and snapping at me.

Welcome home.

A few weeks later I took Cullen shopping for some outdoor sportswear he needed for a hiking and camping trip he was taking with Outward Bound. While trying on clothes Cullen pulled a shirt off and his abdomen was exposed. There was a tattoo emblazoned on his side body. He pulled the shirt down quickly. Too late, I had already seen it.

Now I know lots of people get tattoos and it's not uncommon, but at the time, I didn't know any mainstream kids with tats. From my reference point, only those on the fringe were sporting tattoos. I took a good long look at it as Cullen stood in defiance. I had seen this drawing before. Cullen had created the artwork himself. It was a three dimensional pyramid with a third eye. Above the graphics it read –Question Authority and written underneath the pyramid was –Think for Yourself.

I know I overreacted, but it might as well have read –Question Your Mother's Authority. I felt like I had been slapped in the face. How could my beautiful son deface his body in such a manner? He's a beautiful child of the Creator. He's the physical manifestation of the love shared between his father and me, and he had marred his beautiful body.

I hate the mall. I don't like to shop. It's barely tolerable on the best of days, and Cullen found the whole thing bourgeois and despicable.

Okay, shopping trip over.

We left Eastern Mountain Sports with our purchases and headed across the corridor of the mall to California Pizza. We were supposed to meet Paul, his kids, and Gillian for dinner. They were already seated when Cullen and I walked in. Paul took one look at me and asked, "What's the matter?"

I couldn't trust myself to speak without breaking into tears. So Cullen proudly lifted his T-shirt and showed everyone his tattoo. The kids were impressed by his chutzpah. He was the Pied Piper and the other kids wanted him to know they thought it was cool, and more importantly, that he was cool.

Now I was in tears as Cullen basked in their admiration, and Paul started to laugh. He laughed whenever Cullen or Gillian behaved badly; it took the focus off his kids. I was the fool, and everyone in this so-called family thought my feelings, fears, and sadness were visible proof of what a backward unenlightened geek I really was.

Cullen was angry with me. His grades were falling. I needed to face reality. He was smoking pot all the time. He and I would go to battle nearly every day about it. I went through his room daily like a narc dog on a mission. I flushed his pot down the toilet. Took his pipes, bongs, and lighters, and threw them away in distant dumpsters.

"Mom, where is that bong? It's not mine ... It was Vince's birthday present ... It's a piece of art." He was incredulous that I had the audacity to go into his room, yet alone get rid of illegal things he had spent his own money on.

"If it belonged to Vince, what was it doing here?" I asked as I looked into Cullen's face.

"He can't keep it at his house," he offered this up as if this was an absolutely reasonable explanation why drug paraphernalia would be found in my teenage son's room.

"Well guess what honey, he can't keep it here either. I took it to a dumpster." This type of conversation had become all too frequent as I made the daily sweep of his bedroom.

"What dumpster? Where?" He asked as if he really thought I might tell him.

I just looked at him. "This has got to stop. This is not okay with me. I love you way too much to allow you to travel this path. If you persist on this path, rest assured, I will fight you every step of the way."

So when Cullen violated the house rules, I took his car and parked it in my parents' garage. I became his living nightmare. I wouldn't turn a blind eye to what I knew was going on. If he chose this journey, it wouldn't be with my consent or permission. I love him. I would do anything and everything in my power to keep him safe and well and he may very well have hated me for it, and as painful as that was, I didn't care. I persisted and persevered. I was trying to hold onto him anyway I could.

He had consented to go away with Outward Bound. I left him the literature, but apparently he didn't take the time to read it or I highly doubt he would have agreed to go. He left for Colorado for a substance-free month of hiking and backpacking in the Rockies.

While Cullen was in Colorado, I spent my time cleaning out the O'Shea family basement in order to make a room for my son. I organized years of clutter, threw out dumpsters full of rubbish, and tried to bring some order to the house. The basement was unfinished with poured concrete walls, a cement floor, and no ceiling. Paul contracted to have the basement roughed in with dry wall, a dropped ceiling, and a bathroom. In part this was for Cullen, but Paul was nothing if not shrewd. He knew the basement needed to be finished if he ever hoped to sell his house. In this neighborhood, a finished basement was not optional. In an effort to save some money, in this 2000 square foot basement with a walkout to the river, my parents and I spent weeks priming and painting the drywall and I laid the ceramic tile on my hands and knees. My body ached with fatigue. When Paul returned home from work at the end of the day, all he could see were the flaws. He never acknowledged the efforts I was making to create a home.

In the meantime, Cullen was on a three-day solo mission with only 10 crackers to sustain him. He had a chance to reflect on many things. He is my beloved son and he was traveling his own path. When the month had passed I picked him up at the airport, he was skin and bones. I enfolded him in my arms; we both stood in the baggage claim area and wept.

Later, he would share the details of being perpetually exhausted, cold, wet, hungry and sober for 30 days. He had written me a love letter, from a son to his mother. He said it was the best thing I had ever done for him. He learned to be self-reliant and his personal growth was exponential.

Gillian spent part of that summer at camp and had bonded with some strong-willed young women. She was learning to stand up for herself and speak her mind. She was very unhappy with my decision to marry Paul, and the impact of my decision on her and Cullen. She made that abundantly clear to me. She was more than ready to go to high school and leave the small-minded shenanigans of middle school girls behind. She too was growing in confidence.

I thought about the words of my colleague, Marilee, from Country Day, "I always wanted my daughter to grow to be a strong and independent woman. I just didn't like it when she practiced on me." The truth is you can't have it both ways. People need to practice being assertive and speak their minds so they know how to do it when they need to. I could have used a heaping dose of my own wise words.

Hmmm …

I had made the decision to get married, and I was bound and determined to try and make a go of this for everyone's sake. Blending families is difficult at best. By the time people are in their teenage years, the expectations of home have been pretty well established. Teenagers are difficult, they want to do things their own way and in their own time. Throw in the evil stepmother, and Paul's poor little darlings were off crying to their daddy about the family of ogres that had invaded their home. His alliances resided with his children and my alliances with mine.

We were frequently at an impasse.

Paul never told his children no … about anything. They spent money as if there was an unending supply. Anytime there was something new on the market it was simply, "Daddy I want … " And he denied them nothing, except perhaps the kind of love that provides consistency, training, and discipline.

Gillian found the entire consumer mentality so offensive she began to buy all her clothing at the Salvation Army.

Paul spent money buying his children everything they wanted. But there wasn't enough money in the budget for a cleaning person. Over the course of the first summer it became clear that my responsibilities included cleaning his children's rooms. They were a disaster. They hadn't been cleaned in years and years. Nothing had been thrown away or taken to Goodwill. I didn't know where to begin, but I made a good faith effort on numerous occasions. I thought if I could just get their rooms clean and organized, then they would keep them that way.

His kids expressed gratitude, but within a short period of time they were filthy and messy again. The clear expectation was that dear old Jeanne would clean them up again. They didn't know how to clean their rooms and they had no interest in learning. It had never been their job and it wasn't about to become their job now.

It would've been easier to take a pitchfork and clean manure out of a barn. Horses are incapable of doing that for themselves, and apparently, so were Paul's children.

The only one who had a problem with this was me.

It was now my responsibility to clean the bedrooms, do all the laundry, grocery shop for the family, and cook the meals. But my children hated it there and they were rarely *home*.

And so I did the grocery shopping. One Saturday afternoon, I unloaded the plethora of groceries from the back of the car while Paul and Alex sat on the couch watching TV. I wondered how many trips back and forth I would have to make before someone offered to help. The offer never came but the two of them did get up to peruse the purchases I'd made. There were fruits, vegetables, breads, muffins, and a wide variety of carefully chosen, healthy foods. I carried in the last two bags and placed them on the counter, as Alex blew out of the room in a huff.

Now what? Another teenage tantrum?

"There had better be Blueberry Gushers and chips in that bag." Paul threatened. All the other bags had been emptied out onto the counter, but nothing had been put away.

"No. I didn't buy any today," I responded and I waited to hear about my latest faux pas amongst the growing list of my inadequacies. I had worked all week, and had just spent two hours at the grocery store while these two lounge dogs had been lying around the shanty watching television.

Here it was, the litany of my faults and failings: "You never buy Alex the food he wants. You only buy food that your kids like, but never anything for Alex."

He was just getting started. I had noticed the conversations that started with; "you never" or "you always" were usually the prelude to a tirade. I could tell we were in for a real wingding ... the question was how could I minimize the drama?

I turned my back to him, and started to put the groceries away. "Let's see, here are some banana nut muffins, and some cinnamon bread. I know he likes those. I bought two gallons of milk and he's the only one who drinks it. Maybe he could make some popcorn. There are also beans and cheese and tortillas for burritos." I suggested as sweetly as I could. I wanted to diffuse this situation. I didn't want another battle. But it was brewing.

"He wanted Gushers." The venom dripped from Paul's lips. He stood with his hands on his hips and his feet splayed as he tried to take up more space in the room. Poor little man –he looked like he was ready for the Mexican Hat Dance. I could try to dissipate this with humor but it was probably not a good idea right now as he looked like he wanted to fight. He scowled and waited for a response.

I looked at him and my good humor quickly evaporated. This day I would stand my ground. "No, I did not buy the artificially colored and artificially flavored Gushers ... in this particular flavor of the week ... I did not know that Gushers were the only things that would satisfy Alexander's ever-changing cravings. I didn't get the memo. They weren't on my grocery list. I just spent $250 and two hours of my day off at the bloody grocery store for our collective family. And no, I didn't get the Gushers. And oh, by the way, the last time I checked, your son is able-bodied. He has his own car and a recently reinstated driver's license. Perhaps he can go to the store and get those precious Gushers for himself."

"You're a selfish bitch." Paul snarled at me as he stormed out the kitchen.

Great.

The old Helen Reddy song ran through my head …
That ain't no way to treat a lady,
no way to treat your baby, your woman, your friend.
That ain't no way to treat a lady, no way
But maybe it's a way for us to end.

Whoa. Where the hell did that come from? Stored memory.
I guess I am not any of these …
lady, baby, woman or friend …
at least not to this man …

I puttered around the kitchen and put the remainder of the groceries away. I heard the garage door slam. Paul took Alex to Costco where they proceeded to fill a shopping cart with a private stash of teeth rotting junk food, just for Alex.

I would recall the power play of this particular day every time I would find the candy wrappers strewn about the house or stuffed between the cushions of the couch left there for me to dispose of.

There was so much tension at home that I couldn't eat or sleep.

Paul never touched me.

We had been married less than two months.

Paul's kids didn't like what I cooked and wouldn't eat leftovers. They preferred to go out to eat, but then Paul would complain about how much money he was spending, but in the meantime, the food that I purchased and prepared rotted away in the refrigerator.

He was perpetually angry. He would enumerate the multitude of mistakes I had made in the course of the day. Paul found my faults and failings glaring, and as he yelled I would get quieter, and quieter, until I said nothing at all. I offered no defense and this made him even angrier. How does one fight with the disengaged? He yelled louder and the words became crueler until I felt like I was being badgered, beaten, and bludgeoned.

Whoever said, *"sticks and stones will break your bones but words will never hurt you,"* clearly they didn't know what they were talking about.

In September, I made an appointment with my internist, Dr. Barbara Solomon. She was a lovely woman. I was so emotionally rattled I needed to be certain I wasn't physically ill. In her loving presence, I broke down and cried, "I think I have made the biggest mistake of my life."

In the cold sterile exam room she held my hand and listened. "I thought I wanted to be married again, but really what I wanted was to be married to Fred. But Paul is not Fred." She listened patiently while I told her about my life. At the end of the appointment she wrote me a prescription for anti-depressant medication.

"I don't think I'm depressed … just sad. If there's nothing physically wrong with me, I'll figure this out." I took the prescription, but never had it filled.

The bottom line was: I needed to figure this out.

CHAPTER 8

Blending Families

I reprioritized and tried to reconnect with my kids. It was obvious to them I was suffering in this situation. They let go of some of their anger and began to show me some compassion and kindness.

Paul's house and mine were both on the market, and neither one of them were selling. It was 2004 and the housing market in metro Detroit was unstable as the early signs of problems in the auto industry are emerging. People were sitting tight as they were uncertain if they would continue to be employed.

One day Paul confronted me, "You said your house was worth $600,000 and you thought it would sell immediately." He cast me as the fool as if I had purposely set out to deceive him. I felt terrible as he berated me, and held me personally responsible for the downturn in the economy.

Months and months went by, people stopped to look at the house. But they were only lookie loos, people looking for decorating ideas or those trying to fill some time on a quiet afternoon, but no buyers.

Paul bemoaned the fact the costs of the construction loan were exorbitant, but he resisted all efforts to cut back on expenses at home.

He complained, "Your children are getting a blue ribbon education and my children are getting a blue-collar education." But I rationalized as I had funded my children's education with their father's life insurance money that had been left in trust to me. The tension mounted daily.

The house we were building was enormous. It was a monument to Paul's ego. We couldn't possibly have stayed in my home because according to Paul, "It had no curb appeal." Whereas Paul's house was adequate in size but my children felt like unwelcome guests. The new house was supposed to be neutral territory. The new house would have eight bedrooms and eight bathrooms, a music room, a theatre room, an exercise room, and a wine cellar. It had curb appeal, all 8,000 square feet. This McMansion was being built on ten acres with two ponds.

Over and over again, I expressed my concern about whether we could afford this palace in the woods. Repeatedly Paul offered reassurance, "Don't worry about it, I can afford it."

Every weekend was spent looking for the structural appointments for the new house. One Saturday we sat with the lighting specialist to select the fixtures for the entire house. We were having difficulty coming to consensus as Paul offered an explanation to the saleswoman, "My taste is like Versailles and Jeanne's is like Early Tennessee Holler." She shot me a look that said, "Who is this asshole?" While Paul laughed out loud at his own joke and all I could do was shrug. *This asshole was my husband.*

The longer this process went on the more and more it cost. Paul would bitch at me, get drunk, and keep on spending.

In an effort to escape the madness, I started to walk every day with Duncan, my yellow lab. She and I would be gone for at least an hour every evening. Everyone in my life was angry and often their anger was directed towards me; at least my dog was happy to see me. She was my faithful companion. I loved her and felt loved in return. The walking did both of us a world of good. I felt peaceful after walking. It was a chance to clear my head from the incessant chatter and negativity. When I returned I felt invigorated to deal with the demands of the day, and by nightfall I was tired enough to actually sleep. Walking in the company of my dog did for me what Prozac did for others; it helped me cope and feel better.

Paul had planned a 15th birthday extravaganza for Dana with laser tag and a slumber party to follow. Gillian had a ski meet, so she and I arrived late to the party. Dana was already involved with her friends from school, and we both felt the cold shoulder of exclusion. It was okay. I'm an adult and I know that in the world of teenage girls the only person less interesting than one's own mother would have to be the evil stepmother. This evening Dana was in the company of "her friends."

After the chilly reception, Gillian turned to me, "Hey, I didn't want to be here in the first place. I cancelled plans to be here. She's the one who invited me." But Gillian had been friends with many of these girls since grade school and so even if Dana wasn't particularly welcoming when we first arrived, the others were. So before long Gillian was playing Laser Tag with Dana and the other girls.

I taught ninth graders. I understand the world of teenage girls, give them a minute and the entire social dynamic can change. With sisters, change can occur at the speed of light. Gillian and Dana would work this out.

I sat down with Paul and the tirade began, "Can't you ever get anywhere on time. I'm so tired of this. You are always late. You never leave on time."

Oh great, here it comes. You always … You never … You always … You never …

"I'm sorry, the meet ran over and the cross-town traffic was horrendous." I offered up as an explanation.

"This is an important day for Dana. You're always late and you always have some lame excuse. The girls had already chosen teams and now they had to reorganize to accommodate your daughter." He was surly.

"Her name is Gillian." I was so tired. I had been working all week and had just spent two hours in the car trying to get to this shindig. I was starting to feel stupid. I was trying my best to be a good mom to all the kids and I didn't need his nastiness. It just wasn't warranted, and I felt my fuse burning pretty close to the powder keg. I knew I had better get out of there before I told him off. "I'm going home," I stood up and grabbed my gloves and purse.

"You can't." He informed me.

"Really?" I looked him in the eyes and held his gaze. Good luck stopping me, you asshole. I was incensed.

"You need to drive some of these girls back to the house for the sleepover." He stated this as a matter of fact.

Great. He treated me rudely and yet, I was a necessary functionary in the execution of his plan. "I'm going to wait in the car." He didn't try to stop me.

It didn't speak well for the state of my marriage that I would rather spend a Friday night in January alone in my car, in a strip mall parking lot, in metro Detroit, than have a drink with the man I married only six months ago.

When the party was over, I drove half the girls and Paul drove the others back to the house. I felt like a chauffer.

Oh, the teenage years when the whole universe revolves around oneself.

The only one in the car who spoke to me or acknowledged my presence was my daughter. She knew. She always knew what I was thinking and feeling. No words were necessary. When my transportation services were completed, I excused myself and went upstairs. I was chilled to the bone after sitting in the car for hours.

Paul had pizzas delivered for the 12 girls. The kids picked through the pizzas and stayed up all night hooting and hollering, watching movies, and gossiping as teenage girls will.

In the morning, I went downstairs to clean up. The house looked as if a bomb had gone off. Who did these girls think would be their maid today? I looked around the family room. I counted 40 pizza boxes. Why had Paul ordered 40 pizzas? More than half of the pizza was uneaten and had been sitting out all night unrefrigerated. It was no longer salvageable.

By this time, I was being bitched at on a regular basis because of all the money Paul had to spend now that we lived in his house, yet Paul was the one who needed the big show of wealth.

I was livid. I knew building Paul's Dream Palace was stressing him out so I had been trying to find ways to save money. Yet he continued to be so wasteful.

I should've known that something was amiss. People who worked hard and earned their money were not wasteful like this.

There was a blizzard outside and the driveway was covered with snow, but I needed to get out of there. In spite of the blizzard, I took the dog and we went for a walk. I trudged through the knee-deep snow, and as I walked I tried to let go of the anger, the rage, and sadness. I cried. I knew I could not live like this. I stumbled and fell in the snow, and my dog came to see if I was okay. She kissed my tears away and stayed close. We didn't travel very far as the snow was too deep. I was unable walk my way through the pain.

When I returned home, the birthday party girls were still at the house. The roads had been closed due to the blizzard. I needed some privacy. I couldn't trust myself to speak so I went to our bedroom and locked the door. I had settled in on the bed and had just begun to read when Paul took the passkey from above the molding over the doorway, unlocked the door and came storming into the bedroom. He was wild with anger, and began to rant and rave again. "No one locks me out of my own room!"

I stood to face him. I needed to exert myself and establish a physical presence. I wasn't going to lie passively on the bed. I didn't know how this would play out. He moved into my physical space and then he backed me up against the door as he continued to berate me. He was so close I could smell his foul breath, and feel it on my face while he sputtered with anger. "I don't know who you think you are, but you had best remember that this is my house, and this is my room! Don't you ever lock me out again!"

I stood ... silent and seething. I was waiting for the storm to pass. I knew he wanted to hit me. I could feel the fury.

"What do you have to say for yourself? Nothing? You never have anything to say." He spit the words at me. He taunted me. He wanted me to engage in his battle. He wanted me to give him a reason to hit me so his anger could be justified.

My heart was pounding and my palms were sweating. "I needed a little privacy." My voice was just above a whisper.

"Not from me, not in my own house." He glared at me.

Adrenaline kicked in. It was fight or flight and as usual I opted to flee. I pushed past him and headed down the stairs. I pulled on my boots and grabbed my coat. They were still wet from my earlier outing. I reached into my pocket. My car keys were there. I headed out into the blizzard. The girls in the living room paid me no mind.

My car had four-wheel drive so I ventured out. How in the name of heaven would this marriage and this family ever come together? Paul and I were so different. I could not please him, and my efforts to do so were mocked and ridiculed.

I drove towards home … my old home. I wanted to go home.

It still hadn't sold. The lights were off, the heat was turned down, and the place was cold. I found no comfort there. The life force had gone out of me. I felt homeless and unloved.

I was a million miles from that beautiful, warm, safe place that I once knew as home.

I walked down the street to Shelley and Joel's – Fred's sister and her husband. They were family to me. There were few places I could go uninvited, but I knew they would take me in. Joel made the tea, and Shelley helped me out of my wet things, and wrapped me in a blanket as I was frozen to the core. They sat with me and listened while I described the disaster I had made of my life. I was certain they needed to bite their tongues to keep from saying, "we told you so." But instead they offered only love and not the criticism I deserved for fucking up my life and the lives of my children.

They listened as I spoke about leaving Paul and filing for divorce. The banter that had played on in my head for months was finally spoken aloud. We had been married for a little more than six months.

I elaborated on all my ineptitudes, in the world according to Paul. I didn't know how to load the dishwasher or fold the laundry or grocery shop. He didn't think I was funny and obviously didn't think I was sexy, because he never touched me. I felt unloved and trapped.

I couldn't go home because I had already used my house as collateral to build the new one.

I hated him, and I hated the way I felt when I was with him, and I wanted out.

But I was one of those rare birds who actually took their marriage vows seriously. I struggled with indecision. I was so tired of the daily stress of family life, and trying to make a home, and a life for all of us.

Shelley and Joel just listened as I recounted the horrors of the last few months. They love me and I felt it. I felt better when I left, even if I was still unresolved.

It was late in the afternoon when I finally returned home. We were supposed to go to a party at my friend Cathy's. The birthday party was over, and the participants had gone home, but no one had made any attempt to pick up the house. The girls were sleeping on the couch, and Paul was watching TV when I went directly upstairs and got in the shower. I fixed my hair and dressed for the party in a beautiful floor length brown velvet dress.

Cathy was my friend. Paul knew the only reason he had been invited to the party was because of me. He looked at me as I descended the staircase, all dressed up and going out. The storm had passed. He was quiet and he knew better then to inquire about the status of his invitation. I left for the party alone.

When I arrived Cathy embraced me. From my face, she knew there was trouble in paradise. The party was fun, and provided a temporary hiatus from the realities of my rapidly deteriorating life.

When I returned home Paul had been drinking excessively. He had already gone to bed. I could smell the alcohol emitting from his skin, and the odor permeated the room as he exhaled. He snored and gasped for breath. He rolled away from me as I silently slipped into the king-size bed. We slept on opposite sides and he never acknowledged that I was even there.

I was grateful for this small mercy.

In the morning I got up and got ready for work. Paul was hung-over and we gave one another a wide berth. Neither of us spoke about what had happened the day before. So we moved towards a fragile truce, and I decided to let this sleeping dog lie.

CHAPTER 9

Trouble in Paradise

For the next couple of months the truce with Paul held. I threw myself into my work, wrestled with all the design decisions that needed to be made in the new house –as well as the daily drama of having four teenagers under one roof.

What drama? Well there was Alex and the various members of his concubine frequenting his bedroom as I ever so politely knocked on the door to inform them it was time for dinner.

Then there was the frequent need to beg and cajole the kids to walk the dogs, feed the dogs, and clean up after the O'Shea dog. Paul's kids had begged their father for a puppy, a male husky, but they didn't like to walk him. The dog was untrained and not housebroken. Great.

Of course, we were entertaining our kids and their entourage of teenager comrades at all hours of the day and night. Cars coming and going, the refrigerator emptied on a daily basis and everyone's room looking like a bomb had exploded in it.

This would be enough to send me over the edge on any given day, but to add to the drama, Paul's house was also on the market, and so at any given point and time a realtor would stop by with a potential buyer. It doesn't require much imagination to figure out how Paul responded to the realtor's comment, "Your house just doesn't show well, the dishes must be done, and it really needs to be tidied up."

Despite the fact there were six of us who lived there, and I worked full time and frequently left the house while others were still asleep, it was I who bore the brunt of Paul's anger for my inability to keep the house presentable.

One person, at least, was going to escape the tensions.

At the end of the first semester, Cullen had accumulated enough credits to graduate from high school. He was more than ready to be finished. Like so many very bright young people, he was bored to death by high school, and ready to begin his independent life. I knew from ten years of teaching high school, that once the college acceptances are dispersed that students' motivation to go to class, let alone learn anything, goes right out the window. Teenage shenanigans escalate and Cullen was already the King of Shenanigans.

So he headed off to Ypsilanti to live with a friend who was already in college, and had his own apartment. But the hitch about growing up, and living independently, well it requires one to have an independent source of financial support.

As I recall, my part of the discussion went something like this, "No darling, it doesn't work that way. You have a place to live where I will keep a roof over your head and I feed you. But that offer comes with conditions … as in, my house … my rules. Once you move out and live independently you may make all your own decisions; however, your lifestyle must be independently funded and financed."

It didn't take long before Cullen learned if you don't contribute to the costs of daily living, that you may wear out your welcome rather quickly. Jobs were difficult to come by, particularly the high-paying type or the type that allowed him to do interesting work. And as the month progressed, he learned even low-paying jobs doing uninteresting work were difficult to find –and harder to keep because they interfered with his ability to party like a rock star. So within six weeks he was back home.

He found a job working at a large, high-end nursery called Bordines. He worked from 9 to 5, Monday through Friday in the planting shed. He liked working with plants, but he quickly found the work tedious. He was trying to save enough money to go to Europe during the summer before he headed off to college in the fall.

There is nothing like a low-paying, boring, entry-level job to convince the young and the restless of the benefits of higher education. And the tension at home was no better.

When Cullen was not working, like all teenagers, he wanted to spend time with his friends. This didn't include hanging out with his newly-acquired stepbrother who would like nothing better than to participate in the latest high jinks. Alex tried everything to gain entre into Cullen's inner circle, but he only served to alienate himself further through his acts of desperation. Alex would regularly get drunk and make a fool of himself, and in an effort to redeem himself, he would blame Cullen's friends for sneaking alcohol into the house. Needless to say this didn't endear him to my son.

Cullen was only too eager to find a good out.

In late March, Cullen, Gillian and I took a road trip to look at some of the colleges where Cullen had been accepted. Cullen's only criterion for applying to college was that they have a beautiful campus. He only applied to the colleges on Outside Magazine's list of the *Top Ten Most Beautiful Campuses.* So our road trip took us to Bozeman, Montana, to look at Montana State and Arcata, California, to look at Humboldt State. We were gone for two weeks, my entire spring break.

Driving across the country, with two teenagers, listening to audio books and hours and hours of the Grateful Dead was a welcome reprieve from the ongoing loneliness in my marriage.

I have often joked about the ice fisherman who sits in a drafty plywood shanty, on a frozen lake, looking into a dark hole in the ice in the bitter cold. The punch line is: "If this is his idea of fun … then things must be pretty bad at home."

I know when I told my colleagues at school I was going to spend my spring break driving to California, I could tell from the perplexed looks on their faces that they saw my road trip the same way I saw the ice fisherman. Paul and I had been married less than a year and this was my vacation?

While things were dreadful at home I had another reality to live in: I loved being with my kids. It was more about the time we spent together than where we were or what we were doing. We made our way down the highway laughing, and singing, and discussing the many possible interpretations of the Grateful Dead lyrics.

We howled with laughter after stopping to eat at a roadside diner in Nebraska where Gillian asked the server if they had any vegetarian options. The server suggested the chicken. When Gillian, without missing a beat, politely asked her, "Which part of the plant does the chicken grow on?" And then in an effort to be informative and helpful she said, "If it does not grow on a plant, then it's not a vegetable."

Really Gilly ... we decided to eat elsewhere. "I didn't mean to be rude, but if she thinks chicken is on a vegetarian diet, well, she needed more accurate information."

We discussed the plight of AIDS orphans in Africa, the loss of farmland in rural America, and the pros and cons of biodiesel with equal ease and interest. We skied at Big Sky, hiked in the Tetons, and visited the Redwood Forests in Northern California. We found interesting things to do, listen to, and talk about. Life, in general, has always interested us.

All too soon we'd checked out the colleges and were on our way back to Michigan. My reprieve was over. What a great way to feel about my marriage.

~

Despite the marital tensions, or maybe because of them, I had a very real sense that, in some way, Fred's presence was still with me.

On May 18, 2005, Paul's house and my house sold on the same day, after months of being on the market. It was Fred's 55th birthday, and I believed this was some kind of an omen, a prophetic sign from him. Our financial crisis had been averted. Paul and I would no longer be responsible for making three house payments. The tension and financial pressure eased.

Why then, did I continue to feel uneasy?

In June 2005, my entire extended family went to Hilton Head Island off the coast of South Carolina to celebrate my parents' 50th wedding anniversary. We'd been planning the trip for nearly a year and everyone had cleared their schedules to attend. Fifty years of marriage is something to celebrate! Nineteen of us would be together for the week –no small feat for a family that had scattered to various parts of the country.

Midway through the week, at the height of our family celebration, Paul surprised me. It was a beautiful summer morning, and I was sitting on the veranda having a cup of coffee, and looking over the local paper when Paul emerged from the townhouse with his cell phone in his hand. "I have to leave. I need to make an emergency trip to Germany."

"Now? Can't you get out of it?" I asked. "What is so important that you have to go now?"

"You know I can't talk about certain parts of my job. This is just one of those things. I can't talk about it." His face registered nothing as he looked back at me.

"Can't someone else go?" I asked, hoping Paul could find another solution.

"If I could send someone, you know I would. But I can't." I had asked, and he had answered.

I was disappointed. I thought we were having a nice time. I was having a nice time. It appeared the kids were. Yet Paul didn't appear the least bit distressed he had been called away from our first *family* vacation.

"I've made arrangements to take the two o'clock shuttle to the airport in Savannah. You don't need to drive me. Don't worry, I won't be spoiling your day." He stood and turned to go back inside as I watched from my seat at the table. "I have to pack," he stated.

"When will you be home?" I asked.

"I don't know yet." He responded. "I'll let you know." He looked at me as he opened the door. "Look I'm sorry, but it can't be helped." And then as if it were the first time he had considered how his change of plans impacted the rest of us, he added, "If you can drive all the way from Michigan to California, this drive home should be easy for you."

There it was. Funny, I recalled he didn't think it was such an easy drive when we were driving down here just three days ago. We had to stop overnight. All the time in the car he complained about his back, and how he was bored out of his mind. His son needed an endless supply of junk food, and there was the unending drone of some lowbrow comedy playing on the DVD player in the backseat.

But now, he was leaving and I was to drive the kids the 16 hours back from South Carolina.

Now this may have been an untimely coincidence, but somehow it just didn't sit right with me. I suspected Paul was having difficulty on this vacation because he was not the center of attention. In my family, that is a hard position to capture and a harder one to maintain.

No, in my family, and on this vacation, everyone played tennis, and golf, and went to the beach, and swam in the ocean. By now, I had heard all of the excuses about his injured shoulder, and his injured knee, and how he couldn't play golf or tennis any more, but once upon a time he had been a contender. I think the reality was he didn't want to play, unless he could win, and there was no way he would be able to outplay my father, who is 21 years his senior. I was also beginning to suspect that Paul didn't know how to swim either. He never went in the water, although he never did admit it.

I should've known this vacation was probably not his cup of tea.

All my questions remained unanswered. What was so top secret he couldn't speak of it, not even to me?

I was concerned as he packed his suitcase that he didn't have any clothing appropriate for business meetings. "Don't worry about it," he told me. "I'm flying into Metro and a car will pick me up and take me by the house before I meet the corporate jet at Oakland County International. And then I'll be eating and drinking all the way to Munich with those tall, beautiful, blue-eyed blondes. Ah those beautiful Aryan women." He laughed. "No you don't need to worry about me!"

Was he trying to make me jealous? Whatever. I somehow doubted any of those women would be interested in Paul. He had talked about the flight attendants before, but that wasn't what bothered me. Something didn't sit right with me. He was taking these trips every three to four weeks now, but he could never talk about the reason for them. Yet, he was usually home eighteen hours later. So I checked it out. A commercial flight from Detroit to Munich takes 8 hours, so it hardly seemed feasible to me that he was where he said he was.

So there I was, celebrating a marriage that was 50 years golden. And I was in a marriage that left me riddled with suspicion. I was haunted by the notion I was being lied to. Again, I let it go, as it was easier for all the kids and me when he was away than it was when he was around.

So, with Paul still in Germany, or wherever he was, the celebration ended. I drove the 16-hour trip from South Carolina back to Michigan with the kids in the car.

But still the questions nagged at me. Was I just being suspicious or was I indeed being deceived?

∾

When I returned home, I was faced with the task of packing up and moving the contents of both of our homes. As *luck* would have it, the closings were scheduled one week apart –two months ahead of the time when the new home was scheduled for completion. We would have to cram everything from our two houses into storage and find temporary living quarters.

I was tagged as the person who would pack up the contents of both houses into seven **PODS** and two storage units. We had a colossal amount of stuff. My parents and my girlfriends helped, but the truth was most of the work was done by me.

One evening, in late June while the deadline for the move drew closer and I still had so much more to box and load into the storage containers, I asked Paul, "Do you plan to take any time off work to help me or do you plan to hire someone to help me?"

"So that's how you'd like it to be. I work my ass off while you sit on your ass day after day. You have the whole summer off and I'm working, in case you haven't noticed. If you have so much money just lying around and are too lazy to do the packing yourself, feel free to hire someone. But in the meantime, Princess, I will be working to pay for your new little cottage in the woods." He snarled at me, and went to lie down on the bed for an early evening nap.

We had been married one year. I couldn't help but think about Fred and the way we had worked together. He made it fun. I didn't need to be lavished with praise, but some simple acknowledgment for the work I did would have gone a long way. Fred showed me how much he appreciated me. It was evident in everything he did. To say it wasn't that way with Paul would make me the Queen of the Restraint. The contrast between my two husbands was glaring.

My children packed up their own rooms and did so willingly. Paul instructed his children to do the same. However, the day before we were to vacate his house, both of their rooms were still untouched, and both of his kids had miraculously disappeared.

So the evil stepmother spent hours packing up their clothing, personal belongings, and cleaning out years of filth and debris from their rooms.

When Paul returned from work, he found me on my hands and knees pulling rubbish from underneath Alex's bed: dirty clothing, dirty dishes and unrecognizable half-eaten items of food. Instead of offering any assistance or trying to locate his children and returning the responsibility to them, he took his frustration out on me. "I have been at work all day. All you needed to do was ask them, but instead I get home and yet again you've left the inmates to run this asylum. Just another example for the progressively-expansive list of your personal inadequacies."

He truly believed it was my responsibility to control his children. He saw my inability to do so as yet another example of my weak parenting –that his children were disobedient.

He knew just how to twist the knife where I was most vulnerable. I had sacrificed a great deal to be a good wife and mother, and I did so with love. I had been on the fast track in my own career, but had set that aside when my children were born, and when Fred was ill. Family was my priority. Paul's comments hurt me and he knew it.

In the end, Paul did consent to hire two able-bodied men carry the furniture out of the houses and into the PODS. By the time both houses were packed and all of our belongings were stored away, my entire body ached. My hands were swollen from securing all the glassware, and the precious bits of tchotchke with paper or bubble wrap. My feet and legs ached from carrying the multitude of over-packed boxes and stacking them in precision formation into the PODS. Loads and loads of things that were no longer needed were hauled away to the Salvation Army, and another small mountain was discarded as waste for the landfill. Apparently, all of this was expected of me and thus my efforts went unrecognized and unacknowledged.

At the end of this ordeal, I soaked my sore and aching body in the tub, and I remembered another time when my hands ached from overuse … I had spent the day climbing the trees at my parents' home and picking cherries. I wanted to bake homemade cherry pies while the cherries were at their best – freshly picked. So after spending the day picking the fruit, I pitted gallons of cherries, and then spent the night baking the pies. I can be a little obsessive when I set about a task. The next morning 10 freshly baked cherry pies were on the kitchen counter ready for delivery to our family and friends. My body ached, and my fingers and fingernails were black from pitting the cherries.

I stood in front of the sink trying to remove the stains from my fingers, and Fred kissed me, "Honey, are you sure you don't want to come with me to deliver these?"

"No Fred, I can't. My hands are a mess." I told him as I pulled my blackened fingers from the soapy dishwater. It would be Fred's job to deliver the pies.

When he returned he brought me a bouquet of flowers from the farmer's market, and he had booked an appointment for me at a local day spa for a massage, manicure, and a pedicure. This was not in our budget.

"Oh Honey, thank you, but you didn't need to do this." I looked into his smiling face.

"Oh yes, I did. You have no idea how much everyone loved the pies. You're an amazing woman and I love you. Don't you ever forget." Then he wrapped his arms around me, and looked at my stained fingers. "Besides, it looks like these working hands could use a little love."

He had considered me. His words and his kindness lifted my soul.

It is amazing how a few well-placed kind words can ease the daily struggle. I didn't want to think about how glaringly absent my life was of any kind words now.

Paul and I closed on both houses, and our combined families took up temporary residence in a two bedroom furnished apartment while we waited for the new house to be completed. We were in close quarters because there were the six of us. The girls shared a sleeper sofa in the living area, and the boys had twin beds in one of the bedrooms while Paul and I shared a double bed in the other. All of this forced togetherness only added tension to the already strained relationships.

To ease the stress we decided to take a two-week vacation to St. Maarten where I had arranged for a time-share exchange. This was my first trip to St. Maarten and it was so beautiful. The sun, the sea, and the fresh salt air –it should have provided a beautiful respite from the drama and trauma of the summer. Not so.

One night on our vacation Alex took the rental car without permission, leaving the rest of us stranded at the resort. He returned at 4:00 in the morning. He'd gone to a strip club. Paul blew a gasket –but it was all shouting and bluster, and he quickly got over it. All show and no follow through. Essentially, all he'd done was given Alex a wink and a nod. His attitude was clearly, that "boys will be boys."

Alex seemed to find the cost of his father's anger bearable or maybe the ladies were so desirable, but either way he made plans to go again the next night. The problem was he was out of money.

I had left the unit early and had gone down to get a cup of coffee and read awhile by the pool. Everyone else was still asleep when I left and I had no interest in waking this brood, and rehashing the grit and grime from last night's performance.

I returned to the room to reapply my sunscreen, as it was now mid-day. It was just another gorgeous day in the Caribbean. When I walked in, something clearly was amiss. Cullen who is usually mild-mannered was standing at full alert, pushing Alex up against the wall and screaming in his face. Cullen had caught Alex looking for money in my purse. "You're a fucking thief. How long have you been stealing from my mother?"

Unbeknownst to me, Cullen had suspected for some time that Alex was up to no good. In response to finding Alex going through my purse, Cullen grabbed Alex's wallet from him.

When I walked in it looked like Cullen was about to punch Alex's lights out. Cullen is a strong guy, and could have knocked Alex silly, particularly while he was so enraged. I don't believe I have ever seen my son so angry. "Cullen, step away from him right now." I demanded as Cullen turned to look at me.

"Do you know what this asshole has been up to?" Cullen turned his face towards me, but did not step away from Alex. Alex looked terrified. "Okay you little asshole. Tell my Mom just exactly why you have her credit card information in your wallet. Come on you little fucker, what do you have to say for yourself?" He turned and glared at Alexander.

"Cullen went through my wallet," Alex whined as he tried to shift the blame to Cullen.

"Come on you little *putz*, tell her what I found in your wallet!" Cullen snarled at Alex. "He has all your credit card information in his wallet. He's a fucking thief."

"He had no business going through my wallet." Alex whimpered and looked like he was going to cry.

Cullen handed me a three by five card where all my credit card information was written including my name, numbers, expiration date, and the security code from the back, all written in Alex's handwriting.

I looked at the card in my hand, and I tried to fathom what would possess Alex to steal from me. His father provided for all of his worldly desires. How many times had he used my credit card? And now, how was I going to handle this? My mind was racing, yet I was dumbfounded, and then Paul walked in. "What the hell is going on here?" He roared at all of us.

Oh God, this is not going to go well. Paul was already intoxicated, as he'd been drinking poolside since breakfast.

"Tell him," said Cullen.

"Shut up," Alex said, angrily.

"He had my mom's credit card number in his wallet," he told Paul. And then he turned his outrage back towards Alex. "What were you going to do with it, Alex? Use it at the strip clubs?" Cullen growled with anger.

Paul's face went red. He charged across the room and grabbed Alex by the neck. He raged with blinding contempt for his only son, "You are a lying thief. God help you. You're just like your lying, cheating mother." Comparisons made to Marianne let Paul off the hook. He implied that Alex's issues were deeply entrenched in his mother's contribution to his genetics.

Alex played the role of the *injured party* flawlessly now. He fled the room and we could hear him wailing while he ran down the hotel corridor. "He tried to kill me! You all saw him. He tried to strangle me!"

Paul hung his head and reluctantly admitted, "He shouldn't have gone in your purse, and Cullen shouldn't have gone in Alex's wallet." In return for this admission he wanted me to do the same. He wanted me to say that Cullen was equally wrong for going into Alex's wallet, and he fully expected me to punish him.

He saw both acts as equally culpable.

I did not. I knew Cullen wasn't a thief and Paul couldn't say the same about Alex.

"If he wasn't trying to steal, what was he doing in Alex's wallet?" No explanation by Cullen or me would suffice. My son and I had nothing to apologize for.

Paul left the room and returned to the poolside bar where he drank heavily on into the night.

Later that evening I discovered that Alex had once again taken the rental car without permission.

Cullen, Gillian, Dana and I had dinner together at the hotel restaurant. We tried our best to let go of the suffering and all of the unkind words that had been spoken. I realized the four of us were growing closer together as we built a fortress of loving kindness in an effort to shield one another from all this craziness that was so destructive and damaging. Living with love can help heal past hurts and protect us against future pain. This was all that I had to offer. I hoped it would be enough.

When we returned to our hotel suite, Paul was already asleep, and there was no sign of Alex. I crawled into bed and let sleep close over me. I'd had enough for one day.

Sometime in the early morning hours I awoke to another drunken argument between Paul and Alex. Alex was belligerent and slurring his words. I didn't need this in my life, so I rolled over and put the pillow over my head.

In the morning, I found Dana and Gillian in my bed. Paul was nowhere to be seen.

I got out of bed and followed a horrible smell into the kitchen. There was vomit in the sink, the stench of rancid alcohol in the air, and flies were already swarming. Paul was asleep on the couch. I opened the bedroom door where the boys were sleeping and Cullen looked up at me. The room smelled of vomit, and the sickly odor of alcohol-infused human sweat. Alex was snoring in his bed. He must have been on a hell of a bender last night.

"Come on Cullen, let's get out of here." I stood in the doorway and waited for him. He looked at me and said nothing as he got out of bed. The situation spoke for itself. How could I have subjected my son to this?

He grabbed his swimsuit, I grabbed mine, and we made our way down to the poolside for some coffee and juice.

Cullen had witnessed Alex's early morning homecoming. Apparently, Alex had signed for a bottle of 150 proof rum at the hotel grocery store. No money, no problem. It would be added to the hotel bill.

"Oh good, I'm glad to know I could be the benefactor of Alexander's efforts to drink himself to death." I interjected as Cullen continued his rendition of this early morning saga.

Alex was blinding drunk and from the sounds of things Paul wasn't any better.

"I have never seen anyone so drunk," Cullen said. "Alex's breathing was erratic, then he passed out and started to vomit. I was afraid he was going to aspirate, but Paul just kept on screaming at him." Cullen's face radiated concern. He was clearly disturbed, on so many levels, by what he had witnessed.

Before long, the girls joined us at the pool and they also needed to talk about what had happened. I was heartsick. But Alex was not my problem, and I made a very conscious choice not to get in the middle of this. Paul's problems with Alex were becoming more serious, and it was clear he had as little clue about how to be a father as he did about how to be a husband.

As I tried to lighten the mood for the kids, the small voice that had been whispering in my head grew a little louder. *What have you done? This is not the home and family life you wanted. This is a disaster.*

For the remainder of the vacation, Cullen, Gillian, and Dana hung out with me. We found a way to a peaceful co-existence. On this trip the girls really began to bond and enjoyed one another. They met some other kids about their age and spent the days swimming, hiking, shopping and parasailing. The diversion did them a world of good. Cullen was content spending the time reading, swimming, and relaxing with me.

Later in the week, when we went into town, Paul tried to make amends. Although he never said he was sorry, and in spite of my protests, he purchased some very expensive diamond jewelry for me. I felt like Malibu Barbie. I had all the accoutrements of glamour and wealth, living a plastic life devoid of anything of real value.

How in the world could I be married to this man? He didn't know me. He didn't listen to me. For my sake, and the sake of my own family the voice within was screaming –*get the hell out of this!*

Yet I looked at Alex and Dana. Their pain was palpable. I felt for them. If I left this wretched marriage, I would be just one more transient person in their lives. Another person who couldn't stand and deliver on the promises they had made. Another person who didn't love them enough to stay.

So again, and again, I silenced the voice within and made another effort. At this point in time his children's pain was worse than my own.

CHAPTER 10

A House is Not
a Home

When we returned to our rented apartment in Michigan, life continued along the same rocky trajectory.

Cullen went to Ypsilanti where he lived with Dino, a member of his band. Gillian escaped to the Pacific Northwest for three weeks of adventure travel. And Dana and Alex hung at the mall and around the apartment watching TV day and night.

In mid-August, just before we all returned to school and resumed our lives, Paul extended an invitation for us to attend The Great Corporate Campout in the Poconos. Cullen didn't stop to take a breath before he politely refused the invitation. Instead of saying what I read all over his face –which was "No Fucking Way" –instead he said, "I think I have a show or plans on Saturday. Really, thanks a lot, but I'm afraid I'm unavailable." The last vacation with this so-called family had been quite enough, thank you.

The rest of us were not so clever, so we stammered along, and in the end we had committed ourselves to attend this event none of us had any interest in at all.

Throughout the 10 hour drive we were subjected to the unabridged dissertation about how Paul was the inspiration behind The Great Corporate Campout. How he was solely responsible for seeing it come to fruition, and just in case no one else adequately acknowledged his contribution or sang his praises loud and long enough, he elaborated ad nauseam to be certain we all understood the magnitude of his grandeur.

When we arrived I was speechless. After his glorious build-up, this was a freaking trade show located in some dusty abandoned field at the foothills of the Poconos. There was a portable climbing structure, the likes of which could be seen at our local REI store. There was a scuba event where people stood in long lines to try diving in an over-sized kiddie pool. The water was murky and dirty from the multitude of sweaty bodies that had already taken their turns. *No thank you.* But mostly there were people picking up schwag from the vendors and copious amounts of junk that would eventually find its way to the landfill. The entire event defaced the earth and it disgusted me. I found myself thinking: *I should have known Paul would be responsible for something like this.* My estimation of this man I'd married had sunk to a new low.

We stayed at a beautiful hotel in the Poconos where Paul glad-handed with his old business compatriots. They ate and drank to excess and looked like they had been doing so for years. *This was camp?* Not hardly. I looked about and wondered … *How in the name of heaven had this become my life?*

There was a fly-fishing expedition being offered by Orvis and I wanted to attend. I had watched people fly-fish before, but had never tried it. The people I know who fly-fish have become totally engrossed with it. The solitude and beauty of standing in a river appealed to me. But this interfered with another event where Paul wanted me to put in some face time. So again, I did what was expected of me rather than what I wanted to do.

All in all, I'd done my best to support Paul in his farcical camp. And to boot, I'd given up doing the only thing I had any real interest in. I'd hoped he would notice and say thank you. However, acknowledging the sacrifices of others and expressing gratitude were not in my husband's repertoire of skills.

Ten hours in the car each way, a couple of thousand dollars later, and we were traveling back to Michigan. I was feeling overwhelmingly sad, bordering on desperation after such a disappointing weekend.

Thankfully, we had two audio books to listen to on our trip home, as we had very little to talk about. The first was a mystery about a serial killer with graphic, gruesome descriptions of the brutal murders of young women. This was clearly not my choice.

The second book was <u>Black</u> by Ted Dekkar. We had listened for about an hour. As Paul put in the next disc to continue the story, the kids and I discussed the book. We each offered our opinion as what we thought the story was about.

"I like this story much more than I thought I would. I don't usually like science fiction," Gillian commented.

"Me too," Dana piped up. "Alex, you like sci-fi and fantasy movies, what do you think?" She asked.

"It's cool. I don't really like to read, but I do like sci-fi movies. I didn't think I would like just having someone read a book to me. But I do." Alex said.

"I'm not certain it's just sci-fi, perhaps it's a spiritual story that's heavily veiled in fantasy," I suggested.

"Hmm … What do you mean?" one of the kids replied thoughtfully, encouraging me to expand on my thinking.

"Maybe Tanis is supposed to be Adam, and Elyon represents God, and Teeleh could be Satan," I continued. All the kids had gone to Catholic Schools so they were all well acquainted with the creation scriptures of the Old Testament.

But before any of the kids could even consider this alternative perspective, Paul burst out laughing as if this was the most ridiculous thing he had ever heard.

When I looked at him he was sneering at me. "How absolutely typical of you. You see religion in everything. It's always about good and evil with you. You always try to make everything over in a way you can wrap your little feeble brain around. Why must you always do that? You never just accept things the way they are. You always ruin things for me. Start the Goddamn story. I don't want to hear any more of your stupidity and your narrow mindedness."

"Shut up Dad! You're so rude! Jeanne, don't listen to him. He's a big jerk." Dana was the first to come to my defense and she reached over to hold my hand.

"Don't you ever speak to my mother like that again," Gillian roared at him.

"Or what Gillian. Just what are you gonna do about it?" He challenged her.

"Talk about not leaving a space for anyone else's opinion. What is it with you? You're so arrogant you always have to be right." Gillian was spitting mad, and she too had kept quiet far too long. "My mom always listens to what other people have to say; you might give her the same kind of consideration, every now and again." Now that she had started, there was no stopping her. "And oh by the way, Mr. Brilliance, I think she's absolutely right about this story. You just can't bear the fact she's smart and saw something you missed."

He pushed play and turned up the volume and he turned his eyes back toward the highway.

I had been subjected to his tirades before, but not in the presence of the kids. He painted me into a box that made me look simple and stupid. His comment was so rude and so purposefully hurtful. He knew how I really try to keep an open mind. It was glaringly obvious to everyone in the car what little regard he had for me, and how little he understood my spiritual side. He ridiculed my beliefs, and was demeaning to me as a person. He made these comments in the presence of my daughter and his children. I felt like I had been publicly slapped.

A painful, awkward silence hung in the air while the story played on. Alex kept silent. When we stopped for gas I moved to the backseat and sat between the girls and they each held one of my hands while we looked out the windows. I sat there smoldering with anger, but felt somewhat vindicated as the story played on, and the spiritual references became increasingly obvious.

In addition to his nastiness, when we arrived back at the apartment, Paul made it known that he still expected me to meet my obligation and take his daughter to the oral surgeon the next morning. The surgery was scheduled for 8 o'clock. The office was two hours away, and we would have to drive during the morning rush hour.

I spent the night in the car. I couldn't stand to be in his presence. When Gillian brought me a pillow and a blanket she found me crying. "Mom, oh Mom, I love you so much."

"Oh honey, I love you too," I replied as she wrapped me in her arms and dried the tears from my face. Although it was very late and we had been in the car all day, she didn't go back inside immediately.

She started slowly. She had witnessed Paul and his nastiness, and she had things she needed to say, "You cannot stay with him. He doesn't love you or anyone else. He's just so mean."

"I'm sorry you had to witness that." I knew what she said was true. I had tried to protect the kids from these all too frequent incidents, and from his wicked tongue.

"I can only imagine what he says to you when no one else is around." She paused and took a deep breath. "Why don't you divorce him? We can start over. We don't need that big house and all his *shit*. Cullen leaves for college next week. We can find a place for you, me, and Dana. Let's just leave him." She had thought this through. She had a plan.

"I need to think, darling. I love you so. I will find a way to work this out. I promise." She and I covered ourselves with the blanket, and fell asleep for a little while. When Gillian awoke I sent her back to bed in the apartment, and I spent the remainder of the night in the car.

In the morning, I took Dana to the oral surgeon where she had her wisdom teeth removed. It certainly wasn't her fault her father was an asshole. Once she was home and safely tucked into bed, I went out to my car –*a.k.a.* my private office –to make a phone call. I needed to make an appointment of my own.

∽

The next day Ed met me for lunch at The Fox and Hounds, just down the street from his office. He and I had been friends for a long time. He and Fred were friends since law school, and I was the Godmother for his three children. He was also a divorce attorney.

After Fred had died, Ed had once told me, "You and Fred had it all. I was always so envious of what you had.

Together you were the Alpha and the Omega. I have never known any couple to have what the two of you had."

Ed listened and placed his hand over mine as the story unfolded about the nightmare of my marriage. I remember feeling so much shame for the mess I had made of my life. Ed clearly held me in high regard, and yet I felt like a total fuck up. I was humiliated and rightly so. I explained the mess I had made of my life, and all of the financial repercussions. I had already sold my home and the entire proceeds had been used as a down payment on Paul's Dream Palace in the woods. The new house would be completed in less than a month.

Ed prompted, "And so ..."

I was looking for some very basic information. "Hypothetically, how does one go about getting a divorce?" For me, this was uncharted territory. It was fearful ground to cross. As I sat there, I realized I had hardly eaten a bite. My mouth was dry, my heart raced, my palms were sweating, and my stomach turned. I was concerned Paul would find out I had consulted Ed, and that I was even considering a divorce.

It was in that moment I realized something greater: I, who had always been a brave person, had become afraid. I was afraid of Paul's nastiness, his anger, and his rage. I was afraid of his retribution. How had so much fear grown in me?

Ed listened patiently and gently offered his thoughts. "This will not get better. The only question is –do you want to end your suffering now or later?"

Again, I felt my heart racing. I needed to think. Where would we live? I had given up my home to start a new life … and now I felt like I was *a million miles from home.* It wasn't the house, of course, dear as that place had been to the kids and me. It was the sense of family I deeply missed. Gillian and Dana had bonded like sisters now. I loved Dana. How could I leave her behind with this monstrous father?

I thanked Ed, promising to call if I needed him.

I returned to the safety of my car. I was unable to eat my lunch. I had no appetite. Yet I felt like I had been eating rocks. My hands were moist with perspiration as I gripped the steering wheel. My heart was racing. I needed to regain my composure.

I lowered the visor and looked in the mirror. The few tears I shed during lunch had left the tracks of mascara under my eyes. I fixed my make-up and I took a good long look in the mirror. I was worried. Here I had been in a public place, meeting with a very handsome man, my long-time friend, who happened to be a divorce attorney. What if someone had seen me? What if word got back to Paul? What then?

I didn't put it past him to have me followed. I know in the past he had hired someone to follow two of his ex-wives. Or was I just being paranoid?

In that moment, I understood how victims of domestic abuse feel. They fear their partners. Is that what I was? Was I a victim of domestic abuse? Paul had never hit me. But he had hurt me, repeatedly, by his nastiness, and I was afraid of him.

∾

Paul gave me some space, which he often did after one of his vicious verbal beatings. We treated one another politely, like one might treat a stranger. The next week provided us some reprieve as Gillian, Cullen, and I made another road trip to Bozeman, Montana. It was time to take Cullen to college. He had decided to study music and so he entered his freshman year at Montana State University.

The three of us left for Montana early. We needed this time together. When we arrived we explored Bozeman, rode horseback in the mountains, and spent a few days hiking and exploring in Yellowstone. This was my idea of family time. Perhaps it was because I was with my family, not just the conglomeration of disparate souls who resided in the same house.

When the time came to unload Cullen's things and move him into the dorm, I procrastinated. I didn't want to leave him. That afternoon we went for a hike and it was like old times, just the kids and me, and an afternoon filled with love and laughter. The sun dipped in the sky and the evening came; it was time to leave Cullen behind. I found a few moments to be alone … and cried my heart out.

Where had the time gone? Where had my life gone? How could I leave my beloved son? I had lost so much.

I turned to God and prayed. *Help me! I have lost the life I loved. My son will be far away from me. My home is gone and my family is moving apart. And I'm living a nightmare.*

I found Gillian and it was clear she also felt the pain of Cullen leaving. In our despair, once again we clung to one another.

Then I did what parents everywhere must one day do. I said goodbye to my child and let him walk free into his own life.

And I went back to mine.

∾

When we had returned home, the school year was about to begin, and my work provided me a sanctuary. It was the one place I felt emotionally safe and valued.

After much reflection I decided to make yet another attempt to make my marriage work. I made a pact with God. I would stay and try to be a good influence in Paul's life, and in the lives of his children. So I invited Paul to go to church with me, but he turned me down again and again.

One Saturday night after I had invited him to join me at church in the morning, he cited his reasons. "Me and God are like this," he said, as he held his two fingers side by side.

"Church is for the unwashed masses, but not for me. I have an exclusive relationship with God. And if God loves you, like you so often claim he does, then the way I figure it ... God would want you to be happy, and how could you ever be happy in heaven without me? So the way I see it, even if I'm wrong ... *you'll* get me in."

Huh ... how could I ever be happy without him? The very notion of spending all of eternity with this man filled me with terror. *What the hell was I doing?*

He thought he was funny, but I found his lack of humility repugnant.

So there, I asked and he answered. Most of the time, I went to church alone. Sometimes Gillian worked in the nursery with the infants. Sometimes Dana would come along and help with the little children, but for the most part I went alone. Week after week I would sit in the sanctuary by myself. Church became my lifeline, and I held on.

During those months, Ed's words were never far from my consciousness. "This will not get better. The only question is –do you want to end this suffering now or later?"

But my faith and determination were hard at work, and yet I was in a spiritual no-man's land. Single and alone, yet married to someone who didn't know me and didn't love me. I wrestled daily with the views of my church on marriage, as I am a Catholic, albeit an *àla carte* Catholic.

There were others to consider as well. I pondered the views of my family on divorce, because it was clearly not something my parents condoned. On the other hand, I thought, *I'm 48 years old. At what point in my life am I going to stand up and become a fully functioning adult who takes care of herself and not just everyone else?*

And so the no-man's land started to become an inner war zone, as the ongoing daily banter within my head went back and forth. *For the love of God*, the question tormented me, *should I stay or should I go?* I was my own advocate as well as my inner critic and I became greatly proficient at the art and skill of internal debate.

The time to move into the new house crawled steadily closer.

On Labor Day weekend the new house was ready. It had taken 20 months to build and was magnificent. Paul had wanted a grand home with curb appeal. He certainly got what he wanted. However, the quarter mile long driveway prevented anyone from ever seeing his palatial estate from said curb. The exterior was a combination of red brick, limestone, stucco, and rough-cut timbers. It had old world charm on the outside but the interior was graced with every possible modern convenience. In this 8,000 square foot home there were eight bedrooms, eight bathrooms, five fireplaces, a music room, theatre room, exercise room, wine room, and library. If you could imagine it, we had it. And of course nothing but the finest would do.

I was relieved when Paul suggested I go to church the morning of the move. He had agreed to hire two men to unload the heavy furniture. He implied I would be in the way, so I went to Mass.

Paul and I had already negotiated for hours about the placement of the furniture, and had agreed on the overall decorating plan. When I returned, later that morning, I expected to find things going according to our plan and our agreement.

I was in for a new shock.

Paul's furniture had been moved into the living room, dining room, and family room. In spite of our agreement, Paul had directed the movers to put all of my belongings, and the furniture from my home into the unfinished basement. The basement was still dirty, dusty, and littered with construction debris.

This was the proverbial straw that broke the camel's back. I lost my mind. I yelled, screamed, and cried. I talked about killing myself.

In response, Paul acted like he was baffled and surprised. The movers slipped outside, out of range. Gillian tried to comfort me. He gave her a look, seeking confirmation that I was indeed mentally ill, and that my behavior was totally unfounded. As if my reaction had nothing at all to do with his pushing, pushing, and pushing me closer and closer to the edge.

In the end, Paul took the movers aside, saying just loud enough for me to overhear, "Excuse me, guys, why don't you take a break and give me just a few minutes. I need to negotiate with my *psycho* wife. She gets like this, you know … irrational and unreasonable."

Right. They nodded as if he was the one worthy of compassion and sympathy, and I was a lunatic.

Welcome to my beautiful new home.

Did I leave or go to another part of the house? I don't recall. My mind has protected me from that which was unbearable. Memory has grown hazy and the details of the subsequent hours have been lost. There was so much work to do. Perhaps I went to a distant part of the house and began to unpack boxes and make beds. It was up to me to move the family in. So I did what was expected. I kept my mouth shut, and didn't speak about my feelings. I put my head down and got to work.

A couple of weeks later, I negotiated with the landscapers to move one of my couches upstairs to the music room. A small victory as everything else that was mine, from my previous life, was warehoused in the storage area in the basement.

∾

Somehow, Paul and I reached yet another truce.

The first year in the house, we finished the basement and I worked the next six months as a common laborer, painting walls, and scooting around on my ass on the basement floor cleaning the adhesive off of the wooden floor. We purchased miles of ivory lace and my mother, with minimal assistance from me, made lace curtains for nearly 100 windows. When I wasn't at work or working inside the house, I could be found outside working on the landscaping and in the gardens.

The truce held –I was spending every waking moment in this new house trying to make it a home.

But a house is not a home if there is no love. No matter how I tried, this was a pretty big omission in my book. And still I tried to wrap my head around it.

Paul had been overly affectionate before we married, but now he acted as if he found my body repulsive. He either drank himself into oblivion at the day's end or left me asleep in a chair in front of the TV, only to wake in the early morning hours alone, and to find that my husband had gone off to bed without me ... again.

When he did sleep in the same bed with me, Paul insisted we sleep with our bedroom door open –just in case his daughter might need him. This sounded good in theory except that Dana was nearly 16 years old.

There was no intimacy in the morning either. Morning after morning my dog, Duncan, would wake me for her breakfast and to go outside. Paul pretended to be asleep, because the care of the dog was my responsibility. I would quietly slip out of bed and when she was all taken care of, I was prepared to slip back into bed beside my husband.

On the weekends, our teenaged daughters would be asleep for hours or they were spending the night with their girlfriends –so there was no need to keep the bedroom door wide open.

A man in love with his wife could make love to her as freely as he wanted.

But no sooner had I let the dog back in, there was Paul, out of bed and standing in the kitchen.

This was played out repeatedly, and it didn't take a rocket scientist to figure it out that he was avoiding sex. What kind of man had I married? The kind that wasn't interested in me, that was for certain.

My pride got in the way. I wouldn't beg. I wouldn't plead. If he wanted me … he would have to initiate it.

So I waited, and waited, and he never touched me. The inner war continued.

Stay and be a faithful spouse. Or go?

We moved into months, and months, and months of a sexless co-existence.

CHAPTER 11

The Agony Continues

I kept busy throughout the fall and early winter settling in, and trying to turn this 8,000 square foot palace into a home. It hadn't been easy. There was much to do to transform the space so it didn't feel like something out of a magazine, but rather a real home that was a reflection of the people who lived there. Perhaps that was why the transformation was so difficult, because of the discordant souls who called this abode their home.

Alex was going to college in the next town, and was living in a dorm on campus. He was home occasionally, but I saw very little of him. If truth be told, I was all right with it. I really wanted to like him, but his immaturity coupled with his manipulative behavior made it difficult for me to find a way to relate to him. I tried to remember he was still a kid … a work in progress. But then, weren't we all?

I awaited Cullen's Christmas homecoming with great anticipation. It had been months since he went away to college, and although we had spoken frequently on the phone, it just wasn't the same. I wanted to see him, and just be in his presence. I missed him dearly.

When he finally arrived it was so good to see him. I cut him some slack, because I wanted him to settle in and feel at home. His compatriots visited regularly at the house complete with all the arrogance of the newly independent college students that they were. They were a gang of many, and had been buddies for years and years. Many of these guys had also known Paul's son since grade school, but they had never been friends, and that hadn't changed.

Cullen was cordial to Alex, but less than inclusive. He had a limited amount of time at home, and he didn't intend to spend it with my husband's son. Alex and Cullen had no relationship. Last summer's confrontation had cemented that reality. They were stepbrothers in name only.

The dividing line had been drawn. My family was on one side and Paul's was on the other. There was no cohesion, and Alex sought revenge for being excluded from Cullen and his entourage.

Alex became the self-appointed tattletale. He pointed out all of the rule violations, and there were many. Smoking pot, under-age drinking, eating Alex's special snacks, playing Alex's video games and God forbid, touching Daddy's grand piano.

Cullen was a music major, and at this point he was the only one who knew how to play the piano. Why would someone own an $80,000 Steinway Grand Piano if they didn't know how to play it and didn't keep it tuned? Must have been to impress the neighbors, as it certainly looked lovely sitting in the living room. But that is another story.

So Alex tattled to his father, and Paul characteristically took Alex's side and I came to my son's defense. I argued we should let the boys figure this out and stay out of it. They were no longer children. Paul insisted that I lower the boom on my son and make him abide by the house rules. Good luck making a 19-year-old young man do anything he doesn't choose to do. I wanted Cullen to want to come home, and I wouldn't go to war with him over these things. He knew full well how I felt about the drinking and the pot, and although I'm certain he broke those rules, he did so with discretion. He and his pals would go out for a walk in the woods behind the house. Cullen knew where I stood, we had been down that path so many times, but frankly the rest of Alex's complaints were just chicken shit. There comes a time when a parent needs to choose which battles they intend to fight. Eating Alex's gumdrops didn't even make the list of my concerns.

Cullen had worked hard at school and earned a 3.7 his first semester at college, and after his less than stellar performance in high school, I was exceedingly proud of him. Alex, however, had partied excessively all semester, and didn't pass a single class. But no one told me. At Christmas dinner I told my family of Cullen's accomplishment, and he basked in the praise of his family. Later, Paul would chastise me for making poor Alex feel bad.

Paul had assured that his children's interests were well taken care of. Cullen and Gillian had their own bedrooms and shared a connecting Jack and Jill bath. They had always shared a bathroom and had no problem with the arrangement. Dana had her own room and a private attached bath and Alex had a room on the lower level with his own bath, a private entrance, and access to the theater room, work out room, bar and wine room.

After a repeat performance the second semester, Alexander moved home. He had flunked out of college.

I began to feel like I needed Alex's permission to enter the lower level of the house. He drank excessively and suffered with depression. He slept all day, and partied all night, every night. He rarely bathed, and regularly brought home his new *friends* from the bar.

Paul let it go, and I felt like a visitor in my own house. This wasn't a home. It felt more like a brothel.

Gillian was working at Planet Rock where she taught rock climbing. She had worked full-time all summer. She also worked as a nanny for a five-year-old little girl whose father had custody, and was in the middle of an acrimonious divorce. Her compassion for the hurt and pain of others grew. She was a delight to watch as she grew in grace and wisdom. It broke my heart, but she also felt uncomfortable at home, so instead of coming home she sought refuge at work. She went to Planet Rock even when she wasn't working.

Dana began to invite her girlfriends to the house every weekend, and this gaggle of girls acted as if Dana was the head of the household. I was without any authority in my own home. It didn't feel good.

So I took long walks with my dog. My son had gone back to college, and my daughter was either at school or working, and I felt like an unwelcome intruder in my own home. What was I doing? This was not my home. How had this become my life? I had wanted to be a wife, and mother, and I felt as if I was neither. I was so lonely. My heart was broken, and cried out for love and a different way of being.

Cullen came home that summer after his freshman year.

School was out on June 15th and my teaching responsibilities came to an end. It had been a long year and I was tired. I had a few things yet to negotiate on my contract for the following school year so I had several meetings scheduled for the day after graduation. That morning I awoke with a massive frontal headache. I have only had 2 or 3 real headaches in my life, and this was one of them. But I had an appointment with Glen, the assistant headmaster, about a conference I was supposed to attend in Santa Fe, New Mexico. In addition I had a meeting with the Director of Finance about my compensation for a program I had been asked to chair in the upcoming school year.

The meeting regarding my contract was resolved quickly, and my meeting with Glen was scheduled for 1:00 PM. But by 2:00 PM he was still tied up and

I was feeling sick to my stomach. So rather then wait for him, I headed for home. I was only part way there when Glen called to see if I was still available. But I begged off. I was not well.

Mom was still at the house when I arrived and was still working on those curtains. She asked for my help. I helped her measure, and cut the lace, and she gave me a panel to hem. I tried for about thirty minutes, but I wasn't feeling well so I went to lie down. It was the middle of the afternoon, and taking a nap midday was so unlike me. I knew Mom was frustrated. This was my house, after all, and she had been working on the curtains for months. Since she couldn't get any assistance from me, she decided to go home. We would work on these curtains another day.

At 4:00 PM Cullen came home, and by then I was feeling really rough. I asked him to take me to the hospital. I was really ill. I was doubling over with abdominal pain. I didn't think I could drive myself. He took me to the local urgent care center and at my request, he called Paul to tell him what was going on. Cullen waited with me until Paul arrived. It was now evening.

The doctors were perplexed. They started with a brain scan because of the headache I woke with. It had been plaguing me all day. They gave me some morphine for the abdominal pain, and some contrast fluid to drink because they wanted to get an x-ray of my abdomen.

I began to vomit.

They started an IV. They did not know what was wrong with me. The morphine kicked in, and I began to doze on and off as they took me in for an x-ray and drew some blood.

Sometime during the evening, Paul left and went home. I was still vomiting and incoherent due to the morphine. I don't remember him leaving. I just know that I was dreadfully ill, doped up, and all alone.

Sometime in the early morning hours, the doctor tried to talk to me, but I couldn't hold a conversation. I was so ill. He wanted to admit me to the hospital, but which one? I was so incoherent I couldn't tell him which hospital my insurance would cover. I could not remember, and I began to cry. I asked him to call my husband. He told me he had tried repeatedly, but he was unable to reach him. He didn't answer his phone. They needed to do emergency exploratory abdominal surgery to determine what was wrong.

I couldn't think straight. They decided to send me to St. Joe's by ambulance. I don't remember much from that night. I do remember the siren, and the lights, and it was raining. I remember I was embarrassed because I vomited in the ambulance. I remember apologizing and the paramedics were very kind. It was the middle of the night. I didn't know where I was going. They didn't know what was wrong with me. I was afraid. No one in my family knew where I was. I was alone. I have never felt so alone and vulnerable in all my life.

In the morning, as I was signing consent forms for exploratory surgery with all the elaborate descriptions of every possible outcome, including death or irreparable complications, in walked my husband after a good night's sleep.

"Where were you?" I asked.

"I went home. I was tired. You know I don't like hospitals." He responded matter of fact.

I couldn't believe my ears.

"I went back to the urgent care center this morning. I couldn't find out where they had taken you. No one knew." He offered this up as some type of explanation as the nurse prepped me for surgery.

I was afraid.

In the end, I had an acute appendicitis. My appendix ruptured just as they removed it.

When I awoke, my mother and dad were at my bedside. Paul had gone to work.

Later, my friend Cathy and her husband, *My Keith*, came to the hospital to visit. Cathy knew the sad state of my marriage. Gillian came and crawled onto the bed with me. She stroked my hair and stayed close. Paul showed up later in the evening, and the people who really loved me did not leave. They all stayed until the visiting hours were over. I slept off and on, and within 48 hours I was released. It was my mother who came to take me home.

I healed slowly from the surgery. I needed to rest and take it easy for a few weeks. They loaded me up with antibiotics, which took care of the infection. Physically, I would be okay, but emotionally the trauma and the feelings of fear and abandonment lingered. My dog, Duncan, spent all day, everyday, lying next to my bed. She loved me. I wouldn't have left her if she were as sick as I had been. Yet my husband loved me less, and cared less for me than I loved and cared for my dog. This was the harsh and brutal reality of my life.

The state of my marriage could no longer be denied, and we had been married less than two years. This man didn't love me and it was highly unlikely he ever would.

I had planned to work in the garden that summer, but I couldn't after my abdominal surgery. My children were working and building their own lives, and my priorities were not theirs or anyone else's for that matter.

In late July, I was well enough to go to the *Spiritual and Ethical Education* conference in Santa Fe with my friend Joanne from work. We had a lovely time. I really liked the people I met. It was a workshop where we read, wrote, taught one another, and led discussions. The people in the workshop really seemed to value me, and they listened when I spoke.

I grew.

In my marriage I felt discounted and disregarded, but here among my new acquaintances I felt validated. My work was my refuge. How could I possibly go home?

Joanne listened as I talked about my marriage. She was divorced and she understood. Her strength helped me to see that perhaps there was a way out.

I let the notion percolate.

I felt safe and valued. The week away was very good for me. I played with the notion of moving to Santa Fe. What would it be like to live in a community where I felt loved and respected? The contrast to the life I was living was glaring.

In spite of the fact that my kids were growing up, I was still a mother with responsibilities I took seriously.

I would have loved to stay in Santa Fe and reinvent my life. But now was not the time.

Gillian would be a high school junior that fall. My life belonged to her. My life belonged to Cullen. It was my responsibility to see my children onto adulthood. I honored that responsibility.

When I returned to Michigan, no one had bothered to water the plants in my garden, and in my absence all the plants had died. That which I valued, and worked so hard to create had been disregarded.

The summer drew to an end. One afternoon, while I was at home, the UPS man delivered a couple of boxes. This wasn't unusual because Paul ordered things over the Internet all the time, and the boxes would accumulate in the foyer until he got around to opening them. But these boxes were addressed to me. I was confused. I hadn't ordered anything. I opened them. The boxes contained beer signs and drinking paraphernalia.

I couldn't believe my eyes. What in heaven's name was going on and for how long? I had been getting email from PayPal for months, but I didn't have a PayPal account so I didn't open it. I thought it was spam. Alex had been ordering things on Ebay for months, and had been using my credit card without my knowledge or permission. He had opened a PayPal account with my credit card. Since he didn't work or go to school, and lived in the lower level of this palace; he was the one who collected the boxes from the deliveryman. I was infuriated.

I investigated further, and it appeared he had spent about $500 of my money over the past few months or at least that was as much as I could trace. I closed the PayPal account and reported my credit card stolen.

When I brought this up with Paul, he defended Alex.

What? How could he possibly rationalize this? It was out and out stealing.

"Perhaps Alex feels he is entitled to use your credit card because of all the stuff you buy for Cullen," he suggested this as a possible explanation. "He probably feels you owe it to him as a way to somehow even the score."

Was this guy for real?

"I don't want you to confront Alex," he stated, "you know how emotionally fragile he is right now." And so with that, Paul promised he would deal with his son, and then he recommended that I find a place to lock my purse in my own home.

Seriously.

The days turned to weeks, and still Paul hadn't spoken with Alex so I took matters into my own hands. Paul and Alex were sitting together at the kitchen table while I prepared dinner. I joined them at the table. I gave Paul a look and he shrugged. I interpreted this as permission to go ahead. "Alex," I began, "the UPS man delivered a few boxes. They were addressed to me so I opened them, but I think they belong to you." I waited for him to respond.

Without missing a beat, he said, "Oh good. Where's my stuff?" he looked down at his plate and shoveled in another mouthful of his burrito.

"I have it." I looked him in the eye and waited. "Any idea why they were addressed to me?"

"No." He looked up at me appearing truly bewildered and perplexed. He was such a well-practiced liar.

"Just a minute, I'll be right back." Alexander said as he got up and headed for the bathroom. Paul and I remained at the kitchen table. We sat in silence as we awaited his return. Time passed and Paul went to look for Alex. He had left in his car.

"I told you not to confront him. I told you I would handle it." Paul glared at me.

"That was weeks ago. Just when did you plan on getting around to it?" I was angry now.

Paul tried to blame Alex's behavior on me and I was not having any of it. "It's your fault that my son doesn't want to live in his own home." He was spitting mad by now. "You've created such a hostile environment that you've pushed Alex out of his own home."

Really?

Paul poured himself another large glass of wine, stomped into the family room, and turned on the TV, leaving me with the dirty dishes.

Good-bye and good riddance you sneaky little thief.

Once again, Paul chose to close his eyes to Alex's behavior, but I could not. This kid was crying out for some discipline and boundaries. How much further would he push before he got himself into real trouble? Paul didn't have a clue how to help his son. But I wasn't sorry he was gone. His behavior was becoming increasingly egregious, and once again Paul had given him a pass.

Alexander had driven to northern Michigan to stay with his mother's sister, Aunt Betsy. Alex did not return for over six weeks.

Cullen had made the decision to transfer to a university in northern California. He wanted to study the bass with a world-renowned musician who was a professor there. So at the end of August, Gillian, Cullen, and I embarked on yet another cross-country road trip to take him to college.

I love my son and I believe in him. He owns his own life. It doesn't belong to me.

When we arrived in this university town the housing was limited, and we were late in the game. Most students had made their housing arrangements prior to leaving campus last spring. No university housing remained. We finally found an apartment at a place called the Colony Inn. It was dirty and nasty, and creeped me out, big time. I didn't like it at all. My instinct told me, *no –not here.* But it was all that was available. So he signed a month-to-month lease, and once again, I placed my beloved child in the hands of God. We scrubbed, scoured, and painted to make the place at least tolerable on the inside, and then it was time for Gillian and me to head for home. Again, my heart broke open as I left my son in that hellhole.

What kind of mother would consent to this?

We travelled on and soon Gillian was asleep in the seat next to me. The good-byes had been heart-wrenching for all of us. She needed to sleep to recover from the heartache.

I made my way down the interstate and my thoughts turned to God. I felt so fragile and vulnerable. I feared for my beloved boy. He was so far from home, and I couldn't protect him. I had often turned to God during the darkest points of my life; why did it feel so different to be asking for help now? Was it because so many of the problems I faced in my life were at least partially of my own doing? Bad decisions have consequences, and I had made some real doozies.

That night in the roadside hotel while Gillian was in the shower, in a moment of quiet and solitude, I dropped to my knees, and had a good long heart to heart with God. I thanked God for being an ever-abiding presence. I asked The Almighty to please keep my children safe. I was without pride or shame as I begged for mercy and forgiveness. So many mistakes had been made. I was so lost I wondered if I would ever find a way to right these wrongs, and find my way back to a place of joy and peace.

The message came back to me loud and clear—

I am with you always.
Stop disregarding your instincts.
Your intuition is strong.
Pay attention to it.

So I opened up the dialog, and I prayed for Cullen's safety day and night.

Within a few months, Cullen had moved into a house with some new friends he met on campus. Later, he told me the apartment complex where he had been living was affectionately referred to as the *Felony Inn,* given it was inhabited by tweakers or meth-heads. Lovely.

He had moved on. He was safe and grateful for his new home, and his new friends, and yet, he too was wiser for the experience.

Some people take full credit for the good things that happen in their lives and some see the hand of The Almighty and give thanks. My son was safe, and I thanked God for blessings received. I breathed a little easier.

Meanwhile, back on the home front, I returned to school and Gillian was on the go. When she wasn't at school she was working at Planet Rock. During her freshman and sophomore years of high school she had been a three-season athlete playing field hockey, lacrosse, and competing on the ski team. Now in her junior year she still participated on the ski team, but had decided to move on from the other teams. Now she spent most of her free time climbing, and she was very good at it.

She was disgusted with all the money that Paul spent. To counterbalance this influence in her life Gillian would spend the little free time she had helping to feed the poor in the City of Detroit. She worked with the children growing vegetables at an urban garden center called Earth Works, and on Saturday mornings she delivered food to the poor and the elderly with Focus Hope.

I was so immensely proud of her. She listened to her heart and did what she knew was right. I knew I could learn from her.

Paul never made the connection. Instead, over the course of three years he bought me a $20,000 diamond necklace and three fur coats, and I am a vegetarian! He wanted to dress me like Barbie. I was his arm candy. The logic being … if he had a glamorous wife then he must be a big swinging dick. I was little more than an accessory. He wanted me to make him look good.

I didn't need the jewelry or the furs … I needed love and affection. I needed to be known and valued for the person I was, complete with my faults and failings. I needed someone who could embrace me in my entirety … in my humanity, and in my divinity.

It had become increasingly difficult to put a good face on my marriage. Paul did not know me at all, and had no real interest in learning. I often felt like one of his employees as he tried to impose his will on me.

On more than one occasion I had told him, "Let's be clear here. I don't work for you. I'm your wife and your partner." I could no longer hold my tongue. I was spitting mad. I had listened to his ranting, and been given the lengthy list of things I needed to do or change about myself.

He wanted me to be putty in his hands so he could mold me into some domestic, servile, beauty queen he could take to corporate functions when a spouse was needed.

Did I mention I'm a fiery redhead … good luck with that … and so I listened to my inner voice that said loud and clear–

I am made in the image and likeness of The Almighty.
I am a good person.

I am worthy of love and respect.
Stay true to who you are.

Paul may have heard me, but he never took my words to heart. He continued to try to manipulate me and cajole me into following his lead to a place I had no desire to go.

His world was all about appearances and the acquisition of things. There were times when I felt compassion for him, in spite of how miserable I was in this marriage. For there was an emptiness deep within him, and there would never be enough money, or power, or prestige, or material wealth to fill him up, and make him feel whole. He was trying to fill a spiritual void with material things, and it just does not work that way. His soul was crying out for something more, and he silenced those cries with alcohol, and shopping, and he blamed me for my inability to make everything all right in his world.

So he shopped and shopped and tried to fill the palace with more and more beautiful adornments. He bought Dana a new bedroom set; complete with a king size bed, dresser and mirror combo, chest of drawers, two nightstands, a desk, and chair. The whole set was from the Thomasville Palatial Line. How aptly named.

Gillian slept in her twin bed that she had since she left her crib and it was just fine with her.

Whatever Paul was about, Gillian wanted no part of it.

My beloved daughter could be my guide.

She had found a way to live in this world, but clearly she was not of this world.

If she could do it … maybe I could too.

One night after a particularly brutal day I crawled into bed, and Paul snored loudly on his side. I waited for sleep to release me from my worries and anxieties. I had all of the trappings of wealth. From the outside looking in it may have appeared to be the good life. But I had never felt so alone and lonely.

An old song began to play softly in my brain …

I don't know how to tell you,
it's difficult to say
I never in my wildest dreams
imagined it this way
But sometimes
I just don't know you
There's a stranger in our home
When I'm lying right beside you
is when I'm most alone

Love is why I came here in the first place
Love is now the reason I must go
Love is all I ever hoped to find here
Love is still the only dream I know

I think my heart is broken
There's an emptiness inside
So many things I've longed for
have so often been denied

Still I wouldn't try to change you
there's no one here to blame
There are just some things that mean so much
and we just don't feel the same

Love is why I came here in the first place
Love is now the reason I must go
Love is all I ever hoped to find here
Love is still the only dream I know
True love is still the only dream I know

–John Denver
Seasons of the Heart

I hadn't thought of this song in years. But I supposed it was stored in some distant part of my memory, and yet that night it played on and nudged me.
Is this my intuition?
Is this the voice of God?
In the dark of night I vowed to pay attention.

CHAPTER 12

Listen to the Voices

Little by little, a voice began to resonate from somewhere within my soul, and it would not let me rest. I spent many fitful nights wrestling with my conscience. And the question was always the same: *Do I stay ... or do I go?*

The reality that was so hard to face was that my husband didn't love me. In my heart I didn't think he ever had ... or ever would.

Yet another part of me argued on and on inside my brain. I couldn't quiet these voices. One would speak and offered up an equally compelling reason to stay in my marriage. The voice begged me to consider and reconsider, as ending a marriage and breaking the commitment I'd made was not something I could do easily. And then my heart would speak: *He doesn't love you.* And then, again, my head: *But you made a vow.* So it went, I was tortured and miserable.

But the reality is that I'm a stubborn woman. I'm not a quitter. And I don't like to lose. If I were going to travel down the road to divorce it wouldn't be because I didn't give my marriage the best effort I could.

So I decided to see if there was any possibility of restarting this marriage and coming to some type of reconciliation. I started with what I knew about reconciliation. In the Catholic religion, when one is reconciled with God it is considered a blessed sacrament. I really struggled with the idea of breaking my marriage vows and the destruction of that promise.

One night, lying in bed, with Paul a million miles away from me, yet still sleeping in the same bed, I thought back on the lessons I had learned as a child in catechism.

How is one reconciled with God?

The steps were so simple I could recite them in my sleep:

−first you must own up to what you have done wrong ...
−next you must be truly sorry for your sins ...
−then you ask God for forgiveness ...
−and then one must promise to try to sin no more.

I found myself wondering:

How could I have gone so long without really owning up to the problems and sin in my own life?

Lying there in the dark I thought about sin.

I had grown up Catholic and there had been an emphasis on sin, but now in my adult life I didn't think much about it. Sin had become an antiquated notion, at least in my world. Things had changed. People weren't talking much about sin anymore. People called them choices, mistakes, or our own personal prerogatives. I was one of those people.

Now again, I felt like I'd been eating rocks. Perhaps it was just the undigested emotion making me feel ill. Guilt. Rather than talking myself out of it, I realized I needed to feel the guilt and the sorrow of my broken marriage. I'd made mistakes that had brought me to this place of suffering. Pain, guilt and sorrow are the consequences of making bad choices. These were not emotions that should be disregarded or medicated away. If I sat with these feelings long enough and felt bad enough … it may be an incentive to make the changes that were necessary in my life.

Besides needing to feel the pain that resulted from my own sins, I needed to be honest with myself, and with my Creator … and also with Paul. Oh, that would be difficult. I had played a role in this mess I was in. But if I didn't own my part of this, I knew I would continue to blame Paul, and continue to feel like a victim.

I'm a hardheaded woman, and I didn't play the victim role very well … no, not very well at all.

So there was that to face too. Why did I flee from confrontation? The truth was, I feared my own anger. There had been times I didn't trust myself to speak –and with good reason. So instead of trying to talk things out, like reasonable adults do, I'd fled. I had been running from the conflicts, and the problems in my marriage. There had been times when leaving hadn't been an option, and when I'd been left with no exit, I'd lashed out with my fiery tongue. I used it as a weapon to protect myself, and it hadn't been pretty.

I'd been doing this for a long time and it wasn't working for me. I was miserable.

Staring up at the ceiling in the dark, it was like facing myself in the mirror. I made a conscious choice to change my tactics. Instead of fleeing or lashing out, I needed to start by being honest with myself.

It was painful to admit this fiasco wasn't just something that happened *to* me. I had been an active participant. There was a secret I'd hidden from for some time. And now, here was the raw truth:

Yes, I'd been lonely, that was true enough. But my desires for a life of ease and luxury had led me astray from my place of peace. I had been swayed by the offers of jewelry, furs, and the big house. So I traded a life created out of love, for a life of abject loneliness in Paul's gilded cage. My greed, my selfishness, my faltering, and my failings played a role in the choices I had made. Too often, I had taken the easy way; the path of least resistance as opposed to doing what I knew in my heart was the right thing to do.

Oh dear God, forgive me. There in the night, my tears began to flow as my heart opened to receive the forgiveness I needed so badly.

❧

That was step one.

Next I needed to try to make amends with Paul.

One evening, the kids were out doing one thing or another. I had stopped at the market and bought a filet, as I knew that steak was one of Paul's favorite foods. As I prepared his dinner, I thought about how best to approach him, to ask for his forgiveness. I set the table, and opened the wine, and in my heart I asked God to help me.

When we were seated I started slowly. "Paul I know that things have been pretty rough lately."

He lowered his face towards his plate and continued to shovel his beef tenderloin into his mouth.

I took a deep breath and continued, "I just wanted to say how sorry I am."

No response. Instead, he got up from the table and went to the refrigerator. Returning with a bottle of ketchup, he sat down, and proceeded to cover the remainder of his steak with ketchup.

He didn't say anything so I continued, "You know that I don't like to fight with you, but I know my running away from you hasn't made things any better between us."

Suddenly, he looked up from his plate. "Well, well, well ... " he said sarcastically, continuing to chew as he spoke, with food spilling from his mouth. "Will wonders never cease? This is a first. I didn't know the words ... I'm sorry ... were in your vocabulary."

I paused, shaken. This wasn't exactly how I thought he would respond.

Nonetheless, I took a deep breath and refilled his wine glass, then gathered the courage to continue. "I know that I'm not very good at communicating when you're so angry with me. I know I'm conflict-avoidant. The fighting is hard for me and I truly am sorry."

Silence.

I ran through the steps in my head:

One ... *say you are sorry* ... did that.

Two ... *confess your wrong-doings* ... did that.

I waited for him to react to my apology. I hoped he would accept it.

Finally, Paul put his fork down and took a long pull from the wine glass. "Really. Well, let me tell you something. If you want this marriage to work you had better start paying attention to what I need or I will find someone else who will."

I felt myself go numb inside.

"I give you this beautiful home to live in, and in return you're always running away from me."

Numbness turned to seething.

So this is how it was going to be –after I had asked him for his forgiveness. And what was he saying? –This was my home too. I'd paid for half of it. He didn't give me this home. It was mine just as much as it was his. Did he really believe what he just said?

Still, true to my nature ... again ... I kept my mouth shut and turned the anger in.

Paul had no trouble attacking me. "I'm your husband and I expect you to be here when I get home at night. But no, you're never here. You never live up to your responsibilities around here." He was revved up by then, and food and wine were spraying from his mouth as his voice rose to a shout.

Marvelous. He was drunk and angry. *Same old stuff ... different day.*

"The cleaning woman ... what's her name?" he stared at me.

"Patty." I filled in the blanks of his drunken memory.

"Whatever. She's more of a wife than you are or will ever be." He spat the words at me. But he wasn't done yet.

Gone was the peace I'd felt the night before. I had reconciled with God but it wasn't as easy with Paul.

"This is the first good meal you have made me in months," he rambled on drunkenly. "I'm sick of all that healthy shit you call food."

How had my apology gotten him this wound up and vengeful? On he went, tearing into me, striking at my most vulnerable points.

"You always favor your own kids, and treat my kids like they are the stepchildren …"

The words ran through in my head:

But they are *my stepchildren.*

Countered by: *Bite your tongue. This was supposed to be an apology.*

I took a deep breath to calm the fire in my chest. I didn't want to make things worse. "I just wanted to tell you that I'm sorry," I whispered.

I got up and started to clear the table. I no longer cried when he berated me. I was past that. So I just turned my back, and placed the dirty dishes on the counter.

"Sorry my ass. And don't you turn your back to me. I'm talking to you! I'm sick of this shit and I'm sick of you."

He pushed his chair away from the table, grabbed his wine glass, the open bottle, and stormed down into the lower level. A moment later, I could hear a movie playing in the theater room.

So much for step three.

That night I knew ... there was no chance Paul would offer me forgiveness.

⌁

As Christmastime came I made preparations for the holiday and Cullen's return home from college. A few days before Christmas, Paul obtained tickets for the Bob Seger concert and backstage passes for dinner with Seger and his band. Paul invited me and I declined. I'd heard Bob Seger before, and I didn't want to miss one of the nights when both my kids would be home for Christmas. For some reason, Paul was adamant. I found myself asking, *Why is it so important for him to be seen with me?* He had been given these tickets by one of the big promoters of the event because they had been courting him and his business. By now I knew he got off by wielding his power and influence. When he pitched a fit and insisted, reluctantly I agreed to go.

He picked me up at home the evening of the concert, and he'd already been drinking. Somehow the conversation shifted to the downturn in the housing market in metro Detroit. Given Paul wrote the checks for our bills and handled the finances, I asked him, "So what do we owe on the house?"

"On the first or on the second?" He responded.

"What second?" I asked. What was he talking about? We didn't have a second mortgage.

He turned to face the highway. His hands clenched the steering wheel and he muttered something. I couldn't make out what he had said, and suddenly I felt uneasy. Something was awry. Something was amiss. I didn't trust him to tell me the truth.

It was a very long evening. I felt my muscles tighten and tension was building in my neck and shoulders. My stomach was uneasy.

Just what was Paul up to?

Trust is the foundation upon which all good relationships are built. This is a fundamental truth. And I did not trust this man.

The concert and the dinner were as dreadful as I anticipated. Ancient rockers and banquet cuisine. My mind was racing, and I couldn't let it go. Paul was up to something. I saw it in his eyes.

For his part, Paul drank heavily all evening ... and went directly to bed when we got home. He was snoring soundly before I was finished getting ready for bed. This night was no different then so many others. Alcohol was his mistress. He loved her more than he would ever love me.

When I was sure he was sound asleep I went upstairs to the desk in the music room. The computer was there. I couldn't access the computer as his files were all password protected. The file cabinet where all the financial documents were was securely locked. I didn't have a key. What was he hiding?

Now my heart was racing.

The next day, I left work during my free period and drove to the local branch of Charter One Bank. Charter One held the mortgage on our house. There I made the discovery.

Paul had raided the home equity line of credit on the house. He had spent approximately $350,000 without my knowledge or consent. All of the things he'd been splurging on were being purchased out of the proceeds from the sale of my home.

My stomach heaved. I dropped my head into my hands and I began to cry. I tasted bile, and I was afraid I might vomit. I took a few deep breaths and the feeling passed as I sat there, silently shaking.

The bank manager couldn't believe it. "I've seen this happen before for $5000, maybe $10,000. But never anything like *this*. I'm so, so sorry."

I knew we had a home equity line of credit, it was one of the conditions required to get the loan on the house. It just never crossed my mind that Paul would or even could use that money without my knowledge or consent.

For *25 years* Fred and I made house payments, had foregone everyday luxuries, and invested our sweat equity to provide for a secure future, and improve the value of our investment –our home –and now in two and a half years it had been pissed away and spent by Mr. Paul O'Shea.

I sat with this kind woman in her office. I didn't trust myself to stand. But it was now closing time. She quietly got up and went to lock us in, and then together we tried to determine what Paul had done with the money. It was grossly unclear, but she copied pages and pages of transactions. I would need to try and sort this out. Before I left, under the banker's guidance, I wrote a letter indicating I wanted to close the Home

Equity Line. She notarized the letter and it was closed, effective immediately. No more withdrawals. He didn't consult me when he spent the money, and I didn't tell him when I put a stop to it.

Driving home I was shaking with sickness and rage.

I couldn't stay. I wouldn't stay married to someone I couldn't trust. This was a huge betrayal.

It was as if two tectonic plates had been converging towards one another. So often Paul and I had been at cross-purposes and now this. I had not foreseen this, but perhaps I should have. This is what happens when you build your life on shaky ground. There had been so many smaller rumblings, so many cracks, and so much damage to the foundation of our marriage. But this was the big earthquake that shook my world. I would need to rebuild elsewhere.

What I needed was some time to create an exit plan.

Christmas was days away and my kids were now home. I wouldn't spoil the holidays for everyone. Once Cullen was back in school I would get the hell out of there. All I knew was I couldn't stay with a man who lied to me and stole from me.

If this had happened in a business it would be considered embezzlement, a felony, and punishable by time in prison. But there is no law against marital embezzlement, and I was sick about it.

It's not that I'm a stupid woman, for I'm not. I'd thought about leaving him since our wedding night. But I'm stubborn and prideful. I'd tried to make this marriage work. But no more, I had no more to give.

One day, soon after Christmas I discussed what had transpired with Cullen. "I'm so sorry," I began. "You and Gillian and everyone else tried to tell me, but I thought I knew better. Never in my wildest dreams did I believe he was capable of this. I should have seen it coming but I refused to see."

Cullen placed his hand over mine. His eyes were sad, but sympathetic.

"He kept buying more and more stuff. When I asked if we could afford all of this his answer was always the same … I earned the money and I'll decide how I spend it."

The tears began to flow as I offered my beloved son an apology for the mess I'd made of our lives. I'd dragged my children into this nightmare with me. "I'm so sorry. Please forgive me. I'll make this up to you and Gillian. I will make this all right. I promise."

Not only had Paul stolen from me, but he had also stolen my children's home, and their inheritance. I was racked with guilt and sorrow.

"Mom, this was not your doing. You have a right to be happy. You went into this marriage with only the best of intentions and he betrayed you. You have nothing to apologize for. But where will you go? Will you be okay?" My beautiful son was so gentle and loving towards me when I was so vulnerable and fragile. His face radiated concern.

I shifted from penitent to mother. "Honey, please don't worry. Your Dad, in his infinite wisdom, set things up so that all of the money for your education and Gillian's is safe in a trust account. My retirement funds are also safe. I have a good job, and I'll find us a place to live. None of us have ever needed this kind of palatial estate. Please don't worry. I got us into this mess, and I will find a way out ... and a way home."

I loved that Cullen's concern was for me. But he didn't need to worry about me. I'm an adult and as desperate as I was feeling, this wasn't the biggest hurdle I had encountered in my life, and I knew it wasn't insurmountable.

Cullen could have been angry and self-absorbed, but he didn't think about himself and the implications this loss might have on him. No, he thought of me, and he was kind and merciful at a time when I needed both so badly.

I breathed a prayer of thanks to God for my son. I took comfort and solace in his forgiveness. His words were the salve for my wounded heart.

I invited Gillian to go for a walk at Independence County Park. It was cold, and we were still waiting for snow. We took the path around the lake and held hands as we walked. Gillian is a kind and loving girl. Strengthened by Cullen's support I was certain Gillian would be as eager as I was to move on.

"Gilly, I'm so sorry and I hope you can forgive me for the mess I have made. My marriage to Paul is a disaster, and I know it's as obvious to you as it is to me. I want you to know that I'm planning on leaving him, and I'm going to ask him for a divorce."

She dropped my hand. She was trying to process what I was saying. I filled in the details of his latest transgression and tried to frame the theft in language a young teenager could comprehend.

Watching her face, I could see the anger build. Then, out it came. "You're right –Cullen and I tried to tell you. He's an asshole and he always has been. I didn't want you to marry him. I didn't want to move. I didn't want any of it. But now that I'm here, and in spite of him, I've found a way to live here, and Dana has become my sister!"

She took a deep breath and I knew her heart was breaking. Her face was red, and tears were streaming down her cheeks. She angrily wiped them away with her mittens.

My heart pleaded for her understanding and forgiveness. Then came words I never expected.

"Mom, how can we leave Dana behind?"

I was blindsided.

Dana.

I heard the anguish in Gillian's voice. The girls loved each other, like sisters.

Oh Dana, this poor girl got shit for parents. How I hated Paul at that moment …

"Oh Gillian, I love Dana, too. I'm so sorry … I need to think about this."

Our walk ended, and now my heart –which had just found its way again –was once more confused.

Dear God, I prayed, *what am I to do?*

∾

After the holidays, I avoided Paul as much as possible. I was gone at night, and I left for work before he was out of bed. If I saw him, I knew I would explode.

He wanted to take me to a charity event. This gala was the biggest social event in metro Detroit. All the local celebrities, industrial giants, and the captains of industry would be there. To me it was "Revenge of the Aging Prom Queens," and besides, there was no fucking way I was going to this or anything else with him.

The great dateless Paul O'Shea. Even your own wife can't bear to be in your presence. You made this mess with all your lies and greed and there are consequences for you as well.

This time when he pushed me, I held my ground, "Sorry, I have other plans."

Instead, I went to a restaurant opening with Joel, my brother-in-law. We ate and drank, but mostly we laughed and stayed out until nearly dawn with some of my former neighbors. I couldn't remember the last time I'd had so much fun. I began to see that perhaps I could remake my life. Perhaps, just perhaps I could find a way back to happiness. I felt a spark of hope return.

My anger kept my fear at bay. I held onto it as it provided me the impetus to change my life. Those who loved me best became my co-conspirators. I was fragile, and I needed their love and support if I were going to extricate myself from this living hell. When I would start to waffle, and my resolve seemed to wax and wane, they would throw another log on the fire and douse it with gasoline. All they needed to do was gently remind me of Paul's past transgressions. There were so many to choose from. I had confided in my parents, my sister, and my friends, and their love would see me through this. They loved me, and they wanted what was best for me.

I made my plans to leave him. Locating the key to the file cabinet I copied reams of documents, planning to sort through them later. I was afraid of Paul.

I made arrangements to rent a guest cottage from an acquaintance. Her children had attended grade school with mine. We sat on the cottage floor, and I recounted the horrors of my marriage with this kind, benevolent woman. She commiserated as she recounted the ongoing pain in her own marriage. Her husband lurked in the distance. There clearly was no love lost here. I planned to move mid-week.

I needed to wait until the day after Dana's 16th birthday, which was fast approaching. I owed the dear sweet girl that much, and yet for me, the waiting was interminable.

Knowing Gillian and Dana would be upset; nonetheless I knew I still had to leave. Privately I saw a therapist, who warned me against rapidly executing my plan for fear of Paul's retribution. But the pressure within was growing. I told her I couldn't stay. I was desperate. I was afraid of my husband. I was a coward. I didn't want to face his wrath. I didn't want to talk about this anymore. I just wanted it to be over with. I wanted out.

When I informed my boss why I needed a day off work, he sat across the desk from me and nodded as I cried. "Don't worry about things here," he told me, "just do what you need to do."

And so plans were made: My parents, along with my girlfriends, and two of their husbands, would arrive with their trucks and horse trailers after Paul had left for work.

Two nights before my planned departure, I drove to a local mall to pick up a gift for Dana's birthday. I had ordered a jewelry box, with an engraved plaque that said: "I will love you always."

As I was walking through the center corridor of the mall my cell phone rang. It was Paul. My heart skipped a beat. I didn't pick up. I hadn't been taking his calls for weeks, and didn't trust myself to speak to him.

A few minutes later my phone rang again. This time the call came from Dana's cell phone and I answered. It was Paul. He had tricked me again. Very directly he asked, "Jeanne, are you planning to leave me?"

Never good at subtly, and even worse at deception, I must have fumbled something in my secret planning.

There in the center corridor of the shopping mall, I broke down and began to sob. I was crying so hard, I couldn't catch my breath.

"Please come home," he asked, in a voice so filled with the sweetness and tenderness I'd forgotten he once possessed.

"Okay." It was all I could say between my breathless sobs.

Once again I was in turmoil.

Paul was waiting for me in the master bedroom. He had tidied up the alcove with the bay window where I so often sat to read or write. The room was bathed in low light. And there, on a desperately cold January night, I sat with my husband who hung his head in shame as I cried and recounted the hurts, and betrayal, and the reasons why I wanted a different kind of life … one without him.

"I'm sorry. I do love you and I never wanted it to be like this." His voice was quiet as he looked down at his hands. "I don't want you to stay if you're this unhappy, but I don't want you to go."

He looked me in the eye as he said this, and lifted his hand to wipe away a tear from my cheek.

As he spoke, I was overwhelmed with compassion for this man, my husband, who had suffered losses and sadness of his own. He had been divorced three times before, and now I was leaving him. In that moment, I saw with great clarity: *he would continue to create suffering in his life, as he did not know how to live in a loving relationship.*

He drew a deep breath and continued. "I didn't want you to know about the line of credit. I know I should've told you. I'm sorry. I had planned to pay it back this spring when I got my bonus. The house was more expensive than I planned."

And then … off-track he went, blaming the builder for the expensive construction overages. "He's a Goddamn pirate and you and I got screwed by that bastard," and once more, his anger started to build, and the intimacy that had been building between us was pushed away again by his old hurts and grudges.

He must have seen the look on my face change and quickly he exchanged his anger for remorse. I found it compelling and touching. Or was he just manipulating me? I couldn't be sure.

"Please say you'll stay. I promise I will try to make it up to you." He pleaded.

For so long I'd been consumed with feelings of being unwanted, unloved, and unlovable that I clung to his desire to remain married to me. When he suggested we try marital therapy I agreed. I agreed to go to marriage counseling and I agreed to stay.

Paul wrapped his arms around me and held me as I cried.

And yet, even after this emotional reconnection, my husband didn't make love to me that night. He made no attempt to rectify the lack of sexual intimacy in our marriage.

∞

So I called off my troops of movers and planned a 16th birthday dinner for Dana, with cake, candles and gifts. She was radiant. She was growing into a beautiful young woman. Her father had gifted her with lavish birthdays before. This year for her 16th birthday he bought her a new black BMW convertible. But she too was looking for something else. I had made the decision to stay. She was the reason I couldn't go. She needed to be loved, and I loved her. I always will.

I would not be moving out the following morning.

My girlfriends understood that I wasn't ready. They did not judge me. They stood with me, steadfast, and unfailing in their love. In retrospect, I guess it's a bit like quitting smoking. There are often many failed attempts before you're successful.

I called my Mom and Dad from my private office … my car. I needed my privacy, and I didn't want Paul to know who my supporters were. If he knew, he would find a way to exclude them from our life, and I couldn't bear that.

"Honey, what's going on? Are you okay?" my mother asked when she picked up the phone. She knew me so well. There must've been something in my voice that let her know things had changed.

"Paul found out I was planning to leave him." I could never keep anything from my mother. She needed no words from me to completely size up the situation, but I offered them anyway. "He wants to try again. I'm not going to leave tomorrow."

"My darling girl, I know this is hard for you. Your father and I love you so much, and we will support you in this decision. But let me make this clear to you. Your father and I think this is a bad decision. He's not worthy of you. This man has betrayed you countless ways, and if I know anything it's this –he will betray you again. Mark my words."

When I hung up the phone we were both in tears. My mother is a good and holy woman –soon she would prove to be a prophet.

Maybe Mother's words were the trigger. Or maybe those we love, who have gone before us, really can speak from beyond. Even though I had agreed to stay and try marriage counseling, I began to be aware of something from somewhere in the deep recesses of my being, the voice of my one and only true husband –in a voice that I would know anywhere and always.

From the silent space within, Fred's voice would come to me:

Know what you are worth.

Always remember what you are worth.

How can you explain something like this to those who have never loved and lost? Fred loved me in his earthly body here, and I knew he loved me still from somewhere else. I felt his distress and it woke me. Many nights I lay in bed and offered him my apologies and begged his forgiveness, and in my heart I know he forgave me. In words my children would give voice to later, he also said,

There is nothing to forgive.

I had trouble believing that. Was it just me, though? Was I the one who needed to forgive myself, and couldn't? From the beginning of this marriage I had been receiving a nudge, a very persistent nudge, to claim my own life and to be the woman I had been created to be. But now I was really being pushed. The voice of my consciousness, the Holy Spirit that resides within me, was shouting at me and would not be ignored.

Within only a few days, Paul and I were back to our empty, deadening routines. The complete lack of love and intimacy had invaded this unholy space – *our home* –and I began to formulate an alternative exit plan. I was just buying time for the girls to grow up. I wouldn't disrupt their lives anymore. They were the holy innocents, and they deserved better. I would get them through to graduation and safely off to college. Then I would go and restart my life.

The question that loomed large was:
How could I stand to live with this man until then?
I would have to make the supreme effort.

Paul made the arrangements for the marital therapy. I let him pick the therapist. I was willing to abide by his choice. I was still so angry with him. I could hardly be in the same room with him. The therapy sessions began like this: one week Paul would start and when he was finished I would respond. The next week it was my turn to begin.

His complaints were: I favored my own children, I made all the children do their own wash, and I never cooked things his children liked for dinner.

My complaints were: We never had sex, he spent $350,000 out of the home equity line of credit without my consent, and he was drunk every night.

We went to our weekly therapy appointment for months. Inconceivable as it may be, our relationship went from bad to worse. He was so angry, "Have you no respect for me or yourself? How could you just air all of our dirty laundry in front of a total stranger?"

I thought that was the purpose of therapy.

But after each therapy appointment we didn't speak to one another for days. Nothing improved. Still no sex. I registered this complaint every week with the therapist and in his presence.

Paul's reason, "I'm too angry with her to be intimate."

Strangely, he couldn't even speak my name. I wanted to say *–My name is Jeanne,* but I kept my mouth closed.

By this time, in any case, I suspected the real reason he didn't want to have sex with me. I don't think he liked women. I don't think he was gay. I could have understood that. All I knew for certain was that he didn't like me.

One spring evening, Paul arrived 35 minutes late for our hour-long therapy appointment. Before he arrived, I had a chance to speak with the therapist alone. I asked her for her take on the state of our marriage because she had been listening to us for months.

She paused thoughtfully before she responded. "I've seen couples get past bigger hurdles than you have here." I nodded to indicate I had heard her and to encourage her to continue. "But the difference," she added, "is that they love each other."

"Oh, they love each other," I laughed out loud. "Oh, that little old thing."

She had hit the nail on the head.

And then I confided the therapy sessions were really making things worse at home. He was angry and vengeful now. I told her I was planning to leave him when the girls left for college, and I was just trying to hold on until then. She hugged me and wished me well.

When Paul arrived at the end of our session he was drunk. "She's never home, and she never wants to go to Costco, and there are so many things we need around the house."

The therapist's face registered nothing as she listened to Paul's litany of complaints. And I thought:

Oh God, here we go. More drunken ramblings ... from this drunken fool.

"The bottom line," he said as he slurred his words, "I want her to give me a greater portion of her paycheck."

Since I had cut off the home equity line of credit he didn't have enough expendable income, and he wanted more money from me. He wanted more of my money so he could purchase more things for the house. Things I neither needed nor wanted.

The therapist said nothing. And I thought: *Good luck with that.*

The reality was even though he made four times as much money as I did, no amount of money would ever be enough. The U.S. Government couldn't print enough money to fill the empty hole in Paul's heart.

I knew for sure that I could never fix that for him.

CHAPTER 13

Holding On

My closest girlfriends drew closer as my life continued to unravel. They were the ones whom I had to call off in January when I agreed to try marriage counseling. I had already bared my soul to them. There was no more pretending that my life was fine. They knew differently, so they checked in with me regularly.

Cathy called nearly everyday as I drove home from work, "Everything okay? What are you doing? Do you want to get out of the house?"

Pamela called on the weekends, "Want to have lunch?"

I was fragile, and their love surrounded and protected me.

On my 50th birthday, Cathy called. "I'd like to take you horseback riding. Are you up for it?" She had been riding for years and rode nearly every day. She was forever asking me to join her at the barn.

Nothing was planned for my birthday. I was fifty … half a century old. That in itself seemed worthy of celebration. But Paul and I were barely on speaking terms.

So when I had the opportunity to leave the house, I didn't hesitate. "Yes!" I said, to spending my 50th birthday in a drafty old barn, in late March, in Michigan.

The barn was cold, damp, and dreary. But I was so glad to get out of the house.

Cathy is as chatty a woman as any I have ever met, but her heart is bigger than most. So when I arrived in the tack room, she had orchestrated the welcoming committee. Five women were there to ride –and to help me get ready. First off, I had worn all the wrong clothing because I didn't own any English riding apparel. So these women began rummaging through their trunks, and soon I was outfitted in grey riding pants. They fit like tights, and the inner thighs and buttocks were covered with a darker shade of grey suede. They were designed to keep you in the saddle. They were tight fitting and I felt a bit self-conscious, but sexy in them.

This simple kindness and attention made me feel so welcomed.

"My God, girl you look great for fifty!" Cathy said as she made a minor adjustment in my riding attire.

"So hot and so sexy in those tight pants," Margie laughed as she added a sizzling sound for effect.

How long had it been since I felt sexy or anyone said so?

Patty found riding boots just my size, and as I sat on a trunk to lace my boots one of the women began to braid my long red hair. "She's going to look stunning on Luke." He was Cathy's beautiful quarter horse, and his mane and tail matched my long red braid.

What was it about horsewomen? Perhaps it was because of the love and care they provided for their animals that caused them to develop an extraordinary capacity to understand, that which has been left unspoken. Somehow, these remarkable women understood exactly what I needed. The situation wasn't the same, of course, but the love and care they showed reminded me of being a bride in the company of bridesmaids. They knew this was my special day, in spite of the fact I was in a difficult place in my life. They made me feel loved, pretty, sexy and wonderful. I felt I had come to a place where I belonged and was wanted.

That day I took my first lesson on Luke, Cathy's horse. Margie was my trainer. She was the woman I'd planned to rent the cottage from, so she too was already well acquainted with my story. By the end of the first lesson … I was hooked. I began to understand why these women drove out to a drafty old barn that was cold in the winter and hot in the summer, and shoveled horse manure and groomed their animals. When I was on the back of this magnificent horse, I felt as if I were one with a big beautiful flying machine. It was exhilarating. Working with Luke required love, and patience, and in return I was gifted with the companionship and acceptance that I missed so desperately in my life.

So I leased Cathy's horse, as she planned to spend her summer in northern Michigan, and needed someone to look after Luke. I contracted with Margie to be my teacher and my trainer. And so the seasons passed … and I waited.

∾

Riding became my therapy, and I rode three times a week, all summer long. The company of like-minded loving women helped to balance and heal me. I spent my days working in my garden and riding the horse. The more time I spent at the barn, the more tolerable my home life became –mostly because I was rarely there.

Cullen was taking classes that summer in California to complete his degree. Gillian was still working at Planet Rock and teaching rock climbing.

And as for Paul, he seemed to be looking for a new way to clip my wings and keep me at home under his thumb.

He decided to enhance the entranceway to the house. As part of his plan, he wanted an evergreen hedge to line both sides of the quarter-mile driveway.

Soon he had picked out the perfect evergreens, sea green junipers with prickly foliage, making them deer resistant. These were a rapid-growth species that would reach 6 feet tall, and have a 6-foot spread when fully mature. Small, starter trees would take much too long to grow, Paul decided. So he opted for the largest specimens he could find.

When they arrived, the trees were already 3 to 4 feet high and in 10-gallon pots. Each pot weighed nearly 100 pounds when the soil was moist. And there were hundreds of them.

Not only were the pots difficult to move, they arrived during a heat wave. This represented a large financial investment. We couldn't afford both the plants and a landscaper to get them in the ground, so the responsibility for planting them fell to me. I just couldn't let them sit unattended. They needed to be planted.

I set to work in 90-degree heat to get these plants into the ground. It was back breaking work. The holes needed to be dug. My gardeners' wisdom took over: A ten-dollar plant needs a hundred dollar hole ... and these were not ten-dollar plants. The holes themselves needed to be substantial, and the soil needed amendment. So I hauled the sphagnum peat moss and bags of cow manure home from the garden store, to mix with the soil in each of the holes, ensuring these plants would do well. I planted them with love and care, just as if I would personally be the one who would enjoy them in their maturity. I knew this was not the case, but still I planted them as if it were true. Old habits die hard, and a job worth doing is worth doing well ... and I do love the garden.

On and on the heat wave went, and I hauled the hoses every day to water the new shrubs. When the hoses reached their limit, I filled buckets with water, and carried them to the shrubs at the distant end of the driveway.

The watering alone took hours. And every time I turned around, Paul had located another nursery with more shrubs for me to plant. So I did the planting and the maintenance ... and he just kept on buying more and more.

All the while I counted the days until the girls would be out of high school and I could leave ...

One afternoon, as I was finally putting away the hoses after watering and planting since the early morning, Paul pulled up in his SUV, and the back was loaded with a dozen more shrubs. I had held my tongue long enough.

"Stop!" I said impatiently. "Just stop! Do not buy any more shrubs. I physically cannot plant another shrub *and* care for the hundreds of new shrubs that I have already planted."

I was exhausted. I wanted to spend my days doing something else.

Paul's face went red. "It's your own fault we can no longer afford the landscaper."

My mouth fell open.

The implication was clear to me. He didn't need to say it. There it was ... I was the one who closed the home equity line of credit. And he was punishing me.

"Fine, just let them sit here and die," he spat the words at me.

There was some kind on convoluted logic at work here. Indeed the landscaping would make the house more beautiful. Did he really think that he was doing this for me? For me? Somehow, he expected gratitude, but that was not what I felt. No, I felt manipulated into spending my life and personal resources. My time and energy were being spent to accomplish his goals and dreams. I felt like a functionary, someone to fill his need, someone to get the job done. I felt used and abused.

My 80-year-old father stopped by one afternoon to visit me. He took one look at me and was afraid I was going to have a heat stroke. So he helped me plant the remaining bushes before facing me with absolute clarity.

"It's over 90 degrees today, Jeanne, and the humidity must be over 90 percent. We'll plant again tomorrow when it's cooler." This was non-negotiable, and with that he sent me into the house to cool down.

My Dad came the next day, and the day after that, and the day after that, until the work was completed. Not only did he plant with me, but he also engineered a watering system that ran the length of the driveway covering both sides. He did this at his own expense. He didn't want to see his 50-year-old daughter hauling hoses and buckets of water every day to ensure that the shrubs survived.

To say he was appalled by the way Paul treated me is an understatement.

If I'd had a shred of understanding or compassion for Paul, it was gone.

What kind of man would treat his wife and his father-in-law like this?

It would be one thing if we had been partners in this plan, but I was expected to work all summer long as a common laborer. I'd become the landscaper and gardener of Paul's palatial estate.

࿎

In the spring of the following year, Paul decided that he wanted to have the woods, which were visible from the living room, cleared of debris –all the fallen trees and branches that were under the canopy of new growth. He rented a heavy-duty chipper and parked it at the edge of the driveway.

The message was obvious: Get busy.

Dad and I carried the fallen branches, trees, and scrub shrubs out of the woods, and through the wetlands. Paul stood at the edge of the driveway, and waited there to take the branches from us so he could load them into the chipper. Again, Dad and I did the heavy backbreaking work, while Paul took the job that was significantly easier.

Dad and I carried a heavy tree from the woods, Dad on one end, and me on the other. When we got to the chipper, Paul was nowhere to be found. He had gone to the bar in the middle of the afternoon, and left Dad and me to labor on without him.

Again the issue was raised: *What kind of a man was Paul?*

∾

In August, Paul's son had moved to Los Angeles, Cullen was in northern California in college, Dana was spending time with her mother in northern Michigan, and Gillian was on a trip to the Pacific Northwest with Outward Bound. Paul decided he needed a vacation, and so at his suggestion, we planned a spur of the moment trip for a week in the Caribbean, to the islands of Turks and Caicos.

Despite my resentment at being treated like slave labor, things had become relatively tranquil between us. I was pleased he had invited me. Pleased he wanted to spend his vacation with me. Forever the optimist, I had the audacity to think perhaps, just perhaps, we could work this out.

We landed on the island and took a taxi to the inn. We were staying at the far end of the island. It was beautiful, romantic, and nearly unoccupied as it was the low season and most of the tourists had gone elsewhere. After unpacking, we headed to an island grocery store to buy some provisions for the week.

While I looked for fruit, juice, and bread ... Paul loaded the shopping cart with liquor.

So much for trying to repair our broken marriage, Paul started drinking after breakfast and was drunk every day.

While Paul drank, I went to the beach and went sea kayaking or snorkeling. Under the water with my mask and snorkel I found myself in another world. Swimming over coral reefs, I followed tropical fish, and enjoyed the quiet and solitude. Once more, all alone with my thoughts, I found myself thinking about Paul and all the things he'd told me about his ex-wives: They'd lied to him, stole from him, cheated on him. I had taken him at his word and truly believed he'd been the injured party. While I watched the colorful fish swim beneath me I wondered ... *what stories would he fabricate about me?*

No surprise by now, in spite of the romantic location, Paul never once touched me all week. I had long ago vowed I wouldn't initiate sexual contact again. Too often I had tried, and too often I had been denied. If he wanted me sexually, he would have to come looking for it.

It never happened, so I came to the conclusion perhaps this was exactly what he wanted –a sexless marriage. Some people would say, "That is no marriage at all." And I would be one of them.

I'd wanted to be faithful to the teachings of my church, which believes that marriage is sacred. But in fact, my marriage was an abomination.

CHAPTER 14

Gifts to Help
Me See

When we returned home from our Caribbean vacation things were relatively calm. However, under the surface a sense of restlessness remained.

I started back to work and made the barn my home away from home. Margie and I had become very close over the course of the summer, and she went from being my trainer to being my friend. We took long, long trail rides, and enjoyed the beauty of the changing seasons, but we also enjoyed one another's company. As we got to know one another better our conversations would frequently turn to whose husband was a bigger jerk. No doubt about it Margie had some good stories, and Bryan was a creep ... but hands down, Paul won The Biggest Jerk Award time and time again.

Yet she was ready to make a move ... and I was not.

Over the course of the summer, things had finally reached a breaking point in her marriage, and she moved out of her house. She had struggled to keep her marriage together for years for the sake of her daughters. But they were grown now and living independent lives. Despite her best efforts, she was consumed with overwhelming loneliness.

Now Margie is a stunningly beautiful woman. And I often felt like Pippi Longstocking in her presence, and I'm okay with that as Pippi has a charm all her own. Margie is drop dead gorgeous, but her husband just didn't see it. Instead he doggedly pursued other women. She'd had enough.

That summer, when she moved out, she became my hero. She deserved better, and she had the strength to leave.

I so wanted to be where Margie was. I went to her small rented home on the outskirts of Rochester, and brought a bottle of champagne. I knew this part of the journey would be difficult for her, but once she passed through the darkness things would get better. Together we celebrated her strength.

I knew it would be at least another year before I could leave. Margie had stayed for her daughters, and I was staying for Gillian and for Dana. But at this time, I needed to re-examine my *strengths*. My strengths had set me up to stay. Yet, sometimes my strengths worked against me.

An old song played on in my head.
The strong give up and move on,
and the weak give up and stay

–Dan Fogelberg

He was talking about me. I felt weak and it didn't feel good.

In September, the girls were in their senior year of high school. I was continuing to ride as often as I could. Teaching got in the way of my riding, as work does for many of us, as we try to find time to chase our passions.

Cathy had spent the summer at her cottage in northern Michigan, but now she was home, and would have more time to ride her beautiful horse. I knew I would need my own horse if I wanted to continue to ride. It was a big decision, but going to the barn had become my sanctuary, and riding was my salvation. I feared my life would be incomplete, and I would backslide emotionally without this anchor. So my girlfriends helped me look for a horse of my own.

We searched for a few weeks until I found Poncho. He was an 8-year-old gelded thoroughbred. He stood 16 hands high and was a beautiful chestnut color. Our manes matched, and I liked him immediately. I rode him in the ring with his owner looking on. By now I had learned enough about horses to realize he had good ground manners, and seemed to be a good fit for me. One small problem was that he had limited trail-riding experience. Everything checked out, so I made arrangements to take him for a three-day trial.

To own my own horse felt like a great step towards my independence and building a life of my choosing. One September evening, Margie and I headed out for a long trail ride. It was the test ride for Poncho. I wasn't interested in ring riding, but I loved the trails, and this was how I planned to ride him.

So Margie was on her horse Trinity, and I was settled in on Poncho. We headed up the lane and out across the field. My horse began to act like a teenage boy with a Napoleon complex. Horses are pack animals and they establish a pecking order. Poncho was the new kid on the block. He didn't know the trails and yet he couldn't bear it that he was not the alpha horse.

Trinity was the alpha horse. She was a strong, powerful, and a magnificent creature. Margie held Trinity back, and Trinity respected Margie's authority.

Poncho pulled on the reins. He desperately wanted to lead and I had difficulty holding him back.

"Take control of the situation," Margie called out to me.

I shortened the reins but Poncho was strong, and he continued to give me attitude.

"What's up with him? Take him on down by that stump and let me ride him. You ride Trinity," Margie suggested.

Now I had ridden Trinity off and on all summer when Cathy would be home, as Margie had two horses. Even though Trinity is a powerful creature, I'd not had any problem riding her in the past.

So at Margie's suggestion we switched horses and no sooner than we were seated, Margie called back over her shoulder to me, "Let's canter up the hill."

Trinity heard the word "canter" and without warning, she bolted.

She took off like a bat out of hell.

I reached to grab her mane.

Too late.

I was unseated.

I fell from the horse.

I hit the dry, hard ground and landed directly on my ass.

Instantly I knew I was hurt.

The pain seared through my lower back and up my spine.

Oh God.

I bounced on the earth, the momentum of the fall pushed me over onto my head.

I lay on the ground, stunned, and shaken …

I held my breath to brace against the pain.

"Are you okay?" Margie asked with concern resonating in her voice.

I swallowed hard as I tired to keep from bursting into tears.

"No." I answered.

The pain was now shooting down my legs.

I was sitting on the earth.

I looked around.

I was in a field.

The hay had been harvested.

Trinity was long gone.

Although we were miles away, I knew she had gone back to the barn.

In the midst of the chaos, Poncho reared up on his back legs.

Margie quickly got him back under control.

He was clearly restless and agitated, and wanted to chase Trinity down.

I reached up, and touched the brim of my velvet-riding helmet.

It was crushed.

This could have been worse, much, much worse.

Thank God I was wearing a helmet.

"Can you ride?" Margie asked.

She was thinking through the alternatives. How would she get me out of here?

"No." I kept the answers short.

I was in excruciating pain, and it was the very best I could do at that moment.

"Can you ... walk?" She asked hopefully.

I knew she didn't want to leave me in the middle of this hay field.

"No." I could move my legs –a little.

I was now in agony. My ass was killing me. The pain radiated from the base of my spine up my spinal column and down my legs.

Margie thought for a moment, considering the options ... that were not great. The barn was miles away. I couldn't walk back to the barn. I knew this. I didn't know if I could even stand.

Margie sat atop the horse, and they paced a little ways away.

She couldn't get down to help me.

If she got off the horse, he too would take off and bolt back to the barn.

With every ounce of strength that was in me, I tried to get to my feet.

The pain was nearly unbearable.

I rocked over onto all fours and used my bloodied hands to push myself up to my feet.

A wave of nausea overtook me as I steadied myself.

Now ... could I walk?

"Can you get to the road?" Margie asked.

I scanned the field.

The road was about 200 yards away and there was nothing but uneven ground between the road and me.

"Maybe," I replied, my breath was still uneven.

I could read the dilemma on Margie's face.

Should she stay with me or should she go and get the car?

Later, I would question the wisdom of riding without our cell phones, but we never took them with us because they had a tendency to spook the horses when someone called.

I wasn't thinking clearly.

All I knew was she wanted me to get to the road.

I nodded, and began to move ... slowly ... in the direction of the road.

Margie made her decision, "I'll go get the car."

Margie took off on Poncho back towards the barn.

I hobbled towards the road. Every step was agonizing.

How I got there, I'll never know, but eventually I managed to reach the dirt road.

I stood in the road. Shaking with pain.

A disheveled woman dressed in riding gear. A rider without a horse.

The wait was interminable. I hurt.

I leaned against one of the white wooden posts found on country roads that are meant to keep motorists out of the ditch.

I shifted my weight up against it, and it offered me a bit of support. I waited.

When I thought I couldn't stand a moment longer … there she was.

I was so relieved to see her silver SUV coming down the lane.

She made a three point turn, so I didn't have to walk around to get in on the passenger's side. I hoisted myself into the seat. "I'm hurt." I told her.

"I know." She confirmed.

"Did you find Trinity?" I wanted to think about something else.

Every bump in the road was felt in my buttocks, and radiated up my back. I grimaced.

"Do you think you can drive home?" She asked.

"I think so, I'm more comfortable sitting than standing." I explained.

Comfort was a relative term.

Margie needed to tend to the horses and so I drove home.

My drive home took 40 minutes. I'd told Margie I could make it … I'd be fine … but five minutes down the road I knew it was a mistake. I tried to call Paul to tell him about the accident, but he didn't pick up. I tried Gillian, but she was at work and I couldn't reach her. I called Dana. No answer.

By the time I arrived at home I was in absolute agony. I parked my car in the garage. I slowly shifted my legs out of the car, and placed my feet onto the garage floor. When I tried to stand, I collapsed onto the cold, dirty cement floor. I couldn't bear the weight of my own body.

No one was home. I crawled up the garage stairs and into the house. The master suite was down the hallway of this monstrously large house. I knew I had some Vicodin in my bathroom, leftover from my appendectomy 15 months ago. Using only my arms I dragged the lower half of my body. I inched my way down the hallway. Perhaps the pain distorted my perception of time, but it must've taken me about an hour to get down the hall to my bathroom. I was in unbearable pain. I found the medication, took two and ... passed out on the bathroom floor.

Gillian was gently shaking me. There was anxiety in her voice, "Mom. Mom what happened?"

I mumbled something about a riding accident. She helped me to the toilet, and then carried me to my bed.

Hours later, Gillian was still sitting with me on the bed when Paul arrived home. He'd been at the bar and was drunk. Again.

I recounted the story of the accident. He said, "Look, it's late already. Why don't you take some more pain meds, and I'll take you to the hospital in the morning."

Throughout the night, unable to walk or stand, I crawled to the bathroom twice. Paul slept through it all … or at least he pretended to be asleep.

In the morning, I awoke as Gillian came to kiss me good-bye before she left for school. I called my office, and told Pat, my boss' assistant, about the accident and that I wouldn't be in. She was sweet and dear as she told me, "Don't worry. I'll find coverage for your classes."

When I got off the phone, Paul came back into the bedroom. He was dressed for work.

"I thought you were going to take me to the hospital?" I looked to him for an explanation. "I think I need to be x-rayed."

"Look I forgot, but I have an important meeting. I can't take you this morning. Can't you wait until noon? I'll be home by 12 at the latest." He spoke these words in rapid fire as he was hustling around the bedroom. He was already behind schedule.

There was no room for me in his busy morning. I knew better than to start an argument, and I certainly didn't have the energy for one at this point. It hurt to breathe.

"Could you get me something to drink before you leave?" I asked as he headed out the door. He hesitated long enough to look back over his shoulder with a look that said, *Really? Can't you see I'm in a hurry?*

He disappeared down the hallway, and in a few minutes he came back, standing in the doorway of our bedroom, and tossed two objects across the room. They landed on the bed near me: two cans of warm Diet Coke.

Then he was gone.

Noon came and went, and Paul did not return as promised, nor did he call.

I didn't want to think about moving. I spent the day in bed with Vicodin and two warm Diet Cokes. I hadn't eaten anything since noon the day before. But getting to the kitchen was out of the question. When I absolutely had to ... I crawled back and forth to the bathroom.

Sometime during the afternoon, while I drifted in and out of the painkiller haze, Margie called to see how I was feeling. She wanted to know what I'd found out at the hospital. I told her about the last evening's events, and that I was feeling better, but hadn't been for x-rays yet.

At the other end of the phone line, Margie went crazy. "That piece of shit husband of yours went to work instead of taking you to the hospital? Of course you're feeling better, you're eating Vicodin like it's candy. I'm coming over to take you to the hospital right now!"

She was adamant, but I was able to dissuade her. I promised to call her and let her take me to the hospital, if Paul didn't come home in the next couple of hours. I gave her my word.

The next time I saw Paul it was 6:00 PM. Gillian and Dana arrived home at about the same time. Paul pulled the car up to the front of the house, and the girls supported me —one on each side. They carried me and my feet were dragging behind me. I was in agony as they put me in the car.

The nurses listened to my story. They couldn't believe my husband had left me in this much pain for over 24 hours. They pushed him out of the way and began to care for me. They started an IV and gave me some morphine. I cried with utter relief as the pain began to dissipate.

A CAT scan determined that my pelvis had been fractured. At least it wasn't displaced so there was no need for surgery. By then, I had extensive bruising at the base of my spine. The bruising ascended up either side of my backbone to just below my shoulder blades. I felt grateful. It could have been so much worse.

No one needed to tell me how lucky I was and how I should be grateful. But everyone told me just the same. I thought about Christopher Reeves, the actor who was paralyzed from the neck down after being thrown from a horse. The nurses pulled back my hospital gown to show their co-workers the bruising up and down my spine. Through my drug-induced haze, I heard them whispering about Christopher Reeves and how his riding accident had left him a quadriplegic.

When the ER doc released me to go home, he did so with strict orders. "Absolutely no weight bearing for the next 8 weeks. You may get out of bed only to use the bathroom, but only with a walker." Then he handed me prescriptions for the walker, more Vicodin, and a heavy dose of Ibuprofen.

The nurses carefully and lovingly helped me into the car. Paul drove to the drugstore on the way home to get the prescriptions filled and to buy the walker. It was now after 10 PM. I handed Paul my insurance cards. My insurance was provided by Fred's surviving spouse policy. I drifted in and out of sleep as I waited in the car. I was weary, achy, and in a morphine fog. I was so tired, and I just wanted to go to home to bed.

When Paul returned to the car he put the walker in the back seat. He climbed in the driver's seat and handed me the pharmacy bags with my prescriptions and a receipt. "Your insurance didn't cover the walker. You owe me $89.50."

We drove home in silence. I had nothing to say to him.

I couldn't believe it. Fred's words rang loudly in my head ...

There are people who know the price of everything but the value of nothing.

This man did not value me.

As if I didn't know this before, but just in case I wasn't paying attention —God or the Universe or whoever had lovingly arranged to give me yet another sign, another opportunity to wake up and learn.

In this moment, groggy with pain and medication, I saw clearly ... this was not a loving partnership ... this was not a marriage at all.

Over the course of the next two months I lay in bed alone, day after day. I was alone and I was so lonely.

My mother came by a couple of times each week to help with the laundry and general picking up. She always made me something for lunch. Patty, the woman who cleaned this palatial estate once a week, also made me lunch when she was there. I couldn't walk to the kitchen or stand long enough with my walker to make a sandwich, so most days I didn't eat.

Grocery shopping had been one of my responsibilities. But I couldn't drive or stand, so therefore, I couldn't shop for groceries. Subsequently there was little food in the house.

Paul frequently stopped at the bar on his way home from work. He'd have something to eat before he came home, but most nights he neglected to bring anything home for me. It wasn't uncommon for me to have popcorn for dinner.

Good for health and healing.

Being bedridden for weeks I had ample time to reflect on the reality of my situation. I deserved better than this, and I knew it. I was worthy of love, and my life and my happiness were worth fighting for. I was healing from my fall, and as my bones were mending I was also finding an inner strength. I would need it for what awaited me.

CHAPTER 15

The Perfect Storm

Over the next two months, day after day, I was home alone on bed rest.

The girls were in their senior year of high school, and were rarely home.

I read stacks of books, and when I couldn't read another, I took up painting to pass the time. I could paint while I was seated in bed. I found I liked to paint, flowing color and line together on the canvas. However, I desperately needed a few lessons. Painting was a good distraction. It required concentration and took my mind off the pain and incapacitation ... and off something else that had begun to trouble me.

I had my period. It had started ... but it didn't stop. I'd been bleeding for a couple of weeks. If my circumstances had been different I may not have paid all that much attention, but getting back and forth to the bathroom with a walker was such an ordeal. Initially, I convinced myself that menstrual irregularities were not uncommon as women approach menopause. After all, I was 50. But as the weeks passed, I became concerned something was wrong.

I could barely move, let alone climb onto an exam table and get into the stirrups. My gynecologist reassured me it was probably related to menopause, and not to worry so they scheduled the exam six weeks out.

When I arrived at the gynecologist's with my walker, I had been bleeding every day for 8 weeks. My pelvic exam was normal, but the ultrasound was inconclusive, but it indicated the endometrium was thickened.

Dr. Zinn suggested I have a biopsy in the office. "It is really no big deal, I can do it today. I really don't think this is anything. You certainly don't fit the profile for uterine cancer."

I wasn't that concerned either. I didn't have any of the risk factors. I wasn't overweight, I'd had two children and breastfed both of them for over a year, plus I'm a vegetarian. So I was an unlikely candidate for uterine cancer. Highly unlikely in fact, but I consented to the biopsy just to be certain.

When I finally got home I was exhausted. I went directly to bed. I was weak as a kitten. This was my first outing in weeks. I was convinced I was fine and there was nothing to worry about. I put the biopsy out of my head.

One week later I received a call. Dr. Zinn wanted me to come by the office at the end of the day if I could. Sitting in his office, his words slammed into me.

Highly unlikely … did not fit the profile … I had heard these words before … when Fred was diagnosed with cancer.

This time it was me ... the reality had been confirmed by the biopsy.

I had uterine cancer.

Dr. Zinn wanted to do a complete hysterectomy – removal of my uterus, ovaries, cervix, fallopian tubes, and biopsy some of my lymph nodes near the spinal column, as this is where uterine cancer metastasizes first.

In short, major abdominal surgery.

I sat and listened, shocked beyond words.

Dr. Zinn continued, "Since you have a broken pelvis, you're too great a surgical risk at this time. I'm concerned you might throw a pulmonary emboli ..."

Yeah, yeah, yeah ... this part I understood. I had been on bed rest for over eight weeks. Not good when facing major surgery.

The surgery was scheduled a month later. He wanted me to be stronger.

And so I went home.

Numb.

I sat on my heating pad.

I was stunned and afraid.

I wasn't prepared to face my own mortality.

I had lost my beloved husband, Fred, to cancer.

If I should pass, my children would be orphans.

I was still needed here.

My work here was not yet done.

I began the painful process of calling my family.

Mom and Dad.

Cullen and Gillian.

They all offered love and support.

I know they love me.

I called Paul.

He was in a meeting.

I would have to wait until he came home.

When he arrived I was sitting in the family room crying.

I had only received the diagnosis a few hours earlier.

I gave him the basics.

I really didn't want to talk about it.

Paul nodded and let it alone.

So instead of offering me any comfort or even companionable silence, he turned on the TV and watched CSI –Crime Scene Investigation, complete with graphic images of mutilated corpses.

I hobbled out of the room on my walker. I needed to find some inner peace. Images of mutilated dead bodies wouldn't help me. I thought I might vomit.

So in the morning, Paul took me out to breakfast. Over breakfast, I started to talk about my fears, and I felt myself tearing up.

Paul responded, "You need to stop crying. You need to stop feeling sorry for yourself and find a way to deal with this."

I was speechless. Even after all I had been through with him, I was still surprised by his total lack of compassion for me ... or for anyone else for that matter.

I received permission from my orthopedic doctor to begin physical therapy three times a week. I also walked in the swimming pool every other day for an hour. I was so unsteady on my feet, at least in the pool I didn't worry about falling. I positioned my walker at the edge of the pool so I could get in and out. Every morning for the next month I exercised, and then I would go home and sleep all afternoon. My muscles had atrophied while I was on bed rest and the exercise exhausted me.

A week before my surgery, I graduated from the walker to a cane. I was still so weak and unstable on my feet after eight weeks of bed rest. I couldn't stand without leaning heavily on my cane. But I had things I needed to do before the surgery. I knew that soon enough I would be laid flat again, so I pushed myself hard to try to regain my balance and my strength.

The weekend before my surgery, cane in hand, I flew into Syracuse, New York to visit my sister. Susan was living in the Adirondacks with her husband and her sons. I needed to see her. I needed to lay down my fears. I needed someone to show me some love and kindness. I was a fearful and broken woman.

I feared for my children should something happen to me. I feared for myself. I didn't know what the doctors would find on Tuesday during the surgery. If I didn't survive this I needed Susan to know that I loved her. I needed to know that she would be there for my children. She had become my confidant throughout my rough and rocky marriage.

Fortunately, Susan helped me stay strong and keep my focus on the holy light within. We had a wonderful weekend together.

Now I was ready to face what lay ahead.

The night before the surgery, I couldn't sleep. I needed to be at the hospital by 6 AM. It was going to be a short night. My mind would not quiet and I was filled with anxiety and what ifs. Paul was oblivious to my anxiety and restlessness. He snored loudly beside me.

I needed answers to the questions that disturbed my rest. I wanted to read about the surgery, the treatments, and the prognosis. If I were called upon to make important decisions, I needed to be conversant in the issues. I wanted to know what to ask the surgeon and the oncologist depending on what they found.

The computer was upstairs in the music room. So in the middle of the night, for the first time since my fall, I climbed the stairs. One hand on the handrail, and the other leaning carefully on my cane, I made my way up the stairs.

The computer was in resting mode when I sat down at the desk. I moved the mouse and the screen came to life. The first screen to appear was an online dating site complete with Paul's user name and password.

Really?

I felt like I had been kicked in the stomach. I wanted to puke and purge his poison from my very being.

With everything else I had on my plate, I thought, *now this. Paul was involved in Internet dating.*

I couldn't deal with this tonight. I had bigger fish to fry … I was having surgery for cancer in a few hours.

I made my way down the hallway to Cullen's bedroom. He was back in college and his room was vacant. I lay there quietly in the dark, in prayer, I asked God for strength and healing.

Right now.

In this moment.

It must be all about me.

I woke at 4:30 AM to the sound of my cell phone alarm. I returned to the master bedroom where Paul was still sound asleep and snoring loudly. He didn't even know I had been gone.

I showered, dressed, and dried my hair. Gillian got up early to see me off. I kissed my darling daughter. "I'll see you after the surgery, Mom. I love you."

A lump stuck in my throat.

It was time for me to leave.

Paul waited impatiently. He was ready to drive me to the hospital.

My surgeon's partner, Dr. K, met me in the pre-op area. She was a young, sweet blonde woman … suddenly I had a vision of Gillian 15 years from now. I wondered if I would be here to see her as an adult. Without warning, tears began to run down my face.

Dr. K sat with me on the bed as I signed the consent forms. She hugged me, and offered reassurance. "It will be all right, Jeanne. You will make it through this." Her kindness touched me.

I was ready to go.

My next memory is of my mother. She was standing at my bedside instructing the OR transport team to be careful with me. "She has a fractured pelvis."

In my haze I saw her edge Paul away and back from my bed. Something had happened, but I had no idea what.

Mom bent over to kiss me. "Everything is okay, Jeanne. It's okay."

I'm certain I murmured something, and then nodded off to sleep. I was medicated, and so I slept off and on all evening.

I don't remember much from that first night, except that Gillian was faithful to her promise. She sat at the foot of my bed and kept me company as I slept.

The next day, Dr. Zinn was in to see me. "The tumor appears to have been contained within the uterine wall, but we won't know anything definitive for a couple of days until we get the pathology report on the lymph nodes."

Accompanying the post-operative pain and the nausea was relief. I needed some good news and I was reassured there were no visible signs of metastasis.

Dr. Zinn knew me. He knew I wanted to know if there had been any metastasis. Was the cancer contained or had it already spread? That was still unknown.

Mom spent the day with me and I slept most of it. In the evening, my girlfriends arrived: Jill, Colleen, Margie, Pamela and Janice. Before they arrived, I had been up to the shower, but I was so weak that I had fallen back asleep with the towel still on my head. Colleen sat beside me, and combed my hair and towel dried it. Later, she would tell me how ashen and grey I looked. Colleen had brought me a book, and the others had each brought me flowers. They sat and hovered and kept me company. My angels surrounded me. My friends and my family formed the roof and the walls that protected me from the storm that raged on. They provided a protective barrier that kept me safe.

The question was –How much more could I be asked to bear?

Gillian and Dana arrived, and joined the others. I felt loved.

About 7 PM Paul arrived. I hadn't seen or heard from him all day.

I was still on a morphine drip. I was nauseated. I was still waiting for the pathology report to determine the stage of my cancer. No decision would be made about chemo or radiation until the staging was complete.

The nurse came in and gave me a shot of heparin in my abdomen. They were still concerned about pulmonary emboli because of my fractured pelvis. My abdomen was covered with bruises from the heparin injections.

My girlfriends were not in a hurry to leave. They didn't want me to be alone with my husband. They knew how he hurt me. But I was tired and visiting hours were over. The rules were that only family could remain, and so my girlfriends had to leave. One by one they kissed me good-bye and we made plans to see one another as soon as I was able. Gillian and Dana had homework and tests to study for, so they too headed for home.

Gillian and I have a parting ritual that we have shared since she was a little girl. So before she left, she used her fingers to wipe my forehead clean –three times and said, " 'rase, 'rase, 'rase," and then used her thumb to mark my forehead with the sign of the cross saying, "cross, cross, cross." She leaned her forehead towards me and I did the same for her. And then we said to one another, "I love you infinity infinities and all the extras and even more than that." And this is the way we parted. We had been doing this for years, and it instilled a sense of peace in me.

Paul remained behind after the girls had gone home. Now he was all about his day. He was 57 years old and had been offered an early retirement package. Without consulting me, his wife, he had decided to take it. The package was lucrative. He would be well compensated. He had been coveting a retirement package for over a year now.

"How did all this come about?" I asked.

"I told Human Resources that my wife had cancer and I needed to be home to take care of you. And they agreed to give me a package!" He was giddy with delight.

A wave of nausea hit me. I was appalled. He was using me, and my illness as a ticket to a lucrative early retirement.

I felt sick and tired. I was hurting. Here he was, capitalizing on my misfortune. It didn't sit well with me. I wanted him to go home. He was the last person in the world I wanted to care for me. He was incapable of caring for anyone but himself. Besides, I had every intention of returning to complete health. I pushed the button to infuse another dose of morphine into my veins.

The pain began to subside and I was getting sleepy.

His timing was impeccable as he pulled some papers from his briefcase and handed them to me with a pen, "I need you to sign these."

I was groggy now. "What are they?" I asked. I was in no condition to read through the fine print on these documents right then.

"If you sign these I will get another $1000 every month." He said this as if this was a good thing.

"Why do you need my signature? I don't understand." I was confused. But intuitively I knew something was up.

He took a deep breath. "You are signing away your surviving spousal benefits." He paused.

I looked him straight in the eye. Just what was he up to now?

"Now that you have cancer ... you will probably die before me." He offered this to me as some lame ass explanation.

"Really. We shall see. I'm not signing anything." I gave myself another dose of morphine.

When I awoke next, it was dark. Thankfully he was gone.

I had reached my nadir, the lowest point and the voice of my heart spoke:

You cannot stay.

My heart knew the truth I could no longer ignore. If I wanted a life of health and healing, and I did, then I would need to leave this one behind.

Three days later, I was discharged from the hospital. My mother picked me up and brought me home.

When I climbed into my bed I found that Paul had left the retirement papers that required my signature, on my bedside table with a black pen.

How considerate of him.

Before the end of the week, I heard from Dr. Zinn. The pathology report indicated the tumor had been contained in my uterus and all my lymph nodes were clean. My prognosis for a complete recovery was excellent.

However, my post-operative recovery was rough and complicated. Mom came every day and took wonderful care of me. She was protective and on guard.

Only later, would I find out what transpired while I was in the operating room. My dear friend Jill had come to sit with my mom in the surgical waiting room. Apparently, as soon as I went into surgery, Paul left and presumably went to work. He didn't return until I was out of the recovery room.

He wasn't there while I was under the knife–
When anything could have happened to me.
He wasn't there while the cancer was being staged.
He didn't know the surgery went an hour longer than was expected.
He wasn't there to talk to the surgeon or the oncologist.
He didn't know how the surgery had gone.
He didn't know what they found.
He didn't know if there had been any complications.
He didn't care enough about me to wait.

In this moment my mother glimpsed his true character.

She was unglued by his total lack of caring and his total lack of compassion …

I, on the other hand, was not surprised.

CHAPTER 16

The Leaving

Christmas came and went. I was healing and just lying low.

Over the holidays, Alex returned from California with news that he would be a father in the spring. At 20 years old he had impregnated an 18-year-old girl who already had a one-year-old son.

There are some people who are mature enough for parenthood at 18 and 20 years old. But Alex was not one of them, and neither was this young woman. Neither of them was employed, or had any education, or job skills. Great.

Paul decided to pull some money out of his corporate buy-out to purchase a home for Alex, his girlfriend, her one-year old son, and the new baby that was scheduled to arrive in the spring.

I kept my mouth closed. I had nothing constructive to offer.

In mid-January, I returned to work after being off for four months. I was still a little shaky on my feet. Everyone at work knew about the riding accident, but only my closest friends knew about the cancer and the surgery. I did my best to keep my private life private.

It had been nearly six months since I had been on a horse. I dreamt about riding, the grace, and beauty of the horses. I never dreamt of the fall. I just didn't.

So on the first of March, I thought I was strong enough to return to the barn for a ride on dear gentle Luke. Margie and Cathy were there, and they encouraged me to get back in the saddle. I know there are people who thought I was crazy to ever dream of riding again. But I loved to ride, and I didn't want to give it up.

Margie had been actively looking for a gentle horse for me. She was adamant, she wanted me to start slowly. She found me a loaner. Blair was the eighth horse in a seven-stall barn. His owner, Becky, wanted someone to ride him and board him so she could bring another horse to her barn. We reached an agreement that I would take him, ride him, and board him. And if and when he no longer met my needs, I would return Blair to her where he would be put out to the pasture for the remainder of his days.

Blair was a 26-year-old gelded thoroughbred. He stood 17 hands high and was a bay, which meant he was dark brown, my tall dark handsome older man. I thought he was beautiful. He came to the fence to see me and was so happy to take me on a trail ride. I felt a real sense of peacefulness to be back at the barn in the company of the horses and my women friends. I felt a sense of belonging there that I never felt at home.

I guess if Paul could buy his son a house without discussing it with me, I could return to the barn. Riding was cheaper than therapy, and much more effective, at least for me.

Margie and I began to ride regularly again. Blair was an older horse who hadn't been ridden much in the last few years. We both needed to regain our strength. So we rode one day, and took the next day off to rest. I also took a painting class one night a week when I wasn't riding.

I tried to make a life for myself. I lived with a man who clearly didn't love me. Since he had retired at 57 years old, he sat around the house all day and all night. He rarely left the house. He ate, slept, drank, and watched TV.

This man could not possibly be my husband. This could not possibly be my life.

When it had been one calendar year since the last time we had sex, I asked him, "Are we ever going to have sex again?"

He thought about this for a moment and then responded, "When I lose 60 pounds."

I nodded and left the room. Paul had gained about 60 pounds since we married three years ago. Prior to that time he had been at his dating weight. Given the fact his belly was now el grande, it was probably a simple mater of physics. He couldn't get his male appendage anywhere near me because his protruding belly got in the way. The truth of the matter was that Paul liked hamburgers and French fries more than he liked sex or at least sex with me.

I had waited for a year. That was long enough. I gathered up what was left of my self-respect and moved out of the master bedroom, and took up residence in Cullen's vacant bedroom. The room was peaceful and dark, and I rested well there without the incessant roar of Paul's snoring.

The day of Dana's high school graduation, Gillian had a piano and voice recital. I had to choose. I couldn't be two places at the same time. I was conflicted. I wanted nothing more than to hear my daughter sing. Gillian had been practicing around the house and her voice was beautiful. She was growing in confidence daily. She would be singing The Beatles' song, "Let it Be." I so wanted to hear her sing, but I couldn't miss Dana's graduation, as she was the biggest causality in this disastrous marriage. I love her and I wanted her to know that. Gillian was strong and confident in our love. Dana needed to know, and to be shown, that she was important to me too. So without discussion or fanfare I elected to attend Dana's graduation.

Gillian had been accepted to the University of British Columbia in Vancouver. It was her first choice. I had mixed feelings. On one hand, I was delighted for her, but what would I do without her? Vancouver is so far away. She had worked hard in high school, and all her hard work had paid off. I could not and would not deny her this. She needed to be in Vancouver on August 13 for the International Students' Orientation.

Dana would leave about 10 days later for Miami University in Oxford, Ohio.

The dates were etched in my mind. Once the girls were safely tucked into college, I would be gone. How would I do it? I didn't know. My sleep was restless, but I looked to the light on the horizon.

Yes, a different light was dawning, inspired by women all around me. Gillian and her classmates, all young women, wrote and performed a production about women. The funds they raised would go to Women-to-Women International, specifically the women of Darfur. The vignettes were incredibly powerful. My daughter was amazing and strong. She had found her own way and her own voice. I was inspired beyond words at the power of this production. The strength of these young women gave a voice to the oppressed and they stood up for what was right.

If they could do something brave and amazing like this, I thought, *perhaps I could be brave too.*

As Gillian's high school graduation approached, Paul and I had a fairly major altercation nearly every day. His behavior humiliated me, and he didn't seem to care. He answered his cell phone in the church during the graduation Mass. He felt excluded when Gillian wanted her graduation photo taken with me, her mother. So he up and left me at the post-graduation dinner dance and went home. The incidents were escalating in frequency and there was no more pretense of remorse.

When I arrived home, Paul was snoring like a chain saw. I went upstairs and slept in Cullen's empty room.

In the morning, while he was sleeping off ramifications of way too much alcohol, I got up and went to the barn. I spent the morning riding, and then took some clean clothes to Gillian as her graduation festivities continued. And then back to the barn I went. I was afraid if I saw Paul I would be unable to keep a civil tongue, and I didn't want to get into another round of ugliness with him. So I just stayed away.

I didn't feel emotionally strong enough to take another battering nor did I feel it was necessary to defend my daughter's decisions surrounding the photographs. She made her choice, and I supported her for it. She showed great courage and strength. I could learn a lot from her. So instead of addressing the issues, again I fled from him. No doubt Paul saw things one way, and I saw them another. There would be no meeting of the minds and reconciling over this. I just wanted to minimize the toxic fallout. The best way I knew how was to get the hell out of there.

Sunday morning, Gillian and Dana came to wake me. They were making breakfast because it was Paul's birthday. Paul and Gillian had made peace, as tenuous as it may have been. I decided if Gillian could forgive his transgressions, for the sake of family harmony, I too would let it go.

The next Saturday, we had planned a joint graduation party for Gillian and Dana. Many invitations had been extended and Paul went about doing what he did best ... marketing and promotion. Today, we were being sold as one big happy family.

I had done all of the cooking with assistance from my mother. We had a big spread. We could afford a party for hundreds, but not a caterer. I actually like to cook, and I love the girls, so it was a labor of love.

The party was fun and it was a successful joint venture.

There were times like this, when Paul was charming and on his best behavior, when I actually thought just maybe we might be able to survive this. When I would start to vacillate, my girlfriends came to the rescue, to help me see the errors of my thinking.

The Monday after the party, Margie and I spent the morning riding.

I spent the afternoon working in the garden. The roses needed deadheading, as did the purple coneflower and the stargazer lilies near the lower level patio. Everything needed to be fed. This involved hauling buckets of water and fertilizer. It was an all-afternoon project. The results were paying off. It was a good year for the garden. I found the work satisfying even if no one ever recognized my efforts. No one ever noticed.

Should I stay in this broken marriage, because I love the garden?

I pondered this as I tied up the heavy blue blooms on the hydrangea. I know the notion is preposterous even if I hadn't spoken the words aloud.

No one stays married to a garden, even one as beautiful as this.

I didn't want the solitude of the garden to be disturbed by the incessant ringing of the cell phone. I had purposely left it in the kitchen.

Four missed calls and two voice mail messages from Paul.

First. 3:02 PM "Where are you? Call me back."

Second. 3:04 PM "I'm at the club. I stopped for a couple of drinks. I'll be home by 7 if you still want to go for a bike ride."

We used to ride bikes the summer before we were married. But we hadn't gone for a ride together in almost three years. I'd suggested it in the morning, and now I was surprised that he remembered and was considering it.

I checked the time. It was closing in on 6:30. I began to wash my hands at the kitchen sink and as I did I took a moment to look about this palatial estate.

What an unhappy home. I wonder if Paul will be able to ride his bike? He's probably already drunk.

This chatter filled my head as the peace of the day began to erode. The scent of the orange ginger hand soap filled the room. I paused to inhale.

He has no idea how much pleasure I derived from this simple fragrance.

There was so much he didn't know about me.

It went both ways.

Paul loves the house, the club, the cars, and all the trappings of wealth.

He just didn't love me.

This was not the life I wanted.

I walked into the laundry room and stripped off my dirty gardening clothes.

I wrapped myself in a towel and headed for the shower.

After the shower, I towel dried my hair, and pulled on a pair shorts and a camisole.

I was ready for the bike ride.

I waited for Paul.

He didn't come home.

He'd been drinking since 3:00.

He wouldn't want to ride tonight.

I pulled my bike from the garage.

It was now 7:15. He was 15 minutes late.

My heart confirmed what I already knew.

He wasn't coming.

The beautiful summer evening awaited me.

I mounted the bike, and rode down the tree-lined driveway.

I'm a creature of habit.

I always took the same road, then turned down the country lane, and rode out past the horse farms.

But that night, I took a different route.

I'm uncertain why. I just did.

I crossed the overpass and headed towards the village.

This country road went through the historic neighborhood of the old village.

Near the cemetery, where Fred is buried, Paul's red BMW roadster passed me.

The top was down and there was a pretty young woman in the passenger seat.

Paul was talking and laughing as he passed me on my bicycle.

I stopped, straddled on the bike, and I turned and watched him.

He didn't slow down, but he took the first right turn, and disappeared out of sight.

I called his cell phone.

He didn't answer.

I called again.

He had turned the phone off, and my call went directly to voice mail.

I turned my bike around and slowly rode towards home.

My heart knew – *The time is now*

I spoke the words aloud.

"Thank you Paul. You have just made this so easy for me."

"I'm out of here."

I rode home to our empty, empty house.

I put my bike away in the garage.

I waited.

I tried to wrap my head around what had just happened.

What am I going to do now?

Slipping on my pajamas I crawled into bed in Cullen's room and I tried to occupy myself by reading. I turned the pages, but couldn't focus. I contemplated my next move.

I thought about packing my things, and moving out. But there was part of me that wanted to hear what possible explanation he might be able to offer.

So I waited.

At 10:00 PM I heard the garage door go up. He was home. I could hear him downstairs. I stayed upstairs in Cullen's room. For the first time since I moved upstairs, months and months ago, Paul came upstairs to see me.

He opened the door to the bedroom without the courtesy of a knock.

He was loaded.

"Get out," I told him as I got out of bed and stood to face him. I needed to confront him from a position of strength. Now I was afraid.

He attempted some feeble excuse, "She just needed a ride. I was just giving her a ride. You always think the worst of me." He was slurring his words.

"Oh, I see you had a perfectly good reason to have a pretty, young woman in your car, to drive right past your wife without stopping to make an introduction or offer an explanation as to why you weren't coming home at 7:00 after all … and then to spend another three hours drinking somewhere with your cell phone turned off. You're right … I do think the worst of you. " The words spewed forth like vile toxin being purged from within.

His face went red, and in his drunkenness he moved towards me.

I picked up Cullen's Adirondack hiking stick that was propped up in the corner of the room, with the ends of the stick in each of my hands; I used the stick as a barrier to keep him away from me.

I never touched him with the stick, but Paul was so inebriated that he lost his balance. All on his own he fell flat on his big, fat ass.

Fumbling, he tried to make his way to his feet and then stumbled off to bed.

I called Margie. I woke her. "Can I come over?"

"You know you can. I'm waiting." I offered no explanation and none was needed. She knew what my life had been like.

I left with Duncan, my dog and Luna, my new kitty, and arrived at Margie's in my pajamas.

Margie had turned down the bed in her guest room, and had opened a bottle of wine. She handed me a glass as I walked through the door. We sat in the kitchen and sipped the wine as I filled her in on what had transpired since I saw her in the morning.

"This is it," I said.

Finally.

This was indeed the end.

I talked it through with Margie. She was my sounding board.

She listened while I spoke of my fears. Fear he would find me. Fear he would seek retribution. Fear he would extract revenge.

Where would we live?

What was next?

So many fears.

So many unanswered questions.

And yet I was so relieved.

I wanted to be out of this marriage for so long, and now I had done that which I feared I would be too weak to do. I had left him. I had left this man who had made me so miserable for so long. I had finally mustered up the courage to do so.

I spoke of my sadness and my feelings of failure.

I had failed in this marriage. I was going to divorce this man that I had promised to love until death do us part. My Catholic upbringing fought with my Nordic stoicism. The truth was we had stopped loving each other so long ago, and there was no marriage left, and there was nothing here at all to save, except perhaps the rest of my life.

My life is a gift from God, given to me. I would have to make an accounting for how I chose to spend this gift and I didn't think God would look very favorably if I squandered the days of my life with someone who was not worthy of my time, my love and my life.

Truth was, I was just so relieved to be out of it. I would find a way back to God. It would be easier now that this big obstacle had finally been cast aside.

And yet, I tortured myself, for not only had I failed in my marriage, but I had also failed Paul's children, and I had failed my own. I had disturbed their sense of wholeness and their sense of home.

How could I help them heal from this drama and this trauma that I had willingly thrust them into? I needed forgiveness. I needed to forgive myself. I needed my children's forgiveness. I berated myself for the multitude of mistakes I had made.

I went on and on and Margie listened and refilled my glass while we sat together and watched the sun come up.

Margie is my one in a million friend. There are not very many places that you can go at midnight, in your pajamas, with two animals in tow. I'll always be grateful for her love, compassion, kindness, and generosity that were poured out in abundance at a time when I needed it so desperately.

I woke early in the morning and went back to the house. Paul was sleeping off the indulgences from the day before. I packed a suitcase and threw some essentials into the car. He didn't even know I had gone.

The next day, I met with an attorney and filed for a divorce from Mr. Paul O'Shea.

CHAPTER 17

The Separation

Eventually, Paul sobered up and realized I was gone. Initially, he made no attempt to contact me …

But when I didn't return home the next night he called me on the phone.

I didn't take his calls.

Initially, the voice messages he left were short: "Call me."

I didn't return his calls.

There was nothing more to talk about.

Another day went by, it was the 4th of July and I had been invited to watch the fireworks with Denis and Jill. I was sitting on their boat when I received this text–

"Jeanne,
I know you are hurt and sad and angry. I am sorry that you feel bad. But you know there was nothing untoward going on between me and the woman in my car. I was just giving her a ride.

Please come home. We can work this out. I think we should try marriage counseling again. You should see a therapist—your problem is you're angry and suspicious. You need to get counseling. Call me."

This started out as an apology. But if you read it carefully it was clear, he was only sorry that I felt bad. He wasn't sorry for anything he had done. He admitted no wrongdoing. Instead, he blamed me for my misperceptions and suggested that I was the one who needed help.

He was right about one thing, I did have a problem –I was married to someone who had no concern for me whatsoever –and I was actively seeking a course of action to correct it. It was as if I had been living in a toxic waste dump. I was dumping my husband, and was getting on with the clean-up. I had finally, at long last, had enough.

Gillian had missed the drama of the past few days as she had been vacationing in northern Michigan with her high school girlfriends. When she returned, I made arrangements to rendezvous with her up in the driveway. Paul wasn't home, but I was fearful that he might return at anytime.

I just wanted and needed to get out of town. I was filled with anxiety as I waited for Gillian to return so we could leave. I had already packed my car for a road trip to the Adirondacks to visit my sister, Susan. There was no time for Gillian to repack her bags between adventures, so I loaded her in the car, along with our sleeping bags, my tent, a cooler, and a duffle bag full of her dirty clothes. "But Mom," she protested, "I don't have any clean clothes."

"I can fix that. Have you ever heard of a Laundromat?" I didn't want to delay our departure for one more minute. My anxiety was growing, and I needed to get on the road, and as far away from Paul O'Shea as I could get.

As we drove the 10-hour drive across Canada, I confided in Gillian about the events of the last few days, the state of my marriage, and my plans for a divorce. She knew I was unhappy, and had been for quite some time, but while I elaborated on some of the darkness I had endured with this man, tears of sadness rolled down her beautiful face, feeling my pain as well as her own.

"What a fucker," she said angrily.

She didn't usually speak like that, at least not in my presence. In my eyes she was still a fresh-faced innocent. So I gently admonished her for her language, as only a mother can. "*Gillian.*" My tone said it all.

She looked at me as I drove down the highway, "Sorry Mom, I meant Non-Fuck. That is what he is ... Paul O'Shea, The Non-Fuck. You should be glad that non-fuck never touched you." Her tears gave way to laughter, and we both laughed and cried, while we made our way across rural Ontario. The further away we got from Paul, the closer Gillian and I became, until we were both so enmeshed in the love and comfort of one another.

We would stay only a couple of days in the Adirondacks since Susan's husband Robert had just recently been diagnosed with pancreatic cancer and they were urgently seeking second opinions, and exploring treatment options.

I sat in their living room and faced Susan and Robert while they sat together on the settee. They were joined at the hip. Susan had brought Robert up to speed on the nightmare of my marriage and my decision to leave Paul.

"I'm sorry it's been so tough for you. Maybe the third time will be the charm," Robert said alluding to me remarrying at some point in my future.

"No, Robert … the first time was the charm. Fred and I were so happy together. I know what a good marriage is and my marriage to Paul was not it."

"Oh I know you did. Fred was a great guy. Susan and I had some rough spots earlier in our marriage. Didn't we?" He turned to look at her and she nodded as she reached out and took his hand. "We were able to work through them. I really love your sister. She's so good to me. I can't imagine what my life would be like without her. Our days are peaceful and good here in the north woods."

They continued to hold hands. As I watched them I remembered what it was like to be so close and united with someone that the two of you could speak with one voice. Fred and I had that too, but Paul and I never did, and never would.

"We hope you find love again. It's a hard road to go all alone." Robert looked me in the eye as he offered me his kind words and loving compassion.

The conversation shifted, and we talked briefly about what he was facing. Neither of us needed to share the details of our journeys. It was enough to know there was both hardship and pain on the horizon. We would hold one another in love and prayer for a safe passage.

It was the best conversation I'd ever had with Robert. He validated my experience, and empathized with sadness. Perhaps it was because we were both so vulnerable at that point in time that we were able to cut away the extraneous, and show one another what was really in our hearts.

I am sad to say that this conversation would be our last, as one month later Robert did not survive the surgery.

Gillian and I were nomads that summer. In one month's time she would need to be in Vancouver, British Columbia for college, but in the meantime we traveled to the eastern seaboard and explored the coast of Maine, Acadia National Park, and then went on to explore Nova Scotia, and the Canadian maritime provinces. We laughed a lot and enjoyed one another's company. At one point in time when we were camping out on Camp Breton Island, I was awestruck by the majesty of land as we looked out from a rocky prominence. As the sun burnt through the morning mist you could see miles and miles of the craggy coastline where the mountains reached down to meet the raging sea. I was enjoying the beauty, the peace, and solitude of it all. I remember commenting to Gillian, "I think I could live here. How about you?"

She looked around and then back at me as if I had lost my mind, "No. No, I couldn't live here. You may not have noticed, but there is no one here. No one lives here."

All I could do was laugh. I guess at 18 years old this kind of quiet and desolation wouldn't appeal to her. I, on the other hand, given the pain and chaos in my life these last few years, found this kind of peace and quiet very appealing. "Oh, I suppose you're right," I conceded and of course she was right. As beautiful as it was, this wasn't the kind of place for me to make a home for myself. My daughter was growing with wisdom, grace, and beauty. I needed to heed her words because she has always had the vision to see.

While we were away, I texted Dana a love note. I didn't disclose our location or our plans. I didn't want Paul to know where I was or anything about me. The divorce papers were to be served while I was away. No one leaves The Great and Powerful Oz. I was afraid of him. He terrified me.

He was cold and calculating, and I feared he would seek revenge and retribution for this humiliation. I had seen him in action.

I remembered how he'd basked in the glory of defeating his ex-wife, Marianne, in their divorce. He took great personal pleasure painting her as an unfit mother and a drug addict, so he could get what he wanted … custody of their children. I knew I would be crazy and unbalanced if someone took my children from me. Would I have turned to drugs? Either that or murder.

I was well acquainted with the stereotype: the men always take it up the ass in divorce and the courts favor the woman. As in, she gets everything and he gets taken to the cleaners. I thought about his ex-wife Tina. The stereotype didn't hold in that divorce; Paul retained the house, the furniture, the art, the crystal, the china, and her 4-carat diamond ring. I don't know what she got in the divorce, perhaps just her freedom. Maybe that was enough.

Paul could be so petty and vindictive over things of little consequence. What would he be like now, when there was so much at stake?

I was in uncharted territory. Paul's entire sense of himself was built on the acquisition of power and wealth, and I knew he didn't like to lose face or anything else for that matter.

The very thought of the confrontation that awaited me filled me with trepidation, and I trembled with fear and apprehension. How would he extract his revenge? I couldn't run from him forever. I knew eventually I had to face Paul.

When we returned to Michigan at the end of July, Gillian and I moved into my parents' guest room. The divorce papers had been served, and a strange silence followed. I heard nothing from Paul and was relieved. Maybe he was just over it.

Margie had invited us to stay with her, but Gillian felt more comfortable coming and going from her grandparents' home. I knew my folks would consider it an affront to them, if in my time of trouble, that I didn't count on them to help me. I understood this, and so at 51 years old, I was living, temporarily at Mom and Dad's. They were absolutely lovely and welcoming, but it was hard on my ego to be laid so low. I prided myself on being strong and independent. It was dawning on me maybe it was my pride that got in my way. But after all I had been through it really was nice to be somewhere where people loved me, and were glad to see me.

Gillian and I had been living out of a suitcase. Make that a duffle bag and the trunk of the car for the last month. We needed to return to the house so she could pack up her things for college.

I found my courage and I called Paul. He didn't pick up. So I left a voice mail message, "Gillian and I are coming by the house this afternoon. She needs to pack her things. She is leaving for Vancouver at the end of the week. We will be there between 2 and 3." My hands were shaking as I hung up the phone. I knew he got the call for he never went anywhere without his cell phone. Thankfully, he didn't want to talk to me either.

I pulled into the driveway. His car was parked in the garage. My heart was racing, and I felt a knot in the pit in my stomach. I offered a silent prayer,

Please God let this go well, no more drama and histrionics.

Gillian went in first, and I trailed behind. I could hear the TV in the family room. We took the back stairway and went directly up to her room to pack her things. She needed to be selective, as we were flying to Vancouver. She couldn't take too much. We would get most of what she needed when we got to British Columbia.

I chatted with Dana while we helped Gillian pack. She was ready to go within an hour, and then there was the tearful goodbye with Dana.

"Dana, I love you and I always will, but I just can't stay. When I return from Vancouver, I will drive down to Ohio and see you once you've settled in the dorm." I reached out and hugged her, and we both cried. It broke my heart to leave her but I couldn't stay one moment more. My anxiety level was rising every minute I was in the house. I didn't want a confrontation with Paul, but fortunately he stayed downstairs and out of sight.

I would need to get my work clothes when I returned, but not this trip. I just wanted to get out of there without incident. It went better than I thought it would.

Gillian and I flew to San Francisco to visit Cullen for a few days, and then on to Vancouver. She and I spent a great deal of time together that summer. The reality hit me hard. My role as a mother was changing as both of my children were leaving and living independently on the other side of the continent. I knew I needed to let them go so they could claim their own lives, but that didn't mean this was easy for any of us. Cullen and Gillian and I discussed this at length when we were in San Francisco. I couldn't be the mother who only saw her children twice a year. We vowed that at some point we would reside in close proximity to one another again. But this was the decade of exploration for all of us. I knew this, and I would honor their need to grow and claim their own lives.

As I struggled with leaving Gillian, and the prospect of living alone for the first time in 23 years, I received a phone call from Susan. It was August 5th. We were walking on the campus. Susan was upset. I waved Gillian on, and sat down on the retaining wall around a garden. She was calling from the corridor outside Robert's hospital room. She told me they were doing CPR on Robert. She didn't seem to understand exactly what this meant, but I did. I knew something had gone terribly wrong, and she was going to lose her beloved husband. She was all alone in Boston, and I was in Vancouver: opposite ends of the continent and worlds away. All I could do was wait with her on the phone. All I could offer was an abiding presence. Within the next 30 minutes, they would call the code and stop CPR. Robert had passed on. Susan was a widow. Her sons were fatherless.

This wasn't what had been expected. Pancreatic cancer has a poor prognosis, but no one expected Robert to die from surgical complications. They had been preparing for chemotherapy and radiation therapy. His death was sudden, and Susan and her children had been caught unprepared. My heart was breaking for her. Gillian and I held one another and cried. We cried for Robert, and how his life had been cut short when there was still so much he had wanted to do. We cried for Susan. We cried for their sons, Remy and Rex. As we understood all too well how painful this journey of loss would be. We cried for his parents, and we cried for his sisters. And we cried for ourselves as his loss diminished us, and we would miss him. God help them.

So I changed my plans. My daughter was ready to start this new adventure called college, and my sister needed me. I would fly to Philadelphia for the funeral. And then Susan and I, and her kids, would end the summer at the Jersey shore until I needed to return to work and Susan's kids needed to return to school.

Robert Hazard was a very successful songwriter and musician. His best-known song was *Girls Just Want to Have Fun*. But fame and success do not offer any protection against death and disease.

When we are young we feel as if we have all the time in the world to chase our dreams and create our own realities, but the truth is the days of our lives are limited. The question lingered ... how would I spend my time here on earth? I needed to get on with the business of living, and my continued association with Paul O'Shea was keeping me from doing so ... so let's just get on with this.

With this new insight ...

Once again my school became my haven as I transitioned to my new life as a single woman.

I met with my attorney, and we had a preliminary meeting at the courthouse with Paul and his attorney. Paul's attorney was unbelievably rude and aggressive towards me, and I was feeling vulnerable. I was shaking after the first encounter. People I knew who had been through divorces couldn't believe that Paul's attorney was addressing me at all. They helped me see that my attorney should be protecting me from this unprovoked aggressive confrontation. Although my attorney had been a neighbor and a friend, I didn't feel he would protect my interests or me. I had been emotionally battered by Paul. I didn't need to be beaten up by his attorney. It was abundantly clear after the first encounter that this was their strategy, to attack me as a human being. I should've known Paul would endorse this kind of behavior. He hated to lose at anything. He was a veteran in the world of divorce. He'd been through this three times before, and this would be his fourth battle. This was the third time Harold Williams would be his gladiator. This time I was the foe. I was the one to be conquered and destroyed. Paul wouldn't use the same attorney if he'd not already proven himself in battle.

I strategized with Margie and she suggested that I use her attorney's partner, Don Darkhorse.

Mr. Donald Darkhorse was in his early thirties. He was relatively new to the legal scene but he rapidly convinced me that he was the man for the job. I told him how afraid I was of Paul and his pit bull attorney. I explained how he had bullied me in the presence of my attorney in the courthouse, and how vulnerable I had felt. Don reached across the desk to hand me a Kleenex as my eyes were welling up with tears, and my voice was shaking as I went on to describe the nightmare of my marriage. As the introductory meeting drew to a close, he sized up the situation this way, "You only have one jointly-held asset that is being contested, and your husband spent your investment in the house without your consent. There isn't a judge around that will not be sympathetic towards you. All I need to do is lay out the case." He was calm and confident while he assured me that I was justified in seeking to recover the money I had invested in the house, and if I hired him, when all was said and done, I would have my money so I could purchase another home. I was nervous and uncomfortable spending $300 an hour and handing over a $30,000 retainer to get divorced. I was a single mother, working as a teacher, and I had two kids still in college. $30,000 was nearly half my annual salary. It might not be a lot of money to someone else but it was a lot of money to me and to my family. But this attorney assured me that in the end, it would be Paul who would pay my attorney fees, and that really everything was going to be okay. He would be worth every penny of the $30,000 this divorce was going to cost me.

So I hired the big guns to protect me.

I knew Paul, and I had met his attorney. I was afraid.

I had been assured the divorce would be completed within 6 months ... tops. There were no minor children, and our only jointly held asset was our house. But despite his assurances, there were delays upon delays. The discovery took much longer than expected, and then there were the cancellations for the Jewish holidays, and then there was Thanksgiving, and Christmas and New Year's. I had placed my life on hold. I didn't want to move twice. I figured we would have this resolved before the end of the year, and then I would buy another house with the proceeds from the divorce.

When it became obvious to me that the divorce was going to drag on and on, I knew that I needed to make an alternative living plan. I found a beautiful two-bedroom condo for lease. It was mid-way between work and the barn. It was out of my old neighborhood so I could let go of the fear of running into Paul. I made my plan to move.

Feeling ready to move on, and well-protected by my tough new lawyer, I thought I was ready to face Paul.

I knew better than to just show up at the house, even though it was still half mine. I figured it was the courteous thing to do, so I let him know I was coming to pack my things. The email was sent with three days notice, and the movers were scheduled for the next day.

I had been gone for six months. I thought we'd be divorced by then. I'd been staying with family, friends, and everyone had been gracious, but my kids would be coming home from college, and I needed a place of my own.

I called his cell phone from the driveway. He didn't answer, but instead met me in the garage.

"What are you doing here?" He spewed venom as he spoke.

"My kids are coming home on Thursday, and I've found a place for us to live." I was cautious. I didn't want him to know where I'd be living.

"Did you read my email?" I added trying to keep this civil.

"I said what are you doing here?" Now he was yelling.

"I need my things, some of my furniture, my kid's winter clothes, beds, my wedding crystal from my grandma, and my collection of antique Christmas ornaments. You know just my personal stuff." I passed him and entered the house through the garage door, carrying folded boxes and packing supplies.

I went up the back stairway to Gillian's room. I decided to start there, because she is a bit of a pack rat, and had accumulated the most stuff. There was no sign of Paul.

Thirty minutes passed and my cell phone rang. I answered.

"Jeanne, it's Don Darkhorse." My lawyer. He never called me.

"Yes." I took a deep breath. This couldn't be good.

"What are you doing?" He asked, as if he didn't already know.

"Packing my things, I'm moving tomorrow." I answered matter of fact.

"You should have told me." Great, now I was being chastised by my lawyer.

"Paul has threatened to call the police if you remove anything from the house," my lawyer informed me.

"You've got to be kidding me." I was incredulous. "Sorry," I said, "Let me talk to him and I'll call you back."

I crossed the hall to the music room. Paul sat at the computer and I sat on the couch across from him. The room was a mess.

I took a deep breath and began, "Paul, all I want is what was mine before we married. My kids will be here for Christmas, and I need to have a home for them." I pleaded with him for reasonable behavior.

"You should've thought of that before you left me. If you take one thing from this house I swear I'll call the police," his eyes burned with hatred as he stared me down.

We negotiated and argued. I sat and watched him while he turned his back to me and drafted a document on the computer. He ran a copy. "If you want to take anything. Sign this." He thrust the paper toward me.

I read the document he had prepared. *Does this man think I am an idiot?* It said if I removed anything from the house then I would be responsible for half of the household expenses. It was complete with a line for my signature and was already dated.

"No way am I going to sign that. My lawyer would have a stroke." I tried to pass the buck.

"Call him and ask." He demanded and I agreed.

I read the document to Donald.

"You can't sign that!" Donny was adamant.

"How will I get my things?" I asked in desperation.

"I'll have to go to court next week and file a motion," more lawyer speak.

"Next week is Christmas," I pleaded.

"I'll see what I can do," another promise from our legal system.

Paul had heard the entire conversation. He had swirled the desk chair around to face me and he smirked. *God I hated this man.*

I could see the computer screen from over his shoulder. His screen saver was a photograph of a full-breasted woman in a sheer wet blouse. She moved in and out of focus, and it appeared as if she was moving in closer for an intimate encounter.

"Who is that? " I asked.

"Wynonna Rider," he smiled.

She had always been his proto-type for the ideal sexy woman. Allegedly, he met her once. I thought it was bullshit. He was celebrity obsessed and dropped names and titles like they were confetti on New Year's Eve.

I took a deep breath. "I'm certain she has a picture of you as her screen saver too." Oh my, another snappy retort. Another unfiltered response delivered by yours truly.

Bad idea. Now he was really pissed.

"Do you really expect me to live here with half of the furniture gone?" He turned in the swivel chair and leaned in closer to face me head on. I could smell his foul breath.

"I just want my stuff," I practiced my yogic breathing, and tried my best not to inflame him further.

"I promise you. I will call the police if you try to remove anything," he stared at me. Negotiations were over.

"You fucking asshole." I screamed at him as if a demon were roaring up through my chest.

I was so angry. I couldn't trust myself to be anywhere around him. I left the room and started down the stairs.

"What did you say?" He shouted, charging down the stairs after me.

I reached the door to the garage. I was shaking with rage at the injustice of it all.

"If the dick fits," I bellowed back at him and slammed the door.

I don't know where those words came from. Somewhere deep inside of me I was raging. I had never consciously entertained those thoughts in my entire life. I pondered the old colloquialism. If the shoe fits … if a description applies to you, then accept it … so if the dick fits … then he must be a fucking asshole.

Where in the world had that come from?

And whose voice was that?

Where had that voice come from?

The voice that bellowed, octaves lower and louder than I thought I was even capable of … Was I channeling the voice and anger of all those who have loved me and passed on?

That was exactly what it felt like … perhaps it was true.

I needed to get out of there, but I had nowhere to go. So I drove to the bookstore and sat in the parking lot.

Who the hell was that? That was not exactly a demonstration of my Nordic Stoicism.

I sat in the car and thought about what had just happened. My upbringing had taught me to buck up, behave reasonably and responsibly, not to show my emotions, to be indifferent to pain, grin and bear it, get over it, don't expect too much or be so high and mighty. I had always thought these were virtues. Perhaps in some situations they are.

Why are Nordic people described as stoic? Hmmm … No sense complaining when it is cold and dark and the crops have failed. It's cold and dark and everyone's hungry. Complaining will not put more food on the table. It just makes everyone all the more miserable.

So do I complain when I'm uncomfortable? No, I buck up. I just get over it. I just get on with it. I'm not a whiner. My guess is that people in my family have been like this for generations.

But the rage I felt now had been stuffed down so deep I didn't know it was even there. The notion was brewing within me, that perhaps this was just another form of denial. Denial of what I was feeling. Instead of expressing my long-held rage, I had turned this emotion inward. Perhaps it was this inner rage I suppressed again and again that had made me sick … I recalled the look of disbelief on my gynecologist's face as he told me I had uterine cancer. He looked so perplexed. How could this be, I just didn't fit the profile. Perhaps living with Paul, the lack of love, and all the unexpressed rage had been left to fester within me, and caused me to be sick. I thought I was coping, but maybe I had just made myself sick.

If I wanted to have a healthy authentic life, and I did, I would need to embrace this wise woman within who spoke her own mind.

No more keeping quiet.

Never again the go along, get along Malibu Barbie.

I'd had enough of that bullshit.

Enough.

So under court order, three days before Christmas, Paul released my things to me. The movers were coming in the morning, so my parents and I went to the house the night before to pack my things. Again Paul threatened to call the police. The court order said I could retrieve my things on Friday. Paul wouldn't grant me permission to be in my own house until the next morning. I was furious. He was making this as difficult as possible for me, and I could see the glee in his face. How he enjoyed exerting this control and power over me.

God, I hated him.

And yet the little voice inside my brain admonished me—

Hate is not a family value.

The deep voice from my gut shot back,

But this is not a family and it never was.

The next morning, my parents and my girlfriends descended on the house like a swarm of locusts. We took everything that belonged to my kids and me before this so-called marriage. I had seen Paul in action. I feared anything I left behind would disappear. Everything that was purchased during the marriage was to stay in the house until the property settlement was completed. The movers came to move some of my things to my parents, and some things to the two-bedroom condo I was renting.

Paul skulked around the house. It was December in Michigan and he had the temperature in the house turned down to 55. He wore a down ski jacket. He supervised and didn't speak to me, or to my friends, except to bark out orders. He told me, "Tell the movers to take their shoes off while they're in my house."

This was a ridiculous request as the movers were carrying heavy furniture out to the truck. Did he really expect them to set down what they were carrying to take off and put on their shoes each time they entered and left the house?

I ignored him and although he grumbled, he didn't have a fit and fall in it, as I know he would have done had I been there by myself.

Throughout the winter ...

The proceedings dragged on, and still there was no divorce. My mid-winter break from school was around the corner, and I made plans to go to Mexico with Colleen. Colleen and I have been friends for nearly twenty years. Her husband, Frank succumbed to cancer in the fall, and she became the next one of my friends to endure the loss of a spouse.

We started each morning with yoga on the beach. Followed by breakfast, swimming ... and then a day trip for whale watching, or golf, or an evening sail, or a trip to the spa for a facial and massage.

I was so far off my spiritual path. The years I had spent married to Paul had lead me far from my true north. Could I find my way back? I had reached out to God in my moments of desperation, but my day-to-day life had been filled with anger, alcohol, compromise, and conflict. I was lost and lonely. I tried a variety of churches, but I couldn't find one that really fit. The offerings seemed generic and my issues were specific. I needed to travel inward and reconnect with the indwelling Holy Spirit. This was critical to my finding my way home.

I worked hard at reinventing my life as a single woman. When I returned from my vacation, I joined a yoga studio and began to practice 5 days a week.

I desperately needed to find a way to let go of the anger I had towards Paul. I had lost so much during the years I was married to Paul, but the greatest loss I experienced was the loss of myself. I needed to quiet down all the negative chatter, and try to find my way home, to find a way back to being me. It was not so easy as the reasons for the anger were not without merit, but I learned holding onto the anger didn't hurt Paul. No, it only hurt me. So I needed to find a way to forgive him. But that would require I forgive myself first, and that was much more difficult.

I wallowed around in my thoughts and I worked on letting go. I worked on forgiveness. The yoga helped. The writing helped. I tried to write every day. It helped to ground me. It helped to silence the angry chatter. But now as the divorce drew near, the malevolence threatened to consume me. All the progress I had made to move towards peace and tranquility eroded with a single encounter with Paul or one of our attorneys. I fought daily to keep from being drawn back into this quagmire of nastiness. And it only threatened to get worse.

I practiced my yoga, my breathing, and my faith in the love and mercy of The Almighty.

I took a long walk each day with my dog, Duncan. She loved me and had been my faithful companion.

I went to the barn and rode Blair.

My animals provided me a companionable silence that allowed me the time and space I needed to think and to process what had happened in my life and to my life.

I needed to take a good long look at what had happened. I needed to figure out how I got here.

I needed to own the parts of this that belonged to me.

If I was ever going to forgive Paul, I needed to forgive myself first. This would be the most difficult part.

In so many ways my life was good and full of beauty, and blessings. I needed to remind myself of this and focus on this every day. My life was so much better already. I could endure this. I would survive this. Others have and I would too.

Who's at Fault?
How could I have been so wrong about you?
How could I have been so deceived?
Was I just so lonely?
Just so damn lonely,
That I convinced myself
I could make this work

Did you deceive me?
Or did I deceive myself?
Clearly there were enough warning signs
Was I just not paying attention?

There were so many lies
Lies about your marriages
Lies about your age
You were always the victim
Someone else was always at fault
Someone else was always to blame

This time it was me.

CHAPTER 18

The Divorce

The marriage had been over for a long time. The only remaining issue that stood between me and my legal freedom was the distribution of our property.

Paul's ego matched the palatial estate that was under dispute. He couldn't stand it that I was the one to leave him, and not the other way around. So he counter-sued me for a divorce, and listed himself as a co-plaintive, and painted himself as the injured party. The legal language inserted in his divorce document requested prayers, sympathy, and understanding for the pain and suffering sustained by Mr. Paul O'Shea during the years of our marriage.

Really? No Fucking Way.

Donald, my lawyer, found this laughable but I did not. I now know he grossly underestimated his opponent.

What I wanted was my money back –the $350,000 that I contributed toward the purchase of the house. I would need this money to buy another house and begin again. The issue was that Paul had spent approximately $350,000 out of the home equity line of credit, and the housing market in metro Detroit had collapsed. So when the house was appraised, it no longer appraised for what was now owed on it.

If Paul hadn't spent that money, we would've been able to sell the house. Even in a down market there would've been some money remaining for each of us to start over. But this was no longer the case.

I gave my attorney a copy of all the financial documents. I had spent countless hours trying to determine what the hell had happened to all the money that Paul spent from the home equity line of credit. The paper trail was baffling. It appeared that Paul was "robbing Peter to pay Paul," so to speak. I determined that Paul had 23 different credit cards over the course of our four-year marriage.

He was transferring the balance from one card to the next, making minimal payments on a wide variety of the cards, but not to the tune of $350,000. I did not know where the money had gone. It had just disappeared. On my attorney's recommendation, I turned the financial investigation over to him. Donald assured me, "We know how to track this kind of thing. We do it all the time. This is what you're paying me for." And so I let it go, with the full expectation that he would get to the bottom of it.

My attorney also recommended that we go to binding arbitration. We discussed the pros and cons of this. He said, "I've spoken with his lawyer, and Paul will never settle with you. He will drag this out for years." He spoke with the voice of authority, and I believed him.

It wasn't that Paul wanted to be married to me, but he couldn't bear the humiliation that my filing had caused him.

"Even if the judge were to rule in your favor, I guarantee you that your husband will appeal. This will be even more expensive and time consuming." He assured me, "You'll get a fair shake with the arbitrator."

So I agreed to binding arbitration at my attorney's recommendation.

The waiting continued ...

I soon realized that the $30,000 legal retainer I'd paid upfront was rapidly being spent, and we hadn't yet met with the arbitrator. My attorney was billing me at $300 an hour. Every time I called or sent him an email it cost me at least $75, even if I only needed a yes or no response from him. So I tried to limit my calls to what I considered critical. The end result was that both he and I were ill-prepared for our opponent, and the battle ahead.

The months dragged on and on and *still* we couldn't find a date for the deposition that was agreeable to everyone's schedule. Until at long last we decided on the latter part of March. So much for being divorced in 6 months, this was a marathon, a test of endurance. We were finally getting around to taking depositions 10 months after I had left Paul.

For the love of God let us just get on with this.

The deposition took three full days, and I was more humiliated and embarrassed than I have ever been in my whole entire life. I was required to answer questions about the most intimate aspects of my life, in the presence of these four men: Paul, the arbitrator, and our two attorneys.

I was deposed first. I was sworn in. The question started out innocuously enough. "State your name for the record."

That should have been an easy one. But I have gone by the name Jeanne Marie Selander, my given and legal name, as well as Jeanne Selander Miller as Miller was my late husband's last name. Mr. Williams, Paul's 60 year old, overweight, pompous attorney was off and running about my name. When we finally completed about 35 questions about my name and why I'd never legally changed my name to Miller or to O'Shea for that matter. He concluded by addressing me as, "Ms. Selander or Ms. Miller or Mrs. O'Shea or whoever you may be choosing to call yourself today."

"You may call me Ms. Selander." I stated through clenched teeth.

"Whatever," he snapped back.

Great. 35 questions about my name, this wasn't going to go well. I tried to keep my composure and kept breathing.

The questioning went on for hours and hours about things of so little consequence, but I was beginning to see their strategy. They were going to wear me out, and then the real nastiness would begin.

I had submitted a list of complaints to my attorney about the state of the marriage. I am uncertain why it was necessary as Michigan is a no-fault divorce state. But Donald had requested it, and I had complied with his request. Paul and his attorney were going to systematically try to refute my complaints, as this was the evidence that Paul hadn't been a good husband. My memory is hazy, and I don't recall the order that things were addressed. I believe my mind has done a pretty good job of protecting and healing me from the emotional damage of this ordeal.

I remember feeling particularly humiliated when I was questioned about the lack of intimacy in our marriage.

"Isn't it true that you repeatedly turned down your husband's requests for sex because you were menopausal? Mr. Williams glared across the table. His comments were snide and his tone was laced with malice.

"No sir," *Keep the answers short. Don't embellish.* I tried to heed my attorney's directives.

"No, you didn't turn him down or no you weren't menopausal?" He leaned in towards me.

"No, I did not turn him down." *Oh he is so not going to turn this around like this.*

"You never turned him down?" *He is trying to put words in my mouth.*

"No, I never turned him down because he never asked," I stated. My hands were sweating and the room felt cold and damp. I took a deep breath and exhaled as I tried to stay centered. I was at full alert. I would go the distance. I was in Warrior mode. In my heart I knew that I was worth fighting for.

"What did you want —an engraved invitation?" And then the pig in the suit began to chortle and snort.

"No he never approached me for sex after the first year of our marriage," I could hardly believe I was discussing this with these pigs. Each and every one of them was snickering like they couldn't believe that this was true. Even that asexual bastard of a husband was chuckling like he was Mr. Don Juan.

"Okay, Ms. Selander, tell us about your menopause." He looked down at a lengthy list of questions he had prepared on his legal pad.

Was this guy for real?

"What do you want to know?" I replied. He was supposed to be asking the questions. Why was my attorney letting him talk with me like this?

"When did you go through menopause?" He asked.

"December 1, 2007, when I had a hysterectomy." I answered.

"No, but how long were you in menopause?" He shook his head as if I had answered the wrong question.

Oh he was so smug, and he thought he was so smart. "I think the surgery was about 3 hours, but I cannot say for certain because I was under anesthesia."

"Ms. Selander, I am asking you about menopause, not your hysterectomy. Let me repeat the question, how long were you in menopause?"

"Sir, the answer is the same." I could feel myself flushing fiercely as my blood began to boil. "I went through menopause when they removed my uterus. I no longer menstruate, as I no longer have a uterus. Prior to my surgery, I still had menstrual periods. Menopause is when a woman no longer menstruates."

Now I was spitting mad to be discussing my menstrual history with a bunch of blowhards. Where the hell was my attorney? Why was he not objecting to this line of questioning? Perhaps that little prig was enjoying my sex education lesson as well. I was humiliated … but I was also *pissed.*

Then he launched into a whole line of questions about my surgery.

"So you had a hysterectomy because you had cervical and ovarian cancer, is that right?"

"No." *Where did he get that information? Did Paul really not know what kind of cancer I had?*

"Why did you have a hysterectomy?" He asked.

"I had uterine cancer," I answered.

"Same thing," he muttered to himself, and looked back down at his legal pad.

I could hardly bear this, "No sir. It is not the same thing. They are different parts of a woman's body." I stared him down, and my attorney kicked me under the table.

This hit me pretty hard. This divorce was going to cost me in so many ways, but how could I possibly have been married to someone who knew so little about me, and cared even less. I couldn't believe I was married to a man who didn't even know what kind of cancer his wife was afflicted with.

Later Paul would state under oath, "She told me she had cervical and ovarian cancer. I think she was just looking for sympathy because the prognosis is worse with those kinds of cancer."

Who would do that? What kind of sick manipulation of the facts was this?

"Did you ever consider that your husband didn't have sex with you out of consideration for the fact that you had broken your pelvis, and were going through menopause, and had a hysterectomy, and he thought you were not physically able?" He had changed his tone. He was being dismissive as if I was a frail old woman.

Wrong O Melon Head, "No sir. That would not account for the lack of sexual intimacy in the first three years of our marriage or account for the fact that I'm back riding the horse. If I'm capable of riding a horse, I think I'm physically strong and well enough to have sex with my husband. Why doesn't he want to have sex with me? You'll have to ask him."

My attorney asked for a break. When he got me in the hallway he chastised me for losing my temper. I chastised him for hanging me out to dry. My attorney was unprepared, and I was unprepared. I had never in my wildest dreams anticipated this kind of questioning. Paul's attorney baited me, and I took the bait. It had never been my nature to be sweet and docile. If someone asked my opinion, I would give it, and probably tell you more than you ever wanted to know. I have a low tolerance for ignorance, and an even lower tolerance when ignorance is combined with arrogance. This room reeked of both.

When we returned to the arbitration room, the questioning continued.

"Isn't it true that in the fall of last year that you asked Mr. O'Shea if you could move back in the house and try to reconcile?"

I lost my mind. He was trying to push me over the edge … and he was successful. "That is the biggest bunch of bullshit that I have ever heard!" I nearly shouted it at him.

"I think perhaps we should take a break," as my attorney asked for another recess and escorted me back to the hallway.

"Very nice … 'The biggest bunch of bullshit.' There you have it, right on the record. In the future do you think you could just answer yes or no?"

So there I was –my attorney was worthless, and I was actively engaged in shooting myself in the foot.

The afternoon didn't get any better as Mr. Williams implied that I was selfish, and never cooked or cleaned the house –I was being judged by the standards of a 1950's housewife. Because I'm the woman, these were supposed to be *my* responsibilities.

He offered up criticisms of me as a mother and elaborated on my teenage children's transgressions as proof of my ineptitude as a parent. The lies, the manipulations, and misrepresentations of the truth were crushing to me as a person. Any outsider who listened to this would have been convinced that I was a witch and the world would be far better off without women like me.

My attorney counseled me not to get so emotional, answer only the questions asked, and not offer up any defense. I was smoldering as my character and everything I held dear was tarnished and dishonored. I could've spit nails I was so angry. And yet, while Paul's attorney was actively crucifying me, my attorney sat next to me, and doodled on a yellow legal pad. Paul's attorney was *über* prepared, and my high-priced suit was ill prepared and overmatched. I think I would've faired better if I had represented myself. Instead, for my $30,000, I had hired Mr. Fancy Pants, an attorney who made Detroit Magazine's Best Dressed List, and he drew some pretty good curlicues. I was livid. I felt like I was being mocked by the Old Boys' Club, and my husband, and our attorneys, and the arbitrator were card-carrying members.

Paul and his attorney had conspired to paint me as a conniving, gold digging bitch, and to paint Paul as the innocent victim. They arrived with two 6-inch binders of data that were meant to confuse the financial issues, and to refute any allegations I would make about our loveless union.

Prior to the deposition, Paul and I had been required to submit our financial documents so that the arbitrator had some idea of our current financial situation. During the deposition, Mr. Williams presented a copy of my financial documents from Fidelity Investments. Paul had put a keystroke program on the family computer in the music room and had captured my password. This gave him access to my Fidelity accounts. Over the course of the past 6 months since I had separated from my husband, my parents, who were in their late seventies and early eighties, had asked me to be the executor of their estate. In return, they had given me access to some of their money at Fidelity. The money was to be used in case they needed it for an emergency, if, for example, one of them became incapacitated and needed nursing home placement or end of life care. Paul's attorney spun this in such a way to imply that my parents' money belonged to me, and that I had been hiding my assets and had plenty money.

Now I have always been a saver, but in the divorce, this probably hurt me. Although Paul made significantly more money then I did, I had more money than Paul, because I knew how to hold on to it. Through the course of the financial inquiry I learned that the gifts of diamonds and furs Paul so lavishly bestowed upon me were actually purchased with my money from the home equity line.

In the end, Paul admitted no wrongdoing. My attorney really had no idea where the $350,000 from the home equity line had been spent and Paul and his attorney were silent on the subject.

The deposition was as brutal as the marriage. All aspects of my life had been openly exposed and scrutinized. My marriage, my children, my parents, my friends, my job, my sexuality, my physical health, my mental health, my spirituality, my finances, my role as wife and mother, cook and homemaker. Everywhere I turned, I was found to be lacking. I was poked, prodded and probed and every little festering wound was laid open as a way to embarrass and humiliate me –and if there was nothing there, then Paul and his attorney embellished, elaborated, and manufactured some ugliness that alluded to some rot and deceit that lay just below the surface.

Then it was Paul's turn to be deposed and my attorney asked Paul very few questions. He was unprepared and didn't have a clue what to ask. The depositions were complete.

I had been put through the ringer, but had endured it.

Donald tried over and over again to assure me that justice would prevail, as the arbitrator would see the truth. I had my doubts.

While Paul was under oath I learned that he had made a recent trip to China in search of a mail order bride. *Really? Perhaps if he married for the fifth time, to a woman who needed a green card and didn't speak any English, he might fare better than he had the first four times. What a jerk! He was planning to ruin another woman's life.*

The arbitrator made his final decision. I was granted a divorce. Paul had to put the house on the market. But no one was buying 1.8 million dollar mansions in metro Detroit in 2009. So he would just live in the house until the market recovered, if it ever did. He was awarded all four cars, for in his shrewd and cunning planning, along with my naïveté, he had titled all of them in his name. The bottom line was his debts were his, and my assets were mine. I paid for my attorney, and he paid for his.

When it was all said and done, my four-year marriage to Mr. Paul O'Shea cost me my home, and to put a dollar figure on it, I sustained a loss of about $400,000. This represented 25 years of house payments, and is a lot of money for a single mother who worked as a nurse and a teacher. My head still spins. I cannot believe the injustice. I had trusted the legal system to do right by me … and this was the end result.

Since I was the plaintiff it was my obligation to show up in court with my attorney the day the judge granted me the divorce. The divorce was final as was the distribution of assets.

As we left the courtroom I asked my attorney, "Please tell me how this could have possibly gone any worse for me?"

Donald Darkhorse's response was, "You could be pregnant."

I was incredulous. I couldn't believe what I had just heard. I wanted to slap him. I had just lost my home, and I no longer even had a car. This man, who did not do his job, but did collect a substantial amount of money as payment for his ineptitude, was making a joke at my expense.

Through my tears I told him, "No, Donny that would be impossible. Perhaps you weren't listening through the lengthy depositions, as you may know sex is required to make a baby and we never had sex. And secondly, I no longer have the prerequisite equipment. I'm the one who had a total hysterectomy because I had uterine cancer. Remember?"

I turned on my heel and left the courthouse. I had nothing else to say.

CHAPTER 19

The Healing...
Finding
My Way Home

I spent the next few days trying to get my socks on the right feet. I was a mess. I wanted to run away. I needed to seek cover and lick my wounds. There was one small problem –my car now belonged to my ex-husband and he wanted it back immediately. As if I hadn't made a big enough mess of my life, and to add to my humiliation, I needed to ask for help *again*. So it was that my reliable parents came to the rescue of their 51-year-old daughter, yet again.

I drove what had been my car to my attorney's office. I left the car in the parking lot and the keys with the receptionist. I waited at the curb for my Dad to pick me up and drive me to a car dealership. In my befuddled state Dad researched the vehicles and negotiated the deal. At this point in my life I would've had difficulty thinking my way out of a paper bag. I was so shattered that I didn't trust myself or anyone else for that matter. Except for my family. I bought a Chevy and left the next day for The Adirondacks.

In my gut, I knew I couldn't bear the thought of running into Paul out and about somewhere. He was still living in my house, and walking the streets in what had been my hometown for the last 18 years.

I was a mess. I was enraged at the injustice. If I stayed and had to explain to everyone I ran into what had happened in the divorce, it would be as if I was reliving the nightmare with every retelling. The people who knew me and loved me were burning with anger, and with every encounter I became engulfed in the anger and burned again. I didn't know what I needed, but I did know that the continual reliving of the past would keep me tied to Paul and his toxic existence. If I wanted to heal from the last four years I would need to do it somewhere else.

At some very deep level, I knew I had lost my way, and was far from *home*–

I needed to return to my simple but important foundational values. I needed to heed the wisdom of my own inner knowing, the wisdom of my heart. I had acquiesced to someone else's idea of what was important in life, and I needed to return to the roots of my true self, which I abandoned when I married Paul.

First things first: I needed to get the hell out of town.

I was a very broken woman, and I needed to love and be loved again.

With that in mind, I made plans to spend the summer in the Adirondacks with Susan. She had been widowed ten months before, and was still picking up the pieces of her life. Like me, she was reinventing herself as a single woman and a single mother. I needed my sister and she needed me too.

Cullen had his own life in California now, but he had been with me while I waited for the disposition of my divorce. He had grown into such a wise and gentle man. He was nonplussed and upset about the inherent injustice of what had transpired, but in his indwelling wisdom, he seemed to know what others did not: expressing his anger wouldn't make things easier for me. So instead he offered me reassurance that I was strong enough, smart enough, loving and loveable, and therefore more than able to recover. God bless him, for he helped me see myself through his loving eyes, and I began to believe in myself again.

Gillian wanted to spend the summer traveling, but she'd been away at college all year, and I missed her terribly. I had asked her to spend the summer working at a camp in the Adirondacks. So Gillian put aside her own plans that summer and also stepped up. She would spend the summer just down the road from me, and we would have some time to be together. What a great gift that was.

Dana applied to the same camp, as she and Gillian also needed to be together. They spent their days off with me and with one another. I'm certain if Paul had known she was going to the Adirondacks to be near me, as well as near Gillian, he never would have consented. So she didn't tell him and we spent the summer together –another gift of love.

My mom, my dad, my sister, my kids, and my friends provided the unconditional love, and that was the salve that would begin my healing.

So Gilly and I left Michigan late one afternoon, and crossed the border into Canada. In my new car we made our way to the mountains of upstate New York. Gillian is an easy travel companion. She's always up for the adventure and almost nothing stresses her out. I learn so much from just being in her presence. There were so many people who love me who were ready to burn Paul at the stake, but Gillian thought that would be a waste of some perfectly good trees. Besides, letting him live in the negativity of his own creation was probably punishment enough. So she and I focused on other things.

Perhaps it was the alignment of the stars or perhaps someone out there was looking out for me, and knew how much I needed this, but for whatever reason, this would be a summer of countless blessings.

Susan and I reconnected, and I really cannot remember when I've laughed so much. Perhaps it is because we're sisters and grew up in the same household, but we finished one another's sentences, and howled at one another's jokes. Just being with her helped me beyond measure.

She introduced me to her friends and nearly everyday was filled with some kind of adult frivolity. We hiked, we biked, we boated, we went to yoga, and out to eat, and more nights than not we found someplace to dance. We danced with the men, and we danced with the women, but mostly, we just danced with ourselves for the sheer joy of it. When I danced, I felt connected with my long neglected physical being. I felt sensual and whole. Through dance I found a way to reconnect with myself, this being who had so long been hidden and repressed by living with so much negativity.

My eyes were opening to new possibilities.

During the previous year, I had been keeping a journal, and writing about various aspects of my life. One afternoon, while perusing a course catalog at the local art center, I saw they were offering a class in memoir writing. It was one morning a week, and I was already in *yes* mode. That is, I had quit saying *no* to life and had started accepting invitations. This one sounded interesting. So I went. The weekly writing assignments were given, and were to be read to the group the following week. When I shared little vignettes from my life, people laughed, and people cried, and they encouraged me to keep writing. So I did.

I also signed up for a writer's workshop at the local library, and a weekend writer's retreat with a new friend. I read my essays aloud, initially with some trepidation, as the people at these workshops really were writers, and I was just a fledgling. But through these workshops I found that I had something I needed to say. And the people at the workshops, well, they liked what I said and how I said it. This recognition caused a shift within, for at that moment, I valued their opinions more than I did my own. It was their encouragement that provided the breath of air on my tiny creative spark, and the flame ignited, and I continued to write.

It was in writing about my life and my own experiences that I was able to take a good long look at where I had been. I began to understand why I'd made the decisions I'd made ... difficult as the results had been.

I was beginning to find my *voice.* I was saying things on paper, and reading them aloud ... things I'd harbored inside myself for far too long.

By mid-summer I realized that in body and mind I was beginning to heal ... a little bit every day.

∽

At a deeper level, the healing had also begun.

As I spent time with this lovely young woman, who is my daughter, I learned something from her: Gillian had cultivated the ability to be consciously present in her own life, she wasn't living in the past or preoccupied with the future. She was just being present to what life was offering, with an abundance of gratitude for all of it.

The questions loomed before me:
Who *was* I?
What did I *believe?*
What was important to *me?*

I had been planning my escape from *Alcatraz* for such a long time, planning what I would do to recreate my life, and here at long last I was a free woman. It had been so long since I had been happy *in the present* and I needed to remember how. The time for reawakening my spirit was now.

That summer, Gillian would be my guide. I would watch and learn from her about being consciously present to my own life.

I studied the great spiritual traditions of the world; everywhere I turned, I was reminded about the importance of *staying in the present.*

So I tried to keep my head where my feet were. It kept me in the now. I tried to let go of what had happened in my past. I tried not to worry about things that may never happen.

> *So do not worry about tomorrow;*
> *for tomorrow will care for itself.*
> *Each day has enough trouble of its own*
>
> –Luke 12:34

Somehow I had missed this. It is such a fundamental truth right there in <u>The Bible</u>, the foundation of my own faith.

Since Colleen and I had gone to Mexico in the winter and participated in the early morning yoga classes on the beach, I had continued to embrace the practice of yoga. I wasn't very flexible because I was still healing from being thrown from the horse 18 months earlier ... but I liked it.

I'd found a local studio to continue my yoga practice. Initially, it was about getting some exercise, increasing my strength, and flexibility. I started to feel better. I was getting stronger. I was feeling more centered and more peaceful. I was welcomed into this community at a time when I really needed somewhere I could just be. Soon, I was rearranging my plans and life so I could go to yoga. I continued to practice throughout the summer in the Adirondacks.

It wasn't until my long drawn-out divorce was behind me, that I was able to let go of the fear and feeling of being *on alert* that had overtaken my life. I now was able to take some time and space to think about what I was learning from my life, and to try and get a grasp on the role of yoga in my healing.

The seeds had been planted and they were beginning to take root.

I had attended a Bikram Yoga class. Bikram is also known as *hot yoga*, because the room is heated to 105 degrees. It was the first time I had ever been to such a class. The teacher was talking with me before we entered. She knew I was a newbie. She told me, "Your only goal for tonight is not to leave the room."

The room was so hot. I could hardly breathe.

How in the name of heaven do people practice yoga in this heat?

I spread out my mat and spread a towel over the top as I watched others do the same. As I looked around the room I realized that I was overdressed in my yoga pants and camisole. The men were dressed in shorts and no shirts, and the women wore swimsuits. I did my best to keep up with the unfamiliar routine. Before long, I was slipping and sliding in my own sweat, which had puddled beneath me. Although completely lacking in grace and finesse, I was determined to continue. I watched the clock on the wall.

How much longer?

Five more minutes ... more poses

Three more minutes ... more poses

I can do this. I can do this. This mantra played over and over in my head.

One more minute ...

I'm going to make it ...

I didn't leave the room.

But to my dismay the instructor continued ... on and on. I didn't realize the class was 90-minutes long. I thought it was a 60-minute class. So I turned down the noise in my head, focused on my breathing, focused on my poses, and the time slipped on . . . and the class was over.

Only later would I think about what had happened. I had been extremely uncomfortable in the heat, but for once I didn't leave. This had absolutely been my *modus operandi.* I realized that whenever I'd been uncomfortable in my life, I had fled from the situation in one way or another. I'd pulled away to avoid conflict. I'd stuffed my feelings, thoughts, and opinions inside of myself to avoid arguments and confrontation. I would run away from conflict and pain rather than stand my ground. Spiritually, I'd slipped out the back door.

But by staying in the class I'd stayed with the discomfort, and it didn't hurt me. Reflecting on it, I learned the experience had made me inwardly stronger.

Later, I used this lesson as a lens to revisit the uncomfortable events of my recent past and look at them in a different light.

I'd been telling myself I'd been *victimized* by the deposition, arbitration, and divorce process. But now I found myself reassessing.

The deposition didn't hurt me, difficult though it was. Those men had been trying to break me down. They had played on my weaknesses, and had worn me down … but their ruthless tactics had forced me to turn a corner in my life. I no longer had the luxury to be weak. No, I wanted to be strong. They had tried to break me, but I was learning to be flexible. I was learning to be "The Warrior" –as one of my favorite yoga poses is called –with my feet strongly rooted in the earth, my spine long and lifting from my pelvis, the crown of my head held high, my shoulders back, my heart space open, my arms extended, and my fingers stretched as I looked to the horizon.

What I practiced on the mat and I began to practice in my life.

Yoga was teaching me to look at myself and my life with new eyes and new strength.

Yes, I would need what yoga was teaching me. I learned yoga is far more than the practice of asanas or poses. Yoga means to "yoke with God" or "to be one with God." If God loves me and I believe that to be true, and I am one with the indwelling spirit of God then so is every other living being on the planet … including my asshole ex-husband, and his nasty prick of an attorney, and my limp-dicked attorney …

All right, this was where I still needed more practice. I admit it.

∾

So ...
I began rebuilding the house of my life. I needed to reconnect with my spirit to build the foundation for my life. I no longer felt *a million miles from home.*

∾

That summer another force of healing presented itself. I met an amazing group of women in the Adirondacks. They had been meeting once a week for decades. They're my Miracle Group. They were so loving and immediately welcoming. These women have been students of a wide variety of spiritual teachings for years. I have never known such a group, and yet I felt like I had been looking for them all my life. In their presence and acceptance I found a spiritual home. I no longer felt like a fish out of water while I explored my spirituality. I could speak my mind without the fear that someone would think I was a heretic and blasphemer.

Now I felt strong enough to look into the darkness of my past and was no longer afraid. I began to write, read, and pray on a daily basis.

There are principles that are present in all the great spiritual traditions. It's not that I had not been exposed to them before, but I had become so engrossed in the needs and demands of my physical world I had somehow lost my spiritual direction. So with some quiet time and space I devoted time to study. There was so much I needed to understand:

Non-attachment –Don't get too attached to things because they are just *things,* and things fall apart. For the most important things in life are not things at all.

I thought about what had been taken from me -- only things.

I live in a world of abundance.

Living in the Adirondacks, surrounded by natural beauty, and having a wonderful loving family, and friends, I truly have all I need and more.

There are things that I needed to learn. My marriage to Paul and my subsequent divorce taught me much about non-attachment. Things can be given and taken away. I spent a great deal of my life in the acquisition mode, only to have my money, my home, and even my car taken from me. As devastating as it was at the time, I have learned that I am not my possessions or my bank account.

When it all went away I was still enough, just as I am, because in spirit I am infinite, eternal and whole.

Embrace change –Do not resist change, as change will always come and cannot be stopped. I have held onto situations, even my painfully destructive marriage, out of fear of change. Now, I am learning not to resist change. It is truly a futile endeavor.

Live with a non-judgmental attitude –We are all only players acting in response to the forces that bear upon our lives. People play these roles and behave the way they do because of their life circumstances.

Why did Paul play the roles he did? Why had he made the choices that cost us so greatly, and ultimately destroyed our marriage?

Why did I? Non-judgmental, oh yeah that, I'm still struggling with that one.

So I continued to pray, to study, and practice yoga. I turned inward and in doing so I moved incrementally towards a more peaceful acceptance of what was.

And still the same issues resurfaced again and again. I knew if I were to find my way to a place of peace and love, I would have to find a way to forgive myself for the mistakes I had made. Forgiving myself, I realized, would be primary.

As these newly conscious perspectives were seeded and took root in my life, I knew I wanted more –a way to move forward. A friend in the Miracle Group regularly consulted the <u>I Ching</u>.

I didn't have a clue what this ancient system of divination was all about. I know I had seen a copy of the <u>I Ching</u> on Cullen's bookshelf. And so I began to investigate. I consulted the Internet …

The I Ching is the world's oldest oracle; it's the most loved and revered book of Chinese wisdom; it is the accumulated experience of over 2,500 years of diviners and sages, and beyond that of unimaginably ancient oral traditions; it's the voice that has been offering people help and wise, genial guidance for generations …

But when people ask the I Ching what it is, it responds again and again with great simplicity, describing itself as a well of pure water. This well is always there, standing at the center of the field and available to everyone. Though generations come and go, and the way of life changes beyond all recognition, the well itself never changes, and its water of truth never runs dry.

www.onlineclarity.com

Hmmm … interesting

Why now had this come into my life? I was looking for answers. I hoped that I was wise enough not to disregard that which presented itself in my life.

So I asked the I Ching:

How can I find healing for my heart?

In response I called up the 40th Hexagram.

It read:

The superior person knows that the release is in forgiveness,
Pardoning the faults of others
And dealing gently with those who sin against him

Feel the lightness of being
That results from
Forgiving others and accepting them as they are

There it was again. Asked and answered. I knew I needed to find a way to forgive myself for my participation in this fiasco. I also needed a way to forgive Paul. This was not news to me. I knew it in the core of my being. I had heard these words of Jesus as far back as I could remember:

> *Then Peter came to Jesus and asked, "Lord, how many times shall I forgive my brother when he sins against me? Up to seven times?" Jesus answered, "I tell you, not seven times, but seventy-seven times."*
> – Matthew 18:21-22

Oh shit. I knew that I wasn't off the hook. Would it be possible, in this lifetime, for me to forgive Paul's transgressions? I still had so much work to do.

Sometimes while I had my morning coffee, and looked out over the stillness of the lake, and sometimes I would wake from a deep sleep and write for hours, and sometimes I would sit in the sunshine on the dock just basking in what was.

Passages like this would come from somewhere deep within me:

Why did I keep silent when I should have been screaming?
I know it was in part the way I was raised
To go along and be a good sport
And not make a fuss
Because those that do
Well, they are a real pain in the ass
and everyone knows that
But I now know there are times
and circumstances that require

Standing up for what is right
Screaming and yelling
And being a royal pain in the ass
There were all those times
when you thought I was in agreement with you
but I was not
It had been made abundantly clear to me
That if I looked a certain way
and thought a certain way
and believed what you believe
Then I would be acceptable
Then I would be right and not wrong
Then I would be good
I would be in the inner fold
But if I did not look the right way or wear the right
clothes
Or think the right thoughts and believe the right
things
Well, then, I would be an outsider
If I didn't think like you
then one of us would be wrong
and heaven knows you were never wrong
Your world was very black and white
Right and wrong
People were either with us or against us
Insiders or outsiders
There were no shades of grey
No room for any diversity of opinion
How often did I see you make jokes
and berate those whose thinking

or behavior was outside of the parameters of
acceptability
So I kept my mouth shut
I did not tell you what I thought
I kept it all to myself
God forbid I should be the outsider
I did not want to be subjected to your ridicule
Or your tirades
And to be put out of my home
My place of belonging
So I keep my mouth closed
But my roommate, my inner critic
Oh she rambles on and on
Incessantly
Sometimes her commentary is so loud
She says all the things I think
She says all the things I want to say
But I dare not
Her voice is clear
Her wisdom is valid
She finds her way out through the tip of this pen
Why do I keep quiet when I should be screaming to
make my voice heard?
It is in my training and my upbringing
Is this room really big enough for me?
Is there enough space for my voice to be heard?
Or am I only valid and valuable when I go along
and get along?
How old must I be before I can speak and someone
will listen?

You were looking for the go along and get along
woman.
You were looking for arm candy
Until the atrocities were so outrageous
that I left my marriage screaming
like a woman leaving a burning building
for I knew that if I stayed even one moment more
I would have been burned alive

How do you leave when you have been told
by your church and your family
that divorce is wrong and that marriage is sacred?
Not my marriage and not my divorce
Not my reality
To break with this deeply held convention
was not the mark of a failure
It was an act of courage
Not a failure
but rather a victory
To ultimately do what I know is right

My life is sacred
Not this union called a marriage
It was not sacred
It was an unholy alliance
That I want nothing more to do with

When he degrades me as a person
He defiles the cathedral of my being
My indwelling God space
My Soul

I could not let this defilement continue
If I stayed I may begin to believe
the load of crap you laid on me
Where everything in my being screamed,
"You are a liar!"

What does it mean to live inside myself?
What is home to me?
What do I need to be me?
How will I find my way home?

Forgiveness
I did that over and over and over again in my
marriage
Part of my upbringing
This is what good Christians do
How many times must I forgive Paul?

I am still working on it.
I'm not quite there
yet

So there it was. I knew I needed to forgive myself
and Paul too. I could say the words, and there were
days when I really thought I was making progress
and starting to let it go. But then something would
get triggered in me and I would struggle to push the
myriad of offenses from my mind. Before too long my
anger and resentment towards him was back in full
force. How was I ever going to really forgive him?

When I allowed myself to go deep within –the same questions kept resurfacing:

Was I a victim or just a fool?

What part of this was *mine* to own?

What part *did* I play in the way my past unfolded?

Why *had* I kept quiet when I should have been screaming?

How had I become *the go along and get along girl?*

What the fuck ... I was an adult. I so should have known better. I needed to understand this.

I would wake in the night with anxiety. The questions haunted me night and day. Owning my part, and not just being the victim was critical to my learning. I didn't want to go through these very painful lessons again because I did not look at the truth.

Then one day I came across a film review in *Vanity Fair* of <u>The Girl with the Dragon Tattoo.</u> The heroine was Swedish, as am I, and she bears a variation of my name. She is a Salander and I'm a Selander. That caught my attention because this is an unusual name, and over the course of my lifetime I have met very few. I hadn't read the book, so I decided to see the movie. Or should I say I felt compelled to see it.

The film was dark and at points brutally painful. I began to wonder why I had gone. And then there it was. The bit of wisdom that made me sit up and take notice and if the truth be told ... it kicked me in the ass.

The evil murderer says to the hero, whom he has trapped and was getting ready to kill,

" … the fear of offending is greater than the fear of pain. You knew something was wrong. You knew you would end up strung up in the basement. Yet you came back. And all I had to do was offer you a drink."

—Martin Vanger
<u>The Girl with the Dragon Tattoo</u>

Oh my God, there it was.

Day after day, through so much of my life, I kept my mouth shut. I was afraid to offend you. I was afraid to speak my truth. But somewhere inside, I knew by following Paul's lead I was headed for nothing but misery. I knew I was moving farther and farther away from what was right or at least right for me. I might as well have been strung up in the basement. No, I had let him lead me into that gilded cage, and all he'd had to do was offer me a drink.

Why did I ignore the instinct that said run? That inner knowing that tells us not to go somewhere with someone, it's because we feel socially awkward and so we don't make a fuss. It's the go along and get along overdrive that we have been conditioned to and it puts us in danger. It causes us to disregard our intuition and our gut level response.

How absolutely pitiful … I had been such a fool.

◈

I continued with the process of reinventing my life. I no longer embodied the role of wife or mother. I was divorced, and my children were grown and living independent lives, more or less.

There is a Buddhist proverb that states—

When the student is ready the teacher will appear.

I guess I was now ready.

I signed up for a class at the library. Bette, from my Miracle Group and Mary, her friend from the Presbyterian Church led a book group on Tuesday nights. They were reading, <u>A New Earth</u> by Eckhart Tolle. I had received a copy of <u>The Power of Now </u>by Eckhart Tolle as a gift a few years ago, and I was able to make neither hide nor hair of it. If Bette was leading the discussion, well, that was enough for me. I signed up, and as we systematically took the book apart, another light went on for me.

One evening while we were reading and discussing chapter 6 entitled, *Breaking Free,* I was profoundly struck by Tolle's words.

> *A man who had been an unwanted child and was given no love and a minimum of care and attention by his mother developed a heavy ambivalent-pain body that consisted of unfulfilled intense longing for his mother's love and attention and at the same time an intense hatred towards her for withholding what he so desperately needed. When he became an adult, almost every woman would trigger his pain-body neediness —a form of emotional pain —and this would manifest an addictive compulsion to*

"conquer and seduce" almost every woman he met and in this way get the female love and attention that the pain-body craved. He became quite an expert on seduction, but as soon as the relationship turned intimate or his advances were rejected, the pain-body's anger towards his mother would come up and sabotage the relationship.

Oh my God! Was he talking about Paul? Is this what happened to him? Is this why he was so screwed up?

His mother bore him out of wedlock. He never knew his father and never was close with his mother. He felt that she resented him because she was a young Catholic woman living in Ohio in 1950 when he was born. The world was a different place then, with rigid rules about purity and propriety. The Catholic community was harsh on unmarried single mothers and their fatherless children. The circumstances of Paul's birth had irrevocably altered the course of her life. She never married or finished her education, and they lived with her parents until Paul was grown. Not exactly the fairy tale life that young women in 1950 had been conditioned to dream about.

In his adult life Paul never saw his mother and she only lived 5 hours away. I only met her once, during the first month we were dating. He never wanted to talk about his childhood, and I learned early on not to ask. Occasionally, something would slip out and I knew even into his adulthood he had a great deal of animosity towards his mother.

I have no idea whether Eckhart Tolle is right or not. I haven't read the psychological research to support or refute his claims nor do I intend to, but I do know it was in this moment I began to see Paul in his humanity. Seeing Paul as a member of the human family, and not as a monster, was critical if I were ever to truly forgive him. The seed, be it ever so small, had been planted in my consciousness.

But what the heck was this *pain body?*

According to Tolle:

> *This accumulated pain is a negative energy field that occupies your body and mind. It is an invisible entity that wants to survive. It only survives if you unconsciously identify with it. Then it becomes you and lives through you as it feeds on anything that creates pain such as anger, destructiveness, hatred, grief, emotional drama, violence, and even illness.*
>
> *The pain body feeds on pain. Once the pain body takes over, a person becomes either the victim or the perpetrator. If you do not face it and bring the light of consciousness to the pain, it will be relived again and again. The pain body cannot prevail in the power of your presence. Unconsciousness creates it and consciousness changes it.*

Anger, destructiveness, hatred, grief, emotional drama, violence, and illness caused by unconscious living, this sounded like a recap of the last five years of my life with Paul. I was well acquainted with the roles of perpetrator and victim. Paul played one role, and I the other, and thus pain and suffering filled our lives.

And here Tolle says that pain cannot prevail in the light of conscious living and presence.

Was I truly so unconscious that I allowed this to happen? *Oh dear God*, I thought, *now is the time for me to wake up and take a good long look at this. God knows I must not repeat and relive the destruction, the trauma, and the emotional drama of my past.*

Yet the larger question lingered:

How would I move from unconsciousness and learn to cultivate a conscious life?

Every conscious moment is one less unconscious one – came the reply.

So I moved towards consciousness one moment at a time. Mindfully remembering to breathe and to be present with all that is, to relax, to feel, to watch, and to allow.

In consciousness and mindfulness perhaps I would learn to forgive.

What does it mean to come home?
Home is where they take you in
No reservations needed
There is always room for you
Home is where you are forgiven
In your humanity and in your divinity
Home is where they love you
No matter what

There is nothing my children could do
that would break my bond of love for them
I would forgive them anything
This is the way God forgives me
I am a child of God
And thus always loved
And always forgiven
Paul is a child of God too
Thus worthy of love and forgiveness
God's love is unconditional
Like a parent to a child
So I have found a glorious reunion in the presence
of God
So now I stand in the love,
In the goodness
And in the light

I had a clear understanding that if I were going to restart my life, and have the life I wanted, then I would need to forgive myself. I'm human and thus I make mistakes. God knows I have made some doozies. Making mistakes is part of the human condition and yet, as I attempted to seek peace within myself, and embrace the spirit of God that dwells within me, I learned to recognize with this Divinity that I was capable of forgiveness, of even the most egregious transgressions.

Could I forgive Paul? I acknowledged that with God it was possible and yet I struggled as I felt my pain and anger were justified. Must I really forgive him? I knew the answer, but I didn't like it. My humanity was in battle with the Divine.

I awoke in the night. The room was dark but the full moon shone through the curtains. The voice within was loud and clear–
Embrace the struggle it is part of the journey home ...
I wrote it in my journal. I would need to remember this.

∾

I checked my email. There was a note from Colleen. I took a moment to count my blessings while I waited for the page to load. I missed her. She is someone who knows me and still loves me.

Colleen is another soul sister. She sounded good as her note was light and newsy, the email concluded with a writing from her daughter, Caitlin:

I was working with a spiritual teacher about 13 years ago, and he shared the parable of the two wolves:

An old Cherokee chief was teaching his grandson about life ...

"A fight is going on inside me," he said to the boy.

"It is a terrible fight and it is between two wolves.

One represents anger, envy, sorrow, regret, greed, arrogance, self-pity, guilt, resentment, inferiority, lies, false pride, superiority, self-doubt, and ego.

The other represents joy, peace, love, hope, serenity, humility, kindness, benevolence, empathy, generosity, truth, compassion, and faith.

This same fight is going on inside you - and inside every other person, too."

The grandson thought about it for a minute and then asked his grandfather,

"Which wolf will win?"

The old chief simply replied,

"The one you feed."

Author unknown

And yet again
A voice from the far reaches of cyberspace called out –to give me just what I needed to hear, just when I needed to hear it.

Okay, okay I was paying attention.

∽

The week before I was ready to leave the Adirondacks, as I was saying goodbye to my new friends, Carol Mystic broke down into tears. "I don't know how to tell you this, so I guess I will just come out and say it, I wish that you had been my mother."

Now Carol is not a child, in fact she's probably 15 years older than I am. She and I are both widowed, and we both have been struggling to forgive someone who hurt us.

I was speechless. I think this is the greatest compliment anyone has ever given me.

Carol had met my daughter and Dana, too. For years I had listened to Paul's relentless criticisms of my ability to parent, and of me as a person. I too was moved to tears. What beautiful and loving words this woman had so kindly bestowed upon me. In that moment I felt loved and whole.

The summer drew to a close and it was time for me to return to Michigan. Gillian needed to return to college in Vancouver. I knew I didn't want to go home. I didn't want to leave my sister and she didn't want me to go. We'd had a wonderful summer together and I didn't want to leave Old Forge. I had met people who understood me, and allowed me the space to be at home, at home with myself.

It had been so long since I was comfortable in my own skin, and I didn't want to go back to my old way of being. The question began to take on a life of it's own: how could I figure out a way to stay?

After all the goodbyes had been said. I made a promise to myself to return. I drove back to Michigan to tie up some loose ends, but the seeds of a new life had already been sown.

Over the course of the next few months, Susan and I decided to go into business together. We would open a restaurant and bar, offering small plates with healthy fresh food. I would put my years of teaching nutrition to good use, and all of our offerings would be paired with wine. We bought an old Victorian home on Main Street and renovated our *old grande dame*. She was built in 1902 and when we opened Sisters Bistro in the spring of 2010, she never looked lovelier.

It had been less than one year since my divorce was final.

My new life was beginning.
As I practice my yoga
I think about what I have learned
I think about the fall from the horse
My sitting bones still ache when I sit on the floor
Long since healed physically
Yet the pain remains
Sometimes I am still shaken with fear
Fear of what might have been
No longer broken
But not yet free
There is still that lack of freedom in my movements
As I hold onto old hurts
I know it is time to let them go
Just be with me
Says the voice within
I will heal

Mistakes have been made
But intentions were pure

The time has come
to let go of that which no longer serves me
There is a time for every season
There is a time for forgiveness
of myself for mistakes I have made
I am grateful for my time on this earth
Time to live, love and make mistakes
It is in the making of mistakes that I have learned
Paul forgive me as I forgive you
You have your own journey to travel on
and I have mine

I may have lost my physical home
But my real home is inside of me
And although sometimes it is hidden
by the needs of my body,
my misuse of energy, time and space
and may be drowned out by the incessant chatter
of self-justification or finger-pointing
As in I may have done something right
or something wrong
or been looking for someone to blame

the chatter goes silent
the silence remains
and I am left with
Just me
I know that I am at home
And I am enough
I am complete and whole
Eternal, infinite and light

I embrace my God-given life
And I vow not to waste
the precious moments I have been given

Why did this happen to me?
Why did I allow it to happen?
All the signs were present

Non-attachment
I was so attached to my home
And yet as much as it grounded me
It was also an anchor to my past
My children have flown and have left the nest
They reside on the other side of the continent
The house anchored me in Michigan
To my old life
And as beautiful as that life was ...
Marriage to Fred,
motherhood and family life ...
It is time to transition to something new

A new life with my sister
Ah the laughter
And the love
And the shared purpose
Bring memories of childhood and joy
Returned to me as an adult

A new business
Creating hospitality
Welcoming, generosity and love
In a way that is authentic to my soul

A new home in Florida
To provide sunshine and respite
after a long busy summer in the mountains
Time and place to find my voice
Time and place to write
As I have been called to write for a long time
But the constraints,
real or self-imposed,
Did not allow for this

If not now ... when?
Time for self-exploration
Painting
Gardening
Writing
Yoga
The Beach

And perhaps,
just perhaps,
a new love to dance to
The unstructured dance for myself

Letting go of all the voices
that have told me–
No
Not You
Unchosen
Back of the Line

Now is the time to dance–
Chosen
Sensual
Real
Integrated
Whole

I push away all of the voices that said–
No
or laughed at my self expression
or said do something practical
or said be useful, not just ornamental

Today I embrace all of this
All that has brought me here today
With love and gratitude

Think of all the pain that Paul caused me ...
Or I caused myself
by consenting to be that bird in the gilded cage
The crystal vase on display
But never taken down and filled with water and
flowers
No never enjoyed for its beauty and its purpose

Did I ask for this?
Perhaps
Perhaps once I knew that you were so wrong for me
Perhaps it was I that pushed, pushed, pushed you
away
In an effort to regain my freedom

It is time to return home
To a life of love and gratitude
Leaving the house that was never a home
Was like leaving that burning building
All I could do was run
For I knew if I stayed even one moment longer–
The flames of self-suppression would consume me
and I would die

But no longer–
I live in light
And love
And personal freedom

Yoga is the coming home to oneself
You cannot really teach someone how to do that
It is a complete unfolding process
To learn to be more conscious–
You become less unconscious

As things move
from the unconscious to the conscious
I now know
Even the uncomfortable feelings
such as shame and embarrassment
need to be addressed
it is necessary for integration, learning and healing

Listen to the wisdom of your own heart
The way home is within
At long last
I am home.

If I have been graced with any wisdom through these dark days then it is this–

> *Above all else guard your heart,*
> *for it determines the course of your life.*
>
> *–Proverbs 4:23*

Epilogue

...the endurance of darkness is preparation for great light

St. John of the Cross

Years have past and I now find myself splitting my time between Vero Beach, Florida and Old Forge, New York. I have had plenty of time to reflect on this dark time and place in my life. I think that what I was experiencing was what others have called the *dark night of the soul.*

According to the reading I have done, many seekers find the path to God may involve one or more periods of time where they lose touch with the meaning and purpose of their life and in doing so they feel a poverty of spirit and a disconnection with their soul.

I thought after Fred had died that I had been gifted with insight and understanding about why I was here on the earth. But I lost my way when I married

Paul. I got further and further away from my place of peace. And I have never been so alone and sad in my entire life.

The writings of St. John of the Cross indicate that the dark night of the soul may be necessary for purification if one has lost sight of what is holy. When I met Paul I was not living consciously or virtuously. I was compensating for the loss of my one true husband by accepting Paul and his gifts of material possessions. One misguided attempt to fight the loneliness led to another until I was encased in loss and darkness.

I now see the darkness as a gift. As unwelcome as it was at the time but abiding with the pain and misery has allowed me to be transformed. True transformation is painful and takes time. By learning to forgive Paul and ultimately myself I have been freed to live each day joyously. Enduring the darkness may have allowed me to salvage this beautiful gift of my life.

Made in the USA
Charleston, SC
14 June 2013